Limits to Parallel Computation

Limits to Parallel Computation: *P*-Completeness Theory

RAYMOND GREENLAW
H. JAMES HOOVER
WALTER L. RUZZO

New York   Oxford
OXFORD UNIVERSITY PRESS
1995

Oxford University Press

Oxford   New York
Athens Auckland Bangkok Bombay
Calcutta Cape Town Dar es Salaam Delhi
Florence Hong Kong Istanbul Karachi
Kuala Lumpur Madras Madrid Melbourne
Mexico City Nairobi Paris Singapore
Taipei Tokyo Toronto

and associated companies in
Berlin   Ibadan

Published by Oxford University Press, Inc.,
200 Madison Avenue, New York, New York 10016

Library of Congress Cataloging-in-Publication Data
Greenlaw, Raymond.
Topics in parallel computation:
a guide to the theory of P-completeness /
Raymond Greenlaw, H. James Hoover, and Walter L. Ruzzo.
p. cm. Includes bibliographical references and index.
ISBN 0-19-508591-4
1. Parallel processing (Electronic computers).
I. Hoover, H. James. II. Ruzzo, Walter L. III. Title.
QA76.58.G74 1994 005.2—dc20 94-31180

This book is dedicated to our families,
who already know that life is inherently sequential.

Preface

This book is an introduction to the rapidly growing theory of P-completeness — the branch of complexity theory that focuses on identifying the "hardest" problems in the class P of problems solvable in polynomial time. P-complete problems are of interest because they all appear to lack highly parallel solutions. That is, algorithm designers have failed to find NC algorithms, feasible highly parallel solutions that take time polynomial in the logarithm of the problem size while using only a polynomial number of processors, for them. Consequently, the promise of parallel computation, namely that applying more processors to a problem can greatly speed its solution, appears to be broken by the entire class of P-complete problems. This state of affairs is succinctly expressed as the following question: Does P equal NC?

Organization of the Material

The book is organized into two parts: an introduction to P-completeness theory, and a catalog of P-complete and open problems.

The first part of the book is a thorough introduction to the theory of P-completeness. We begin with an informal introduction. Then we discuss the major parallel models of computation, describe the classes NC and P, and present the notions of reducibility and completeness. We subsequently introduce some fundamental P-complete problems, followed by evidence suggesting why NC does not equal P. Next, we discuss in detail the primary P-complete problem, that of evaluating a Boolean circuit. Following this we examine several sequential paradigms and their parallel versions. We describe a model for classifying algorithms as inherently sequential. We finish Part I with some general conclusions about practical parallel computation.

Because of the broad range of topics in the rapidly growing field of parallel computation, we are unable to provide a detailed treatment of several related topics. For example, we are unable to discuss parallel algorithm design and development in detail. For important and broad topics like this, we provide the reader with some references to the available literature.

The second part of the book provides a comprehensive catalog of P-complete problems, including several unpublished and new P-completeness results. For each problem we try to provide the essential idea underlying its P-complete reduction, and as much information and additional references about related problems as possible. In addition to the P-complete problems catalog, we provide a list of open problems, a list of problems in the class CC, and a list of problems in the class RNC.

Using the Book in a Course

The book has been designed so that it will be suitable as a text for a one semester graduate course covering topics in parallel computation. The first part of the book provides introductory material and the problems can easily be converted into numerous exercises. The book would be ideal for use in a seminar course focusing on P-completeness theory. It can also be used as a supplementary text for a graduate level course in complexity theory. Several of the chapters in the book could be covered in a graduate level course or the book could be used as a reference for courses in the theory of computation. This work could also be used as a rich source of sample problems for a variety of different courses. For the motivated student or researcher interested in learning about P-completeness, the book can be used effectively for self study.

Additional Problems and Corrections

In producing this book over a period of many years we have tried to be as accurate and thorough as possible. Undoubtedly, there are still some errors and omissions in our lists of problems. In anticipation of possible future printings, we would like to correct these errors and incorporate additional problems. We welcome suggestions, corrections, new problems, and further references. For each of the P-complete problems, we are also interested in references to papers that provide the best known parallel algorithms for the problem.

Please send general comments, corrections, new problems, bibliography entries, and/or copies of the relevant papers to

Ray Greenlaw at `greenlaw@cs.unh.edu`

Corrigenda and additions to this work can by found in the directory

`pub/hoover/P-complete` at `ftp.cs.ualberta.ca`

and via the World Wide Web at

`http://web.cs.ualberta.ca/~hoover/P-complete`

Research Support

The authors gratefully acknowledge financial support from the following organizations:

Ray Greenlaw's research was supported in part by the National Science Foundation grant CCR-9209184.

Jim Hoover's research was supported by the Natural Sciences and Engineering Research Council of Canada grant OGP 38937.

Larry Ruzzo's research was supported in part by NSF grants ECS-8306622, CCR-8703196, CCR-9002891, and by NSF/DARPA grant CCR-8907960. A portion of this work was performed while visiting the University of Toronto, whose hospitality is also gratefully acknowledged.

Acknowledgments

An extra special thanks to Martin Tompa who helped keep this project alive when it was close to dying. Martin has provided us with many useful suggestions over the years — all of which have helped to make this a better book.

A special thanks to Anne Condon and Alex Schäffer for carefully reading drafts of the book. Their suggestions helped to improve specific sections.

We wish to thank the following for contributing new problems, pointing us to appropriate literature, and providing us with corrections and suggestions on drafts of the manuscript: Richard Anderson, José Balcázar, David Barrington, Paul Beame, Erik Brisson, Anne Condon, Stephen Cook, Derek Corneil, Pilar de la Torre, Larry Denenberg, Sergio De Agostino, John Ellis, Arvind Gupta, John

Hershberger, David Johnson, Marek Karpinski, Tracy Kimbrel, Dexter Kozen, Luc Longpré, Mike Luby, Jon Machta, Andrew Malton, Pierre McKenzie, Satoru Miyano, Christos Papadimitriou, Teresa Przytycka, John Reif, Alex Schäffer, Roger Simons, Jack Snoeyink, Paul Spirakis, Iain Stewart, Larry Stockmeyer, Ashok Subramanian, Eva Tardos, Shang-Hua Teng, Martin Tompa, H. Venkateswaran, Joachim von zur Gathen, and Thomas Zeugmann.

We want to thank the reviewers who provided us with general comments about the organization of the book as well as detailed comments. We have tried to incorporate as many of their suggestions as possible although not all of them were feasible for us.

We want to thank Don Jackson at Oxford University Press. Don has been very helpful at each step in the production of this book and has been a great person to work with.

Finally, we would like to thank Mike Garey and David Johnson whose book *Computers and Intractability: A Guide to the Theory of NP-completeness* [113] has served as a model for this work.

November 1994   Ray Greenlaw
                                                        Jim Hoover
                                                       Larry Ruzzo

Contents

Limits to Parallel Computation

Part I:
Background and Theory

Chapter 1

Introduction

1.1 Bandersnatch Design

The subject of this book is best illustrated by the following scenario.

Suppose that you are employed in the halls of industry. More than a decade ago your company entered the highly competitive "bandersnatch"[1] market. While other companies thought that bandersnatch design was an intractable problem, and spent millions on supercomputers to search for possible designs, your company had the foresight to employ a few theoretical computer scientists. They discovered that there was a feasible algorithm for designing a bandersnatch directly from its specification. Your company can take an n-word specification of a bandersnatch and, in about n^3 steps, can test if the specification is reasonable and design an optimal bandersnatch that meets it. With your algorithm, a typical 15,000 word bandersnatch specification takes about one month to design. Construction only takes a week, so design dominates the bandersnatch building process.

Your competitors, on the other hand, do not have a fast algorithm for producing optimal bandersnatch designs. The best that they can do is an exhaustive search through the approximately $2^{n/150}$ possible different designs that meet the specification looking for the best one. Since this exhaustive search for the typical size of specification would take a while (say, 10^{16} years, assuming one design per microsecond)

---

[1] **bandersnatch.** A fleet, furious, fuming, fabulous creature, of dangerous propensities, immune to bribery and too fast to flee from; later, used vaguely to suggest any creature with such qualities. Lewis Carroll, Through the Looking Glass, 1871.

your competitors must be content with the suboptimal designs that they can produce in about the same time as you. At least that was until yesterday. Seeing the value of research, your competition formed a consortium and also invested in computer science. They too have discovered the feasible optimal bandersnatch design algorithm.

Since design dominates the production process, your bosses decide that the way to regain your company's competitive advantage is to reduce the design time. They give you the task of dramatically speeding up the design process.

Like most modern computer scientists you begin working on the problem by reading the news on the Net. One day an ad catches your eye.

ADDICTED to SPEED?

Is your single processor too slow? The Concoction
Machine Mark-1 parallel computer is just for you!
No matter what your problem, solve it faster with
the Mark-1's many processors working in parallel.
In fact, we promise that with enough processors,
any reasonable problem will run exponentially
faster on our machine. Send us e-mail for more
information.

Inconsequent Machine Co.
"We trade processors for speed."

Sensing its corporate salvation, your company orders one of the machines. When it arrives you unpack it and discover that its architecture is very simple. A very large collection of identical processors is attached to a very large shared memory. Processors can read and write simultaneously to the shared memory for essentially unit cost. Input and output are performed by loading data into memory before the computation and reading it out afterward.

You decide to try it on a simple problem that often occurs in bandersnatch design: Given n items, sort them according to their keys.

Your first algorithm uses a very simple divide and conquer strategy. Divide the n items evenly among processors, sort each subset with one processor, and then merge them. Not being sure of how many processors to actually use, you parameterize your algorithm so that the number of processors $p(n)$ is a function of the number of items n. Since you have lots of processors, so long as $p(n)$ is a small polynomial in n you will not exhaust the capacity of your new machine. Even if you do have to order more processors, your rate of expansion will be reasonable.

You assume that the items to be sorted are already in shared memory, stored in locations labeled $x_1, \ldots, x_n$. The first phase of your algorithm assigns disjoint equal-size subsets of the items, one subset to each processor. In the second phase, each processor (in parallel) sorts its subset using a good sequential algorithm, in time $O((n/p(n)) \log(n/p(n)))$.

The final phase is to merge the sorted subsets into one ordered set of items. This is the most complicated part of the algorithm. The idea is to do simultaneous merges of pairs of subsets of items into increasingly larger ordered subsets. The first stage uses $p(n)/2$ processors to merge $p(n)/2$ pairs of subsets, each of size $n/p(n)$. The next stage uses $p(n)/4$ processors to merge these $p(n)/4$ pairs of subsets of size $2n/p(n)$, and so on. The final stage uses 1 processor to merge 1 pair of subsets of size $n/2$. Each merge is done sequentially, and it turns out that the time for the last stage dominates this phase of your algorithm, taking $O(n)$ time.

Adding the times of all phases in your algorithm, you get that in asymptotic terms, a parallel sort using $p(n) \leq n$ processors takes time

$$O\left(n + \frac{n}{p(n)} \log \frac{n}{p(n)}\right).$$

The actual performance of your parallel algorithm depends on $p(n)$. When $p(n)$ is a constant independent of n, the time simplifies to $O(n \log n)$, which is asymptotically no faster than the sequential case.

You then consider what happens when the number of processors is small relative to the problem size, as when $p(n) \leq \log n$. In this case, the time simplifies to $O(n(\log n)/p(n))$, and you note that the parallel sort exhibits an "optimal speedup" in the sense that

(number of processors) $*$ (parallel time) $=$ (sequential time).

Unfortunately, for your algorithm, whenever $p(n)$ exceeds $\log n$, the time simplifies to $O(n)$, so additional processors help little.

This is discouraging, for although you obtain some speedup, it is not enough to produce a dramatic reduction in sorting time. It is certainly not of the kind of exponential reduction promised by the ad. For that, you must be able to sort n items in $O(\log n)$ time steps, although you would be happy with some polynomial version of that, such as $O((\log n)^2)$.

Thinking a bit more about the problem of sorting, you realize that its essence is to compute the position, or rank, of each item in the final sorted list. If the items stored in locations $x_1, \ldots, x_n$ have ranks $r_1, \ldots, r_n$, then in one parallel step n processors can rearrange the items by having processor i do the assignment $x_i = x_{r_i}$, assuming that the items are distinct.

Can ranking be done independently for each item? If so, then the time to compute the rank of every item would be the same as the time to compute the rank of one item. The time to sort would then reduce to the time to rank one item.

You next realize that you can do the ranking quickly by using n^2 processors. Since you have lots, n^2 is not an unreasonable number to apply to the problem, unless you are sorting a very large set.

The ranking algorithm has two phases. In the first, a processor is assigned to each pair (i, j) where $1 \leq i, j \leq n$. Processor (i, j) determines whether the value stored in location x_i is greater than that stored in x_j and stores a 1 in location $c_{i,j}$ if so, and a 0 otherwise. In the second phase, for each item i, the n processors $(i, 1), \ldots, (i, n)$ compute the sum $\sum_{j=1}^{n} c_{i,j}$. This sum is the rank of item i, and is stored in r_i. The sum can be computed by using the processors to mimic a fast addition tree. Overall, the ranking takes $O(\log n)$ time.

So by using n^2 processors your new algorithm can sort n items in time $O(\log n)$. This is a very dramatic speedup, of the exponential kind promised in the ad.

You summarize your discoveries in Table 1.1. (Although this will suffice for our story, a visit to your local University library, assuming it has not been closed during the latest wave of budget reductions, will uncover even better parallel sorting algorithms; see Leighton [228], for example.)

Buoyed by your success with sorting, you go on to develop fast parallel algorithms for many other problems. You notice that all of your solutions have two common characteristics — they use a *polynomial number* of processors, and have a *polylogarithmic* running time. That is, on an input of size n, your algorithms use about n^k processors and take time $(\log n)^l$, for some constants k and l. These algorithms are *feasible*, in the sense that they only use poly-

Algorithm	Processors	Time
Sequential Sort	1	$O(n \log n)$
Naive Divide and Conquer Sort	$p(n) = O(1)$ $p(n) \leq \log n$ $p(n) > \log n$	$O(n \log n)$ $O(n(\log n)/p(n))$ $O(n)$
Parallel Ranking	$p(n) = n^2$	$O(\log n)$

Table 1.1: Summary of Bandersnatch Sort Subroutines.

nomial numbers of processors, and they are *highly parallel* in the sense that their running times are polynomial in $\log n$ (polylogarithmic for short). You also notice that all of the problems have polynomial time sequential algorithms; that is, they all have feasible sequential solutions.

You formulate the following question.

Does every problem with a feasible sequential solution also have a feasible highly parallel solution?

With confidence gained from your initial successes at developing good parallel algorithms, you begin work on the core of the bandersnatch design problem.

After a few weeks, your office filled with crumpled paper, you have yet to develop a fast parallel algorithm for bandersnatch design. It appears that the design problem contains an inherently sequential component that defeats your, by now, rather sophisticated algorithmic tricks for obtaining highly parallel computations. You are faced with the prospect of announcing failure to your boss. Discussing your troubles with a colleague at lunch, she observes that what you need is a theory for parallel computation similar to the theory of *NP*-completeness for sequential computation. With that theory, showing that a problem is *NP*-complete is evidence that an always fast and exact sequential algorithm is probably not possible. You would like a similar method to show that a fast parallel algorithm is probably not possible.

Fortunately, your colleague has just read this book. What you need, she says, is to show that bandersnatch design is *P*-complete. By doing so, you will be showing that it is probably inherently sequential; thus, a fast parallel solution to every instance of the prob-

lem is probably not possible. With this evidence, you can go to
your boss and suggest that the design problem be relaxed somewhat
in the interest of speed, and that it makes sense to continue your
employment.

1.2   Informal Background

When this book's distinguished ancestor *Computers and Intractability: A Guide to the Theory of NP-Completeness* by Garey and Johnson [113] was published in 1979, complexity theory was not often a part of the algorithm designer's toolkit. Today every graduating computer scientist is at least aware that problems whose worst case time complexity is in the class P have feasible solutions, and that problems that are *NP*-complete are probably difficult to solve in general. Accordingly, we have relegated many standard definitions to Appendix C and concentrate our formal definitions on the basic notions relevant to parallel computation. Before embarking on such a detailed treatment, however, we will introduce the material in an informal way.

1.2.1   Feasible, Highly Parallel, and Inherently Sequential Problems

As a general rule we want our algorithms to be feasible. By feasible we mean the ability to solve the desired instances of a problem within our available resources. In practice, feasibility is very dependent on context and is not particularly portable between different problems and situations. But one common principle holds throughout almost all situations: an exponential growth rate in consumption of some resource required for a computation limits application of the method to all but the smallest of instances. Thus, feasibility has come to mean that the growth rate for the resource is bounded by a polynomial in the input size. This gives us the common notion that a problem has a feasible sequential solution only if we have a polynomial time algorithm, that is, only if any size n instance of the problem can be solved in time $n^{O(1)}$. Although widely acknowledged as being very simplistic, the dichotomy between polynomial and nonpolynomial time algorithms has proved to be a powerful discriminator between those computations that are feasible in practice and those that are not.

The same broad notion applies to parallel computations, except that processors are also considered as a resource. So we consider a parallel algorithm to be feasible only if we can find solutions to size n problem instances in time $n^{O(1)}$ using $n^{O(1)}$ processors. However, this definition of feasibility is not universally accepted, primarily because hardware appears to be a qualitatively different resource from time. But if we are not allowed to use a polynomial numbers of processors, how many should we be allowed to use?

The most compelling justification for using this polynomial notion of processor feasibility comes from considering what is involved in trading processors for speed. Parallel computation provides the potential of achieving a qualitative change in the time required to solve a problem by reducing polynomial sequential time to subpolynomial parallel time. So the goal of parallel computation is to develop algorithms that use only a reasonable number of processors and are extremely fast.

Regardless of the number of processors available, this goal is fundamentally limited by the speedup equation:

$$(\text{best sequential time})/(\text{number of processors}) \leq (\text{parallel time}).$$

The obvious consequence of this is that to achieve any subpolynomial time algorithm, a polynomial number of processors must be used. Thus, using the term "highly parallel" as we do does not even make sense unless we are willing to invest (at least conceptually) in a number of processors roughly equal to the best sequential time for the algorithm.

Still, what constitutes a reasonable number of processors and what is very fast remain debatable issues. We tend to think of time as an easily obtainable resource in the sense that any machine is capable of using arbitrary amounts of time if we are willing to wait. To handle a bigger problem we simply let the algorithm run longer. Clearly this is not the case for processors. Any given machine is finite, and to add more processors means at the very least that we have to acquire them and integrate them into the interconnection network of the machine. Thus, at first glance, it seems unreasonable to entertain a model in which the number of processors is not fixed. On closer inspection, however, this viewpoint is instructive.

There is a useful analogy to memory requirements in sequential complexity theory. In reality, computers have memories of some fixed, finite size. Virtual memory may stretch that bound a bit in

practice, and (budget permitting) more memory chips can be bought
and installed, but fundamentally memory is a fixed resource whose
quantity is not subject to algorithmic control. This hard reality not
withstanding, it has proved very fruitful to study the space complexity of algorithms as if space $s(n)$, like time $t(n)$, were an arbitrarily
flexible commodity. This patently unrealistic assumption does not
make the theory either wrong or irrelevant; it just means that the
application of the theory is slightly indirect. If the space consumption $s(n)$ of some algorithm for a given problem exceeds available
memory, it usually does not mean that we should jog to the corner
hardware store to buy more. Rather, it means that we must scale
back the problem size we expect to solve, or find a better (more
space efficient) algorithm.

Similarly, it has been fruitful to view the processor requirements
$p(n)$ of parallel algorithms as growing functions of n not because
the machines are flexible, but because the viewpoint allows us to
focus on important intrinsic issues, like parallel decomposition of
problems, and yet still be able to translate those insights into answers
to pragmatic questions, like "how big a problem can I solve in this
amount of time with this number of processors."

The debate over appropriate models will undoubtedly continue.
Further opinions on these and related issues can be found in Sanz
[315]. Fortunately, in this work, we can ignore most of this debate
since we are concerned with problems that apparently have no subpolynomial time feasible parallel algorithms at all. In other words,
rather than being highly parallel, these problems appear to be inherently sequential in any reasonable model of parallel computation.

Thus, without creating much controversy, we can adopt the following informal definitions.

- A problem is *feasible* if it can be solved by a parallel algorithm
  with worst case time and processor complexity $n^{O(1)}$.

- A problem is *feasible highly parallel* if it can be solved by an
  algorithm with worst case time complexity $(\log n)^{O(1)}$ and processor complexity $n^{O(1)}$.

- A problem is *inherently sequential* if it is feasible but has no
  feasible highly parallel algorithm for its solution.

Note that the class of feasible parallel problems is synonymous with
the class P, and we will use the two terms interchangeably.

1.2.2 Why is *P*-Completeness Important?

What can we do when faced with a problem that appears to be inherently sequential? One is to demonstrate at least a single instance of the problem whose solution by a parallel algorithm requires more than $(\log n)^{O(1)}$ time. This bad instance would then provide a lower bound for the worst case time complexity of the problem. Unfortunately, nontrivial lower bounds are notoriously difficult to establish. In fact, we know of no provably inherently sequential problem.

An alternative approach to understanding the difficulty of a problem is based on our usual experience with problem solving. Rarely do we solve a problem from scratch. Instead, we usually attempt to break the problem into subproblems that we already know how to solve, and whose answers when suitably combined give us a solution to the original problem. That is, we *reduce* the original problem to simpler ones that we know how to solve. For example, in the introductory scenario we reduced the problem of sorting a set of items to the problem of computing the rank of each item in the set.

Even in the absence of an *absolute* lower bound, we can exploit this idea of reduction, using it counter to its normal problem solving role, to establish *relative* lower bounds. Suppose that many others have worked on highly parallel algorithms for solving some problem B and all have failed. The general, but unproven, consensus is that problem B is inherently sequential. Further, suppose that we begin working on a new problem, B', that we know to be feasible and for which we seek a fast parallel algorithm. After a small amount of work, we fail to show that B' has a highly parallel solution, and we begin to suspect that it also is inherently sequential.

Unfortunately, our small efforts on B' are hardly convincing evidence for the difficulty of B' — perhaps we are just too slow at seeing good parallel solutions. But suppose we also observe that the hard problem B can be reduced to B'. Now our case for the inherent sequentiality of B' is as follows: B' must be difficult because if we could solve B', then we could solve B, and B has resisted numerous attempts by many experts.

How strongly does this argue the difficulty of B'? If B was actually provably inherently sequential, would the reduction of B to B' be irrefutable proof that B' was also inherently sequential? The answer depends on how the reduction was performed. Usually we describe the reduction of B to B' in terms of an algorithm that makes calls to a procedure for solving B'. The complexity of the reduction is defined to be the complexity of the reducing algorithm under the assumption that the cost of procedure calls for solving B' are not significant. So if the reduction of B to B' was highly parallel, then a highly parallel algorithm for B' would translate into a highly parallel algorithm for B. This would contradict the inherent sequentiality of B, so B' must itself be inherently sequential. The argument would fail if the reduction was merely feasible, that is, accomplished by a polynomial time *sequential* algorithm. Since in this case, the reduction composed with a solution to B' would not produce a highly parallel algorithm for B.

Unfortunately, no such proof of inherent sequentiality for B exists, so the fact that B is reducible to B' is rather a weak case for the difficulty of B'. After all, maybe reducing B to B' is in fact the route to a better parallel algorithm for solving B. One weakness of the argument lies in the fact that we only reduced a specific problem to B'. Suppose, instead, that we can capture the nature of *all* seemingly inherently sequential problems. If every such problem was reducible to B', then the argument favoring B''s difficulty becomes much stronger. For example, finding a highly parallel solution to B' would imply that there are *no* inherently sequential problems after all.

The way of showing that B' contains within it all of the important characteristics of every problem that might be inherently sequential is to prove that every feasible problem can be reduced to B' using a highly parallel reduction. Since every inherently sequential problem is feasible by definition, this would show that if there are any inherently sequential problems, then B' is one. Equivalently, this shows that if B' has a highly parallel solution, then there are no inherently sequential problems. When we show how every problem having a feasible sequential algorithm can be transformed into an instance of problem B', we have established that B' is *complete* for the class of feasible parallel problems. That is, B' is complete for P.

We leave details of reductions and completeness to the next chapter, but two remarks on the implications of establishing a body of complete problems are in order.

Every time one shows another problem to be complete, we get a larger body of problems that are diverse, yet of equivalent difficulty. The entire body of P-complete problems then provides a rich characterization of the difficult parallel problems. The hope is that some common essence of inherent sequentiality can be extracted from the collection. Even more optimistically, one might hope to show that they are in fact not inherently sequential at all.

For the algorithm designer, perhaps the more important implication is in guiding one's search for good parallel solutions. Often, the particular difficult problem is only one component of some larger problem. Knowing that the subproblem is complete strongly suggests that the decomposition of the larger problem should be reformulated. For example, Linear Programming (Problem A.4.3), Maximum Flow (Problem A.4.4), and Maximum Matching (Problem B.9.7) often play a role as key subroutines in the solution of more complex combinatorial optimization problems. The former two problems are *P*-complete, while there is a feasible highly parallel probabilistic algorithm for the latter. Thus, an algorithm designer seeking a highly parallel solution to a novel combinatorial optimization problem would be well-advised to avoid formulating his solution in terms of Linear Programming or Maximum Flow subproblems, and perhaps to cast it as a Matching problem, instead.

Alternatively, it may be that the particular instances one wishes to solve are weaker than the general *P*-complete problem, and so may actually have highly parallel solutions. For example, although Linear Programming and Maximum Flow are *P*-complete, restrictions of them such as Two Variable Linear Programming (Problem B.2.2) and 0-1 Maximum Flow (Problem B.9.6) do have highly parallel solutions. Additionally, *P*-completeness theory can guide algorithm designers in cases where a particular function has a highly parallel solution, but certain algorithmic approaches to its computation are not amenable to such solutions. Computing breadth-first level numbers via queue- versus stack-based algorithms is an example (see Chapter 8 for more details).

1.3   Some History

The notion of *P*-completeness appeared at roughly the same time as that of *NP*-completeness, but for a very different reason. The motivation was to study the relationship between sequential time and space. In particular, Cook raised the question of whether everything computable in polynomial time is also in polylogarithmic space. That is, the motivation was to ask whether a Turing machine running in time $n^{O(1)}$ could in general be simulated by one operating in space $(\log n)^{O(1)}$. Cook did not answer this question, but his 1973 conference paper [63, 64] did show that this question was equivalent to the question of whether a single, specific language, Path Systems (Problem A.6.8), could be recognized in space $(\log n)^{O(1)}$. That is, he showed Path Systems to be complete for P, obtaining the first P-completeness result! Like all fundamental complete problems, the reduction Cook gave was a generic one for simulating a polynomial time-bounded Turing machine, using Path Systems in this specific case. The exact relationship between P and polylogarithmic space remains open, although we do know that polylogarithmic space cannot equal P; see Johnson [177] for more details.

Since space complexity was the focus, Cook used a space-bounded form of reduction, logarithmic space reduction (independently introduced by Cook [63], Jones [179], and Stockmeyer and Meyer [344]). It required that the algorithm accomplishing the reduction be restricted to using $O(\log n)$ space on inputs of length n. Subsequent work followed this lead; the parallel time-bounded reductions discussed in Section 1.2.2 were not introduced until much later. We discuss reductions in more detail in Chapter 3.

The year after Cook's paper, Jones and Laaser [180, 181], and Galil [111, 112] presented more P-complete problems, still motivated by the issue of polynomial sequential time versus polylogarithmic space.

In 1975, Ladner showed that the Circuit Value Problem (CVP) was P-complete [225]. In 1972, Savage had shown that any Turing machine with time bound $T(n)$ could be simulated by a Boolean combinational circuit of size $O(T(n)^2)$ [317].[2] Ladner's proof hinged on the observation that the transformation of the Turing machine into a circuit could be accomplished in logarithmic space. Ladner also remarked that CVP provided a simple example of a P-complete language of the type identified by Galil [112]. Later, Goldschlager showed that the more restricted monotone, and planar versions of CVP were also P-complete [122]. CVP and its variants have turned out to be among the most useful of the P-complete problems, and will be discussed extensively in Chapters 4 and 6. These results established the relationship between polynomial time sequential computations and the parallel model of polynomial size circuits.

Around the same time period, numerous parallel models of computation were being introduced, and evidence was accumulating for

---

[2]In 1973, Pippenger and Fischer improved this result to size $O(T(n) \log T(n))$ and depth $O(T(n))$ [289].

the *Parallel Computation Thesis*, which states that sequential space is polynomially related to parallel time. In other words, what can be computed in $f(n)^{O(1)}$ sequential space can be computed in $f(n)^{O(1)}$ parallel time, and *vice versa*. The thesis first seems to have appeared in the work of Chandra and Stockmeyer [50]. It was crisply stated and further elaborated on in Goldschlager [123]. In addition, Goldschlager's dissertation seems to be the first place to make the connection between P-complete problems and problems that are unlikely to parallelize. In light of the Parallel Computation Thesis, P-complete problems can be solved in polylogarithmic time in parallel if and only if every problem in P can be solved in polylogarithmic space.

One weakness in the Parallel Computation Thesis, from the standpoint of formally capturing the notion of "feasible" parallel computation, is that the fast parallel simulation of anything more than sequential $O(\log n)$ space came at the expense of a superpolynomial number of processors. Similarly, anything more than an $O(\log n)$ depth circuit required superpolynomial time to simulate with a small space sequential machine. Borodin raised the question of sharpening the Parallel Computation Thesis to consider simultaneous resource bounds [40]. For example, is the class of problems that simultaneously use polynomial time and polylogarithmic space equivalent to the class that simultaneously use polynomial numbers of processors and polylogarithmic parallel time? Pippenger did not answer this question directly, but showed that similar simultaneous resource bounds did in fact hold when Turing machine time and reversals were compared to circuit size and depth, and when Turing machine time and space were compared to circuit size and width [285].

Another important contribution of Borodin's paper was to introduce the notion of uniformity conditions for the construction of families of circuits. Various notions of uniformity were subsequently explored by Allender [9], Barrington, Immerman, and Straubing [24], Goldschlager [126], Pippenger [285], Ruzzo [308], and others.

Considerable interest was raised in this class of problems that used polylogarithmic time and polynomial size circuits, much of it originally due to Nick Pippenger. Cook indicates that Pippenger studied these types of circuits during his 1978 visit to the University of Toronto [65]. This prompted the naming of the class by Cook to be "Nick's Class" or *NC* for short [65]. Now the question of whether all feasible problems had highly parallel algorithms could be succinctly stated as whether P equals NC. A flurry of works soon appeared showing that various polynomial time sequential algorithms had corresponding NC algorithms.

Goldschlager, Shaw, and Staples were some of the first authors to state the importance of P-completeness in the parallel setting [128]. As usual, completeness arguments were used for those problems that seemed to defy attempts to place them in NC. Since the issue was now one of how a sequential computation could be transformed into a parallel one, the reduction changed from a sequential one (logarithmic space) to a parallel one (NC). This did not render the previous logarithmic space reductions obsolete, because Borodin's paper [40] also showed that any $O(\log n)$ space computation could be simulated by an $O((\log n)^2)$ depth and $n^{O(1)}$ size transitive closure circuit. Thus, any such reduction was also in NC. In many cases more direct and depth efficient reductions do exist.

The phrase "inherently sequential" was used frequently in connection with hard to parallelize problems after it appeared in a paper by Reif entitled *Depth-first Search is Inherently Sequential* in 1985 [300].

Since then, the explosion in results on parallel computation has made this book necessary.

We note that several early papers applied the term "P-complete" to what are now called NP-complete problems. Additionally, the term *p-complete* is used in another domain, involving projections; see for example Valiant [357] or Geréb-Graus, Paturi, and Szemerédi [115].

1.4   Related Works

The goal of this book is to provide a comprehensive overview of the theory of P-completeness. Because of the sheer size of this subject, we are unable to cover other important aspects of parallel computation in any detail. Indeed, topics such as parallel algorithm design and analysis warrant their own books. We list a few references to some of these other topics. Our intention is not to be complete, but simply to note a few that we are familiar with.

The book *Efficient Parallel Algorithms* by Gibbons and Rytter has a brief discussion of parallel models of computation followed by substantial material on parallel algorithms [117]. It also has a short chapter describing *P*-completeness.

JáJá's book *An Introduction to Parallel Algorithms* devotes a chapter to discussing parallel models and then extensively delves into parallel algorithms [172]. The book also has a brief section on *P*-completeness.

The large work *Introduction to Parallel Algorithms and Architectures: Arrays, Trees, Hypercubes* by Leighton contains a detailed discussion of many different types of parallel models and algorithms for them [228].

Synthesis of Parallel Algorithms, edited by Reif [302], contains twenty chapters organized around parallel algorithms for particular types of problems, together with an introductory chapter on *P*-completeness (Greenlaw [138]), and one surveying PRAM models (Fich [105]).

The chapter *Parallel Algorithms for Shared-memory Machines* by Karp and Ramachandran [195] in the *Handbook of Theoretical Computer Science* [360] describes a variety of highly parallel algorithms for shared memory machines.

In the same handbook, the chapter *A Catalog of Complexity Classes* by Johnson is a thorough overview of basic complexity theory and of the current state of knowledge about most complexity classes [177]. It is an excellent reference for establishing the context of each class and its established relationships to others.

Miyano, Shiraishi, and Shoudai's 1989 paper also surveys *P*-completeness theory, as well as providing a catalog of most of the then-known *P*-complete problems [268].

The papers (Kindervater and Lenstra [210, 211], Kindervater and Trienekens [213]) provide extensive bibliographies of papers about parallel algorithms and parallel algorithm development for combinatorial optimization problems.

1.5 Overview of This Book

The remainder of this book is organized into two main parts. The first part is devoted to the theory of *P*-completeness. The second part is a compendium of *P*-complete and open problems.

Part I is directed to the reader who may be familiar with the notions of *NP*-completeness and parallel computation but who has only seen some, if any, of *P*-completeness theory. The reader familiar with these topics will probably find much that can be skipped. Part I is divided into the following chapters.

Chapter 2 introduces the two main models of parallel computation: the parallel random access machine, or PRAM, and the uniform Boolean circuit family.

Chapter 3 gives precise complexity class definitions for the notions of feasibly parallel and inherently sequential problems, and formalizes the notions of reducibility and completeness.

Chapter 4 deals with two prototypical hard problems for parallel computation — Generic Machine Simulation and the Circuit Value Problem.

Chapter 5 discusses evidence suggesting that P-complete problems are in some sense "inherently sequential."

Chapter 6 addresses the original Circuit Value Problem as described by Ladner [225] in more detail, as well as giving several restricted versions that are also P-complete.

Chapter 7 examines the greedy algorithm — a simple sequential paradigm that gives rise to many P-complete problems.

Chapter 8, motivated by experience with the greedy algorithm, presents a model that deals with inherently sequential algorithms.

Chapter 9 introduces two other notions of strong and strict P-completeness.

Chapter 10 discusses approximations to P-complete problems.

Chapter 11 provides a wrap up of Part I of the book, addresses recent developments, and contains conclusions.

Part II of the book contains the reference collections of P-complete problems in Appendix A, and of open problems in Appendix B. To make this part as self-contained as possible we provide definitions and background material for each problem. In most cases, we provide a brief sketch of the P-completeness reduction. From our sketch, a reader familiar with P-completeness theory should be able to deduce the full reduction without it being necessary to track down the original references. In addition, a number of the reductions we present were previously unpublished and appear here for the first time.

Finally, the various notations are collected in Appendix C, and the complexity classes used are briefly defined in Appendix D.

Chapter 2

Parallel Models of Computation

2.1 Introduction

Before we can discuss the difficulty of solving a problem, we must first choose a suitable machine model in which to describe our computations. A machine model is a parameterized description of a class of machines. Each machine in the class is obtained from the model by giving specific values for the parameters. For example, a Turing machine is specified by giving the number of work tapes, symbol set, and program. The choice of model that we make depends on how we wish to balance such factors as simplicity, generality, historical use, novelty, plausibility of actual implementation, and ease of programming. This flexibility inevitably leads to a proliferation of different models, and parallel computation is no exception to this tendency toward diversity.

The menagerie of parallel models includes bit vector machines (Pratt and Stockmeyer [293]), Boolean circuits (Borodin [40]), parallel random access machines, or PRAMs (Fortune and Wyllie [109], Goldschlager [126]), k-PRAMs (Savitch and Stimson [323]), alternating Turing machines (Chandra, Kozen, and Stockmeyer [49]), parallel pointer machines (Cook and Dymond [68], Dymond [98], Dymond and Cook [99, 100]), aggregates ([98, 99, 100]), conglomerates (Goldschlager [126]), and a large variety of machines based on fixed interconnection networks, such as grids, hypercubes, and shuffle-exchange (see Leighton [228]).

Such variety makes it difficult to compare competing models. At the qualitative level, models can be distinguished by their processor granularity and their interconnection pattern. One important distinction among models is in the granularity with which they treat parallel operations. A model can be fine-grained and treat bit operations as the basic unit of parallel computation, or it can be coarse-grained and, for example, treat local subcomputations on processors as the fundamental unit. In addition the model can be structured, in which case the machine can only manipulate atomic data objects and cannot access their representations (as bits for example).

Another important qualitative difference among models is the nature of the communications between processing elements. Some models allow unrestricted communication between processing elements at any time. Other models require a fixed communication pattern. In some models there is no charge for the communication pathway between elements, in others there is.

These kinds of qualitative distinctions are difficult to make precise, and so a more useful way of comparing models is via mutual simulation. If any machine from model A can be simulated by some machine from model B, then we know that any problem solvable by a model A machine is solvable by a model B machine. But this is not enough, as we also need to know how the resources used by model A compare to those used by model B. Fortunately, despite the diversity of the models, each parallel model has some computational resources that correspond to our intuitive notions of running time and processing hardware. This enables us to compare the simultaneous time and processor requirements of a machine from model A with its simulation from model B, and vice versa. If the requirements are roughly the same, then we can consider the models to be essentially equivalent.

For feasible, highly parallel computations, most parallel models are equivalent to within a polynomial in both time and hardware resources, simultaneously. By this we mean that if the size n instances of some problem can be solved in time $t(n) = (\log n)^{O(1)}$ and processors $p(n) = n^{O(1)}$ on a machine from model A, then there exists a machine from model B that can solve the size n instances of the problem in time $t(n)^{O(1)}$ and $p(n)^{O(1)}$ processors. Thus, if a problem is feasibly highly parallel on one model, it is so on all other models, and the theory of P-completeness becomes very robust and insensitive to minor variations in the computational model.

Not all parallel models possess the property described above.

Models with limited interconnection schemes can be too weak to simulate other models. For example, for the tree connected parallel machine, although any two processors can communicate via short paths, there is a bottleneck at the root that limits the bandwidth of the communication between processors. The mesh connected parallel machine can only communicate directly with its neighbors, and this results in an average path of length $\sqrt{n}$ for n processors (see Leighton [228]). On the other hand, some models of parallel computation are simply too powerful to be simulated by the more common models. This includes most machines that can generate exponentially long values or activate exponential numbers of processors in polylogarithmic time. More discussion of the relationships among various models can be found in the excellent surveys by Cook [66], Fich [105], and Karp and Ramachandran [195]. Additional papers surveying other aspects of parallel models and parallel computing include Johnson [176], Kindervater and Lenstra [211], Spirakis [338], van Emde Boas [359], and Vishkin [364].

Since our choice of model is relatively unimportant for a discussion of inherently sequential problems, we can chose simply on the basis of convenience. For high level discussions our preferred model is the parallel random access machine (PRAM). When we are concerned with more detailed questions of implementability and small resource bounds, we will use the more low level uniform Boolean circuit model. These models are presented in the next two subsections.

2.2 The PRAM Model

In sequential algorithm design the favorite model of computation is the random access machine, or RAM. Each RAM consists of a computation unit with a fixed, user defined program; a read-only input tape; a write only output tape; and an unbounded number of local memory cells $R_0, R_1, R_2, \ldots$ with each cell capable of holding an integer of unbounded size. The computation unit is very simple. It has operations for moving data between memory cells, either directly or indirectly; comparisons and conditional branches; and simple arithmetic operations such as add, subtract, multiply, divide, and so on. A RAM program is a sequence of these instructions. Execution starts with the first instruction and ends when a halt instruction is encountered.

Typically, all operations in the RAM model are assessed one unit of cost regardless of the length of the numbers being manipulated by the operation. The usual complexity measures of interest for RAM computations are time, in the form of the number of instructions executed, and space, in the form of the number of memory cells accessed. To prevent this notion of time from distorting our notion of feasibility, the model prohibits (either by *fiat* or by careful choice of instruction set) rapid generation of very large numbers. For example, the model will prohibit numbers of superpolynomial length from being generated or tested in polynomial time. Aside from these considerations, the power of the RAM model is essentially unchanged throughout a broad range of variations in the instruction set.

The natural generalization of the RAM model to parallel computation is the parallel random access machine introduced independently by Fortune and Wyllie [109], and by Goldschlager [126]. The PRAM model consists of a collection of RAM processors that run in parallel and communicate via a common memory.

The basic PRAM model consists of an unbounded collection of numbered RAM processors $P_0, P_1, P_2, \ldots$ and an unbounded collection of shared memory cells $C_0, C_1, C_2, \ldots$ Each processor P_i has its own local memory, knows its own index i, and has instructions for direct and indirect read/write access to the shared memory.

Rather than being on tapes, inputs and outputs to the computation are placed in shared memory to allow concurrent access. Instructions are executed in unit time, synchronized over all active processors.

A typical PRAM instruction set is given in Table 2.1, with the addressing modes described in Table 2.2. Note that in this simple machine, local memory cell R_0 serves as an accumulator so that at most one read and one write to shared memory occurs for each instruction. Also, observe how the multiply and divide instructions only take a constant operand in order to prevent the rapid generation and testing of very large numbers.

Two important technical issues must be dealt with by the model. The first is the manner in which a finite number of the processors from the potentially infinite pool are activated for a computation. A common way, although often unstated in the literature, is for processor P_0 to have a special activation register that specifies the maximum index of an active processor. Any non-halted processor with an index smaller than the value in the register can execute its program. Initially only processor P_0 is active, and all others are sus-

Instruction	Description
$\alpha \leftarrow \alpha$	move data between cells
IDENT	load the processor number into R_0
CONST c	load the constant c into R_0
ADD α	add contents of α to R_0
SUB α	subtract contents of α from R_0
MULT c	multiply contents of R_0 by constant c
DIV c	divide contents of R_0 by constant c and truncate
GOTO i	branch to instruction i
IFZERO i	branch to instruction i if contents of R_0 is 0
HALT	stop execution of this processor

Table 2.1: Sample PRAM Instructions.

Address α	Description
R_i	address of local cell R_i
R_{R_i}	local cell with address given by contents of R_i
C_i	address of shared cell C_i
C_{R_i}	shared cell with address given by contents of R_i

Table 2.2: Sample PRAM Addressing Modes.

pended waiting to execute their first instruction. P_0 then computes the number of processors required for the computation and loads this value into the special register. Computation proceeds until P_0 halts, at which point all active processors halt. Goldschlager's SIMDAG model is an example of a PRAM using such a convention [126]. Another common approach, used, for example, by Fortune and Wyllie's PRAM, is to have active processors explicitly activate new ones via FORK instructions [109]. Again, this issue makes relatively little difference in the power of the model, provided numbers are not allowed to grow too quickly.

The second technical issue concerns the way in which simultaneous access to shared memory is arbitrated. In all models, it is assumed that the basic instruction cycle separates shared memory reads from writes. Each PRAM instruction is executed in a cycle with three phases. First the read (if any) from shared memory is performed, then the computation associated with the instruction (if any) is done, and finally the write (if any) to shared memory is performed. This eliminates read/write conflicts to shared memory, but does not eliminate all access conflicts. This is dealt with in a number of ways, including:

CRCW-PRAM — The concurrent-read concurrent-write PRAM permits simultaneous reads and writes to the same memory cell. Some method of arbitrating simultaneous writes to the same cell is required. For example, in the PRIORITY version only the write by the lowest numbered contending processor succeeds. (Goldschlager's SIMDAG is a model of this type [126].) In the COMMON version the write succeeds only if all processors are writing the same value; in the ARBITRARY version any one of the writes succeeds.

CREW-PRAM — The concurrent-read exclusive-write PRAM permits simultaneous reads of the same memory cell, but only one processor may attempt to write to the cell. (Fortune and Wyllie's model is of this type [109].)

CROW-PRAM — The concurrent-read owner-write PRAM is a commonly occurring restriction of the CREW-PRAM. It preassigns an owner to each common memory cell. Simultaneous reads of the same memory cell are allowed, but only the owner can write to the cell. This restriction ensures exclusive-write access. (This model was introduced by Dymond and Ruzzo [101].)

EREW-PRAM — The exclusive-read exclusive-write PRAM requires that no two processors simultaneously access any given memory cell.

All of these variants of the PRAM are deterministic, except for the ARBITRARY CRCW-PRAM. In this model it is possible that repeated executions on identical inputs result in different outputs.

The taxonomy above originates in Vishkin [364]. See Fich for an in-depth discussion of PRAM models [105].

Any given PRAM computation will use some specific time and

hardware resources. The complexity measure corresponding to time is simply the time taken by the longest running processor. The measure corresponding to hardware is the maximum number of active processors during the computation.

Our standard PRAM model will be the CREW-PRAM with a processor activation register in processor P_0. This means that processor P_0 is guaranteed to have run for the duration of the computation, and the largest value in the activation register is an upper bound on the number of processors used.

Note that no explicit accounting is made of the local or shared memory used by the computation. Since the PRAM is prevented from generating large numbers, that is, for $t \geq \log n$ no number may exceed $O(t)$ bits in t steps, a computation of time t with p processors cannot store more than $O(pt^2)$ bits of information. Hence, for our purposes p and t together adequately characterize the memory requirement of the computation, and there is no need to parameterize it separately.

To compare models, and later to introduce the notion of a reduction, it is important to identify what we mean by a computation of a machine. This means specifying how the inputs are provided to a computation, how the outputs are extracted, and how the cost of the computation is accounted. For PRAMs we adopt the following conventions.

Definition 2.2.1 *Let M be a PRAM. The* **input/output conventions** *for M are as follows. An input $x \in \{0, 1\}^n$ is presented to M by placing the integer n in shared memory cell C_0, and the bits $x_1, \ldots, x_n$ of x in shared memory cells $C_1, \ldots, C_n$. M displays its output $y \in \{0, 1\}^m$ similarly: integer m in shared memory cell C_0, and the bits $y_1, \ldots, y_m$ of y in shared memory cells $C_1, \ldots, C_m$.*

M computes in **parallel time** *$t(n)$* **and processors** *$p(n)$ if for every input $x \in \{0, 1\}^n$, machine M halts within at most $t(n)$ time steps, activates at most $p(n)$ processors, and presents some output $y \in \{0, 1\}^*$.*

M computes in **sequential time** *$t(n)$ if it computes in parallel time $t(n)$ using 1 processor.*

With these conventions in place, and having decided on one version of the PRAM model to be used for all computations, we can talk about a function being computed in parallel time $t(n)$ and processors $p(n)$.

Definition 2.2.2 *Let f be a function from* $\{0,1\}^*$ *to* $\{0,1\}^*$*. The* function f is **computable in parallel time** $t(n)$ **and processors** $p(n)$ *if there is a PRAM M that on input x outputs* $f(x)$ *in time* $t(n)$ *and processors* $p(n)$*.*

All of the various PRAM models are polynomially equivalent with respect to feasible, highly parallel computations, and so any one is suitable for defining the complexity classes P and NC that we present in Chapter 3. However, the subclasses NC^k of NC are not defined using PRAMs — for that we will require the Boolean circuit model, described in the next subsection. (The reasons are largely historical, but note that the set of functions computable in parallel time $O((\log n)^k)$ is probably different for each of the four PRAM types listed above. Defining NC^k in terms of circuits thus avoids this sensitivity to details of the PRAM model, as well as, arguably, making the definition more firmly based on technological realities.)

The final important point to note about the PRAM model is that it is generally not difficult to see (in principle) how to translate an informally described parallel algorithm into a PRAM algorithm. Consider, for example, the parallel sorting algorithms described informally in the introduction. There and as is typically done we assume the input is specified by integers rather than bits. The significance of this point is that it makes the PRAM a convenient vehicle for parallel algorithm design, just as the RAM has proved to be a convenient model for sequential algorithm design.

2.3   The Boolean Circuit Model

Although the PRAM model is a natural parallel extension of the RAM model, it is not obvious that the model is actually reasonable. That is, does the PRAM model correspond, in capability and cost, to a physically implementable device? Is it fair to allow unbounded numbers of processors and memory cells? How reasonable is it to have unbounded size integers in memory cells? Is it sufficient to simply have a unit charge for the basic operations? Is it possible to have unbounded numbers of processors accessing any portion of shared memory for only unit cost? Is synchronous execution of one instruction on each processor in unit time realistic?

To expose issues like these, it is useful to have a more primitive model that, although being less convenient to program, is more closely related to the realities of physical implementation. Such a model is the Boolean circuit (Borodin [40]). The model is simple to describe and mathematically easy to analyze. Circuits are basic technology, consisting of very simple logical gates connected by bit-carrying wires. They have no memory and no notion of state. Circuits avoid almost all issues of machine organization and instruction repertoire. Their computational components correspond directly with devices that we can actually fabricate.

The circuit model is still an idealization of real electronic computing devices. It ignores a host of important practical considerations such as circuit area, volume, pin limitations, power dissipation, packaging, and signal propagation delay. Such issues are addressed more accurately by more complex VLSI models (Lengauer [229]), but for many purposes the Boolean circuit model seems to provide an excellent compromise between simplicity and realism. For example, one feature of PRAM models that has been widely criticized as unrealistic and unimplementable is the assumption of unit time access to shared memory. Consideration of (bounded fanin) circuit models exposes this issue immediately, since a simple fanin argument provides a lower bound[1] of $\Omega(\log p)$ on the time to combine bits from p sources, say by OR, a trivial problem on a unit cost CRCW-PRAM.

A circuit is simply a formal model of a combinational logic circuit. It is an acyclic directed graph in which the edges carry unidirectional logical signals and the vertices compute elementary logical functions. The entire graph computes a Boolean function from the inputs to the outputs in a natural way.

Let $B_k = \{f \mid f : \{0,1\}^k \to \{0,1\}\}$ denote the set of all k-ary Boolean functions. We refer informally to such functions by strings "1," "0," "$\neg$," "$\wedge$," "$\vee$," among others. For the sake of readability, we will also frequently use "NOT," "AND," "OR," and other common descriptive words.

Definition 2.3.1 *A **Boolean circuit** α is a labeled finite oriented directed acyclic graph. Each vertex v has a type $\tau(v) \in \{I\} \cup B_0 \cup B_1 \cup B_2$. A vertex v with $\tau(v) = I$ has indegree 0 and is called an **input**. The inputs of α are given by a tuple $\langle x_1, \ldots, x_n \rangle$ of distinct vertices. A vertex v with outdegree 0 is called an **output**. The outputs of α are given by a tuple $\langle y_1, \ldots, y_m \rangle$ of distinct vertices. A vertex v with $\tau(v) \in B_i$ must have indegree i and is called a **gate**.*

---

[1] The notation $\Omega(\cdot)$ is used for lower bounds, analogously to $O(\cdot)$ for upper bounds; see Appendix C.

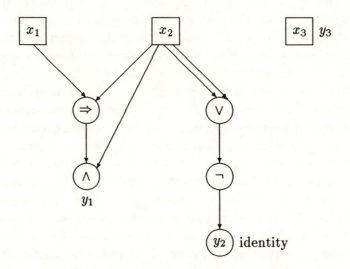

Figure 2.3.1: A Sample Boolean Circuit.

Note that fanin is less than or equal to two but fanout is unrestricted. Inputs and gates can also be outputs. See Figure 2.3.1 for an example. The circuit depicted there has inputs x_1, x_2, and x_3; and outputs y_1, y_2, and $y_3 = x_3$. Input x_2 has fanout four. Gate y_2 has fanin one.

Each circuit computes a well-defined function of its input bits as specified in the following definition.

Definition 2.3.2 *A Boolean circuit α with inputs $\langle x_1, \ldots, x_n \rangle$ and outputs $\langle y_1, \ldots, y_m \rangle$ **computes a function** $f : \{0,1\}^n \to \{0,1\}^m$ in the following way: input x_i is assigned a value $\nu(x_i)$ from $\{0,1\}$ representing the ith bit of the argument to the function. Every other vertex v is assigned the unique value $\nu(v) \in \{0,1\}$ obtained by applying $\tau(v)$ to the value(s) of the vertices incoming to v. The value of the function is the tuple $\langle \nu(y_1), \ldots, \nu(y_m) \rangle$ in which output y_j contributes the jth bit of the output.*

When the logical function associated with a gate is not symmetric, the order of the incoming edges into the gate is important. See Figure 2.3.1 for example, where there is an $\Rightarrow$ gate. Orientation can be ignored in the usual case in which only symmetric functions like AND and OR are computed by the gates.

The resource measures of interest for a circuit are its *size* and *depth*.

Definition 2.3.3 *The **size** of α, denoted* size(α), *is the number of vertices in α. The **depth** of α, denoted* depth(α), *is the length of the longest path in α from an input to an output.*

The circuit shown in Figure 2.3.1 has size eight and depth three.

Each circuit α is described by a string denoted $\overline{\alpha}$. This description can be thought of as a blueprint for that circuit, or alternatively as a parallel program executed by a universal circuit simulator. In any case, although we speak of circuits, we actually generate and manipulate circuit descriptions (exactly as we manipulate programs and not Turing machines). Thus, we need a circuit description language. We adopt the one described below, although many alternative descriptions would work equally well. Ruzzo discusses a number of different ones [308].

Definition 2.3.4 *The **standard encoding** $\overline{\alpha}$ of a circuit α is a string from $\{0,1\}^*$ grouped into a sequence of 4-tuples (v,g,l,r), one tuple for each vertex of α, followed by two sequences of vertex numbers $\langle x_1,\ldots,x_n \rangle$ and $\langle y_1,\ldots,y_m \rangle$. Within the encoding, the vertices of α are uniquely (but arbitrarily) numbered in the range $1,\ldots,$ size$(\alpha)^{O(1)}$. The tuple (v,g,l,r) describes a vertex v and its oriented connections to other vertices as follows. Vertex number v is a g-gate, where $g \in \{I\} \cup B_0 \cup B_1 \cup B_2$. The left (right) input to v, if any, is numbered l (respectively, r). The vertex number of the ith input is given by x_i, and that of the jth output is given by y_j.*

The main point of this definition is that circuit descriptions are simple objects to generate and manipulate. Note that the 4-tuple is actually a binary string, although for ease of presentation we have described it as a string over the alphabet consisting of parentheses, comma, decimal digits, and the like. Each 4-tuple can be encoded in binary as a string of $O(\log($size$(\alpha)))$ bits. The length of $\overline{\alpha}$ is $O($size$(\alpha)\log($size$(\alpha)))$.

Note that in the Boolean circuits defined above, all gates have fanin at most two, but there is no *a priori* upper bound on the fanout of a gate. Hoover, Klawe, and Pippenger show that conversion to bounded fanout entails at most a constant factor increase in either size or depth [160]. On the other hand, we could also consider circuits allowing gates of unbounded fanin. In this case it is common to restrict the set of allowable gate functions to elementary symmetric functions like AND or OR, or perhaps other threshold functions like MAJORITY. Usually, the size of an unbounded fanin circuit is defined to be its number of edges. For unbounded fanin circuits, conversion to bounded fanin entails no great size increase (at worse squaring the size), but may increase depth by a factor proportional to the logarithm of the size. In the other direction, any bounded fanin circuit may be replaced by an unbounded fanin circuit of slightly smaller depth (a factor of $\log\log(\text{size})$) but polynomially greater size (Stockmeyer and Vishkin [345]). Even greater depth reduction is also possible, all the way down to depth two, but only at the expense of a superpolynomial increase in size by converting the circuit into disjunctive or conjunctive normal form.

2.3.1   Uniform Circuit Families

An individual circuit with n inputs and m outputs is a finite object computing a function from binary strings of length n to binary strings of length m. Consequently, different circuits are required for different length inputs. This is in contrast to our usual notion of computation: one algorithm handles all possible lengths of inputs. How can the notion of circuit be generalized to functions on strings of arbitrary length?

The simplest generalization occurs when the output length m is a function, possibly constant, only of the length of the input. That is, we are only considering the simple case of functions f where the length of $f(x)$ is the same for all n-bit inputs x. Call this length $m(n)$. In this case we can represent the function

$$f_\alpha : \{0,1\}^* \rightarrow \{0,1\}^*$$

by an infinite sequence of circuits, $\{\alpha_n\}$, where circuit α_n computes f restricted to inputs of length n. Such a sequence is called a circuit family.

Definition 2.3.5 *A **Boolean circuit family** $\{\alpha_n\}$ is a collection of circuits, each α_n computing a function $f^n : \{0,1\}^n \rightarrow \{0,1\}^{m(n)}$. The **function computed by** $\{\alpha_n\}$, denoted f_α, is the function*

$$f_\alpha : \{0,1\}^* \rightarrow \{0,1\}^*,$$

defined by $f_\alpha(x) \equiv f^{|x|}(x)$.

The special case where the length of the output is always one is particularly important for defining formal languages.

Definition 2.3.6 *Let $\{\alpha_n\}$ be a Boolean circuit family that computes the function $f_\alpha : \{0,1\}^* \to \{0,1\}$. The* **language accepted by** $\{\alpha_n\}$*, denoted L_α, is the set $L_\alpha = \{x \in \{0,1\}^* \mid f_\alpha(x) = 1\}$. We say L_α is* **recognized by** $\{\alpha_n\}$.

When the output length varies with the value as well as the length of the input, some additional output bits must be computed by the circuit to indicate which of the remaining output bits are valid data. This is a technical complication that we will not explore.

How does one describe an infinite collection of circuits? With no constraints whatsoever, we get the so called *nonuniform* circuit families. Nonuniform circuit families are unexpectedly powerful, in that they can "compute" non-computable functions. For example, consider the circuit family $\{\alpha_n\}$, where circuit α_n consists of n inputs, all ignored, and a single output gate v that is a constant function. Gate v is defined to be the constant 1 function if the nth Turing machine halts on its own description, and is defined to be a 0 gate otherwise. Thus, the circuit family $\{\alpha_n\}$ computes a function f_α that is uncomputable in the usual sense, since it can be used to solve the Halting Problem.

Nonuniform circuit families are widely used as objects of lower bound proofs, where their unexpected power merely serves to strengthen the significance of the lower bounds. However, the example above shows that they are a somewhat unsatisfactory model in which to consider upper bounds. In particular, there is no effective way, given n, to obtain a description of the nth circuit α_n. The obvious approach to addressing this difficulty is to provide an algorithm for generating the members of the family. That is, a circuit family is defined by giving a program in some computational model that takes n as input and then outputs the encoding $\overline{\alpha_n}$ of the nth member. In doing so, an infinite object, the family, is effectively described by a finite object, the program. The question then becomes, how much computational power is permitted in producing the description $\overline{\alpha_n}$?

Guided by the intuition that the circuit constructor should have no more computational power than the object it constructs, Borodin introduced the notion of *uniformity* [40]. One example of a weak circuit constructor is a Turing machine that is limited to only $O(\log n)$ work space on inputs of length n. Few problems of interest can be solved in this limited amount of space, yet such machines can describe a wide class of useful circuit families.

Definition 2.3.7 *A family* $\{\alpha_n\}$ *of Boolean circuits is* **logarithmic space uniform** *if the transformation* $1^n \to \overline{\alpha_n}$ *can be computed in* $O(\log(\text{size}(\alpha_n)))$ *space on a deterministic Turing machine.*

Note that the complexity of producing the description of α_n is expressed in terms of the size of the resulting circuit, instead of the usual method of expressing it in terms of the input length. For polynomial size circuits, and by using the technical device of supplying n in unary, the complexity is also logarithmic in terms of the length of the input.

Logarithmic space uniformity is sometimes called Borodin-Cook uniformity, and was first mentioned in Cook [65]. This notion of uniformity has the desirable property that the description $\overline{\alpha_n}$ can be produced in polynomial time sequentially, or in polylogarithmic time in parallel with a polynomial number of processors. Thus, the circuit constructor is reasonable from both sequential and parallel perspectives.

Just as there is no general agreement as to the best model of sequential or parallel computation, neither is there general agreement as to the best notion of uniformity. Different notions are appropriate to different purposes. For example, if one is willing to give up fast parallel construction of the circuit descriptions, in essence trading construction time for circuit size or depth, one can use P-uniformity. Introduced by Beame, Cook, and Hoover [26], and further examined by Allender [9], a family $\{\alpha_n\}$ is *P-uniform* if the transformation $1^n \to \overline{\alpha_n}$ can be computed by a deterministic Turing machine in time $n^{O(1)}$.

As another example, although logarithmic space sequential computations (hence logarithmic space uniformity) can be simulated efficiently in parallel, it is not known whether they can be simulated in parallel time $o((\log n)^2)$. Thus, logarithmic space uniformity is generally considered inappropriate for circuit families of depth $o((\log n)^2)$. For depths down to $\log n$, the definitions proposed by Ruzzo are preferable [308], and subsume logarithmic space uniformity at and above $(\log n)^2$ depth. These definitions are based on alternating Turing machines, another reasonable parallel model (Chandra, Kozen, and Stockmeyer [49]). For still smaller depths, including constant depth unbounded fanin circuits, the definition of Barrington, Immerman, and Straubing is preferred [24]. The definitions of [24, 308] also have the virtue of having natural, uniform characterizations that are completely divorced from circuits and from any ancillary notions of uniformity. For example, Ruzzo defines U_E-uniformity and shows that any language is recognized by a U_E-uniform family of polynomial size, $(\log n)^k$ depth circuits if and only if it is accepted by a logarithmic space, $(\log n)^k$ time bounded alternating Turing machine. Barrington, Immerman, and Straubing give a similarly clean characterization of uniform constant depth, unbounded fanin circuits in terms of "First Order Definability" [24]. Other definitions of uniformity are considered by Goldschlager [126] and Pippenger [285].

Given these conflicting definitions, which should we use? It seems that in practice it rarely matters which definition is used, but in the interest of precision we must choose one, and logarithmic space uniformity seems the simplest to understand, even though the other definitions cited above are often preferable on technical grounds. Thus, hereafter the unqualified term *uniform* will mean logarithmic space uniform.

2.4 Circuits and PRAMs

We have alluded to the fact that many parallel models are equivalent when we consider feasible highly parallel algorithms. That is, if a problem has a feasible highly parallel solution on one model, then it also has one on any equivalent model. Originally the notion of feasible and highly parallel came from the observations that certain problems had polylogarithmic time and polynomial processor solutions on many different models. In a triumph of circularity, all the models that support feasibly highly parallel algorithms became the "reasonable" parallel models. In order for any new parallel model to be considered reasonable, it must be able to simulate some existing reasonable model and vice versa.

To give the reader some feel for how these simulation arguments are constructed, we now sketch the equivalence between CREW-PRAMs and logarithmic space uniform Boolean circuit families. These kinds of simulation results are quite technical, and sensitive to the precise details of the models involved. The actual details of the subsidiary algorithms used in the simulations, such as the parallel prefix computation, can be found in Karp and Ramachandran [195], for example.

The first result concerns the simulation of a circuit family by a PRAM.

Lemma 2.4.1 *Let $\{\alpha_n\}$ be a logarithmic space uniform Boolean circuit family, such that α_n computes the function $f^n : \{0,1\}^n \to \{0,1\}^{m(n)}$, with $\mathrm{depth}(\alpha_n) = (\log n)^{O(1)}$ and $\mathrm{size}(\alpha_n) = n^{O(1)}$. Then there exists a CREW-PRAM M that computes f in parallel time $(\log n)^{O(1)}$ and processors $n^{O(1)}$.*

Proof Sketch. The simulation consists of two phases. The first phase takes n (the size of the input) and constructs the standard encoding of the circuit α_n. The second phase actually simulates α_n on the input.

First phase: The first phase must generate $\overline{\alpha_n}$ using a feasible highly parallel algorithm. Since the circuit family is logarithmic space uniform, there is a Turing machine M_α that on input 1^n uses work-tape space $s(n) = O(\log n)$ and generates $\overline{\alpha_n}$. Because the meaningful input to M_α consists only of n 1's we can assume that the Turing machine has a one-way, read-only input tape. We can also assume a one-way write-only output tape on which the encoding is written. For convenience we also assume that the tape heads advance one cell to the right after an input or output operation. How can such a machine be simulated quickly in parallel?

The first thing is to observe that the state (here meaning configuration) of M_α can be completely described by the tuple $\langle q, i_{pos}, w_{pos}, w_{data} \rangle$ that specifies the internal state q of M_α, the input head position in binary (relative to the start position), the work tape head position in binary (relative to the start position), and the work tape contents. The size of the state tuple is $O(s(n)) = O(\log n)$ bits, and so there are only $n^{O(1)}$ distinct states. Call the set of such states Q.

Next, we construct the state transition function $T_\alpha : Q \to Q$ for M_α. Note that neither the input nor the output tape contents are explicitly included in the state tuples. In constructing the state transition function, however, we can ignore the input tape contents, since when we simulate M_α on input 1^n, a read will deliver a 1 if the head position is less than n and a 0 otherwise. We can also ignore the output tape contents since they cannot affect the computation, and, as described below, we can deduce later what was written by examining the sequence of states occurring in the computation. Constructing T_α can be done quickly by assigning one processor to each state tuple in Q.

Given the initial state $Q_0 = \langle q_0, 0, 0, \epsilon \rangle$ we can simulate the execution of M_α for t steps by computing

$$Q_t = T_\alpha^t(Q_0). \tag{2.1}$$

That is, we compose the state transition function with itself t times and apply it to the initial state.

Since M_α is logarithmic space bounded, it cannot run for more than polynomial time, and so it has a polynomial length state sequence $Q_0, Q_1, \ldots, Q_{t(n)}$. This sequence can be computed efficiently by using the parallel prefix algorithm of Ladner and Fischer [226] to compute the functions

$$T_\alpha^t, \ 1 \le t \le t(n),$$

then applying (2.1).

The encoding of α_n can be extracted from this sequence by locating every Q_i that writes a bit to the output tape, and then doing parallel list contraction to produce a single string composed of these bits.

Second phase: It is a simple task for a CREW-PRAM to simulate the circuit α_n given its encoding $\overline{\alpha_n}$. The basic idea is that the gate numbered i in the circuit is assigned to processor $P_{\rho(i)}$, and the output value of gate i is written to shared memory cell $C_{\rho(i)}$. The renumbering function ρ is used to allocate processors and cells to the circuit gates. It is simply $\rho(i) = i + n + |\overline{\alpha_n}|$.

Processor $P_{\rho(i)}$ executes a very simple loop that reads, from shared memory, the value of the inputs to gate i, computes the logical function associated with the gate, and writes the result to $C_{\rho(i)}$. It takes some time for the correct logical values to propagate from the inputs through to the output, so the loop has to run for depth(α_n) iterations. At this point the loop halts, and the values of the output gates are compacted, using list ranking, to the first $m(n)$ memory cells $C_1, \ldots, C_{m(n)}$. Recall $m(n)$ is the output size of α_n; it is easily obtained from the circuit encoding. Finally, the value $m(n)$ is placed in C_0.

One problem is that this phase needs to know the depth of the circuit. This can be computed in a feasibly highly parallel way by doing $(\max, +)$ transitive closure on the circuit graph. Alternatively, the algorithm could stop the simulation when the state of the gates is no longer changing.

Complexity: Each of the phases is feasible and highly parallel, thus so is the simulation. $\qquad \square$

How can a PRAM be simulated by a circuit? The main problem is that the PRAM has a potentially unbounded number of memory cells, each one with contents of potentially unbounded length.

Lemma 2.4.2 *Let M be a CREW-PRAM that computes in parallel time $t(n) = (\log n)^{O(1)}$ and processors $p(n) = n^{O(1)}$. Then there exists a constant c and a logarithmic space uniform Boolean circuit family, $\{\alpha_n\}$, such that α_n on input $\langle x_1, \ldots, x_n \rangle$ computes output $\langle y_{1,1}, y_{1,2}, \ldots, y_{i,j}, \ldots \rangle$, where $y_{i,j}$ is the value of bit j of shared memory cell i at time $t(n)$, for $1 \leq i \leq p(n) * t(n)$ and $1 \leq j \leq c * t(n)$. Furthermore, $\mathrm{depth}(\alpha_n) = (\log n)^{O(1)}$ and $\mathrm{size}(\alpha_n) = n^{O(1)}$.*

Proof Sketch. Since combinational circuits have no memory, they must simulate the computation of M step-by-step, with the output of one step becoming the input of the next step. Thus, the circuit will have $t(n)$ layers, one for each time step of M's computation on an input of length n.

Without additional information, the circuit must be designed to handle the worst case estimate of the number of local and shared memory cells used by each processor, and the number of bits used by each cell. The time and processor bounds guarantee that no more than $t(n)$ local memory cells per processor, and no more than $p(n) * t(n)$ shared memory cells in total are accessed. In both cases, no more than $c * t(n)$ bits are generated per cell. Therefore, each layer of the simulation must maintain information on $p(n) * t(n)$ local memory cells and $p(n) * t(n)$ shared memory cells, each containing $c * t(n)$ bits.

The only problem is that, because of indirect addressing, the accessed memory cells can be spread over an address space of size $2^{c*t(n)}$. Thus, it is not possible to simulate every cell that could be accessed. Instead the simulation must dynamically allocate memory cells from a pool of cells, each cell tagged with its address. Stockmeyer and Vishkin show how this can be done in a feasible highly parallel way [345]; see also Karp and Ramachandran [195]. For the sake of simplicity we will assume that no indirect addressing occurs outside the first $p(n) * t(n)$ cells.

A layer consists of $p(n)$ copies of a circuit that simulates one step of a single processor. The circuit simply implements the basic operations of the PRAM processor, which can all be done with $O(\log(p(n) * t(n))) = O(\log n)$ depth, polynomial size subcircuits.

The circuit for a single step of one processor takes as input its own local memory bits from the previous layer, and all shared memory bits from the previous layer. The shared memory bits from all processors must be merged together using a tree that allows the bits from the (at most) one processor that wrote to each shared memory cell to replace the existing bits.

The total depth of the simulation is at worst $O(t(n) * \log n)$, and the circuit is polynomial size.

Finally, we claim that the description $\overline{\alpha_n}$ can be generated by a logarithmic space Turing machine. The overall circuit is very regular, and the main issue is picking a simple numbering scheme for the blocks that form a layer, and then for the individual layers. □

These two results combine to give the following theorem.

Theorem 2.4.3 *A function f from $\{0,1\}^*$ to $\{0,1\}^*$ can be computed by a logarithmic space uniform Boolean circuit family $\{\alpha_n\}$ with $\text{depth}(\alpha_n) = (\log n)^{O(1)}$ and $\text{size}(\alpha_n) = n^{O(1)}$ if and only if f can be computed by a CREW-PRAM M on inputs of length n in time $t(n) = (\log n)^{O(1)}$ and processors $p(n) = n^{O(1)}$.*

Similar simulation results among the various models of parallel computation allow us to observe that if a problem is inherently sequential on one reasonable parallel model, then it is inherently sequential on all other reasonable models.

Chapter 3

Complexity

The goal of this chapter is to provide the formal basis for many key concepts that are used throughout the book. These include the notions of problem, definitions of important complexity classes, reducibility, and completeness, among others.

3.1 Search and Decision Problems

Thus far, we have used the term "problem" somewhat vaguely. In order to compare the difficulty of various problems we need to make this concept precise. Problems typically come in two flavors: *search problems* and *decision problems*.

Consider the following search problem, to find the value of the maximum flow in a network.

Example 3.1.1 *Maximum Flow Value (MaxFlow-V)*
Given: *A directed graph $G = (V, E)$ with each edge e labeled by an integer capacity $c(e) \geq 0$, and two distinguished vertices, s and t.*
Problem: *Compute the value of the maximum flow from source s to sink t in G.*

The problem requires us to compute a number — the value of the maximum flow. Note, in this case we are actually computing a function. Now consider a variant of this problem.

Example 3.1.2 *Maximum Flow Bit (MaxFlow-B)*
Given: *A directed graph $G = (V, E)$ with each edge e labeled by an integer capacity $c(e) \geq 0$, and two distinguished vertices, s and t, and an integer i.*
Problem: *Is the ith bit of the value of the maximum flow from source s to sink t in G a 1?*

This is a decision problem version of the flow problem. Rather than asking for the computation of some value, the problem is asking for a "yes" or "no" answer to a specific question. Yet the decision problem MaxFlow-B is equivalent to the search problem MaxFlow-V in the sense that if one can be solved efficiently in parallel, so can the other. Why is this?

First consider how solving an instance of MaxFlow-B can be reduced to solving an instance of MaxFlow-V. Suppose that you are asked a question for MaxFlow-B, that is, "Is bit i of the maximum flow a 1?" It is easy to answer this question by solving MaxFlow-V and then looking at bit i of the flow. Since we can examine bit i of the output of MaxFlow-V quickly in parallel, any feasible highly parallel solution to MaxFlow-V yields a feasible highly parallel solution for MaxFlow-B.

Next, consider how solving an instance of MaxFlow-V can be reduced to solving a number of instances of MaxFlow-B. Suppose that you are given an instance of MaxFlow-V to solve. First compute an upper bound on the maximum flow in G, such as the sum of all the capacities of the edges of G. This can be done quickly in parallel. The resulting limit on the flow gives a limit, m, on the number of bits in the maximum flow. Then we solve m instances of MaxFlow-B, one for each of the bits of the maximum flow, to obtain the value of each bit. Finally, combine all the bits to compute the value of the maximum flow. Thus, any highly parallel solution to MaxFlow-B implies an highly parallel solution to MaxFlow-V. That is, MaxFlow-V can be reduced, efficiently in parallel, to MaxFlow-B.

Thus, if we are interested in studying the intrinsic parallel complexity of maximum flow, it is sufficient for us to look at this particular decision variant. This idea generalizes to any situation in which one is computing a function. For example, any function $g : \{0,1\}^* \rightarrow \{0,1\}^*$ induces the associated "bitwise" decision problem "Is bit i of $g(x)$ equal to 1?" Provided that we have a bound on the length of $g(x)$, we can determine the value of $g(x)$ bit by bit. Consequently, the complexity of computing $g(x)$ cannot be substan-

tially greater than that of deciding the value of a particular bit of
$g(x)$.

Therefore, when it comes to assessing the difficulty of a problem,
it is usually sufficient simply to consider the problem's associated
bitwise decision variant. Other related decision problems often work
as well, but one must be somewhat careful. For example, consider
the following variant of maximum flow.

Example 3.1.3 *Maximum Flow Threshold (MaxFlow-T)*
Given: *A directed graph $G = (V, E)$ with each edge e labeled by an
integer capacity $c(e) \geq 0$, and two distinguished vertices, s and t,
and an integer k.*
Problem: *Is the value of the maximum flow from source s to sink
t in G less than k?*

It is possible to reduce the computation of MaxFlow-V to the
decision problem MaxFlow-T, but the reduction seems to be impossible to do in a feasible highly parallel way. Suppose that the flow
has at most m bits. Then the flow can be determined in m steps using a binary search. For example, the high-order bit of the flow can
be determined by asking if the flow is less than 2^{m-1}. If the answer
to this question is no, bit m of the flow is 1. Assuming a negative
answer, the next bit can be determined by asking if the flow is less
than $2^{m-1} + 2^{m-2}$. In this way, solving m instances of MaxFlow-T
yields all bits of the flow.

This results in a reasonably fast sequential algorithm. Unfortunately, it does not give a fast parallel algorithm since each particular
instance of the decision problem to be solved depends on the answers
from the previous ones, and so they apparently cannot be solved
in parallel. It is conceivable that MaxFlow-T has a feasible highly
parallel algorithm while MaxFlow-V and MaxFlow-B (see Problem
A.4.4) likely do not.

The reader is referred to (Abrahamson, Fellows, and Wilson [2]
or Karp, Upfal, and Wigderson [197]) for further discussion of "parallel self-reducibility," that is, determining the parallel complexity
of a search problem assuming the availability of an oracle for the
corresponding decision problem.

Another possible area of concern is whether the specification of
the problem is functional or not. That is, whether each instance
has a unique solution, or admits many possible solutions. In the
case of MaxFlow-V the problem was functional. The special case of
a search problem where the solution is unique is called a *function*

problem. Below we provide an example of a search problem that is not a function problem.

Example 3.1.4 *Maximum Flow Pattern (MaxFlow-P)*
Given: *A directed graph $G = (V, E)$ with each edge e labeled by an integer capacity $c(e) \geq 0$, and two distinguished vertices, s and t.*
Problem: *Compute a flow pattern. That is, a flow on each particular edge of G that overall achieves the maximum flow from source s to sink t.*

There may be many flow patterns attaining the maximum flow; MaxFlow-P produces just one of them. It is possible that successive solutions of the same instance of MaxFlow-P result in different flow patterns. Thus, reductions to MaxFlow-P must be carefully designed. They cannot assume, for example, that parallel solutions deliver the same answer as was done in the MaxFlow-V to MaxFlow-B reduction above. Nor can they use the technique of recomputing the solution in order to save space. One simple way of making these kinds of relational problems into functional ones is to require an additional property of the solution, such as it being the lexicographically first among all solutions.

3.2 Complexity Classes

A complexity class is a collection of problems (usually decision or function) of some characteristic worst case difficulty — the most famous being the class P of decision problems with polynomial time sequential solutions. Within a class, some problems may be easier than others, but all of the problems can be solved within the resource bounds associated with the class.

An important consideration when defining a complexity class is the type of objects it will contain. It is convenient to compare complexity classes using the usual terminology of sets — we speak of one class being a proper subset of another, or of one class being the intersection of two other classes. Thus, if possible, we want all of our complexity classes to contain the same kind of object. We also want to perform computations that manipulate members of a class, such as reducing one problem in the class to another. So an additional consideration when defining a class is that the members of a class be easy to code as strings from $\{0, 1\}^*$.

For these reasons, most complexity classes are defined in terms of formal-language acceptance problems. This means that the members of a complexity class are languages, each language being a set of strings from $\{0, 1\}^*$. Hence, every complexity class contains the same kind of object — a set of strings.

How can we make the jump from decision and function problems to language recognition problems over the alphabet $\{0, 1\}$? There are two issues we need to confront. The first is how problems are encoded over the binary alphabet; the second is how to view decision and function problems as languages. First, we address the coding issue.

Decision and function problems are normally phrased over an alphabet having many more than two symbols. For example, it is often convenient to use delimiters such as #, (,), and the digits $0 - 9$ when expressing a problem. When passing from our usual informal description of a problem to a language recognition question, we would like to preserve the amount of information contained in our original description. Therefore, we introduce the informal notion of the size of a problem. The size of an instance of a problem is naturally measured by the number of symbols in the full problem specification.

There are many ways of coding a specific decision problem, such as MaxFlow-B, into a language recognition problem. Any encoding that meets the following guidelines is acceptable. First, it must be easy to produce the encoding of any instance of the problem. This prevents encodings from containing the answer to the problem as part of the encoding.

Next, the coding should be compact. The length of the binary encoding should roughly correspond to the size of the problem instance, say by being polynomial in the original instance size. This way we can express the complexity of a problem either in terms of the size of the problem instance, or the length of the instance encoding, and both measures will be equivalent to within a polynomial factor.

For example, a directed graph G on n vertices can be coded as an adjacency matrix of roughly n^2 bits. The complexity of an algorithm for finding a spanning tree of G can be expressed either in terms of n or in terms of the length of the encoding of G. In either case the complexity will be polynomial time. On the other hand, the size of an integer is usually expressed in terms of the number of digits in its binary or decimal representation. By encoding an integer x

in unary, it becomes possible to factor x in time polynomial in the input length — something we do not know how to do if x is coded in binary. Such cases where the length of the encoding is exponentially larger than the instance size are considered unreasonable.

Finally, the encodings being considered should all be interconvertible within the computational resources that we are studying. That is, no one encoding contains more computational hints than any other.

Now we return to the issue of how to view decision and function problems as language recognition questions. When problems are expressed in decision form, they immediately provide an associated language L consisting of those strings that encode the "yes" answers to the problem. Membership of a binary string x in L is then equivalent to an affirmative answer to question y for the decision problem, where y is the original unencoded version of x.

Suppose L is the language corresponding to a particular decision problem. We may think of coding an instance of the problem with its answer. For example, $x\#1$ means $x \in L$ and $y\#0$ means $y \notin L$. Consider the language $L' = \{x\#1 \mid x \in L\}$. This language provides an alternative view of L.

When we want to consider function problems as language recognition questions, the approach described above turns out to be useful. Fix an encoding of instances for a specific problem. A function problem F can be viewed as a language recognition question using the language

$$L(F) = \{x\#i\#j \mid \text{bit } i \text{ of the function at } x \text{ has value } j, j \in \{0,1\}\}$$

Note that if we can compute the solution to a function problem, we can easily recognize its corresponding language, and vice versa.

The reader may have noticed that in our descriptions of languages we have been using the delimiter $\#$. By applying a homomorphism h such that $h(0) = 10$ and $h(1) = 00$, and coding $\#$ as 11, we obtain a language over $\{0,1\}^*$.

To specify precisely the complexity of a decision problem and of its associated language, we need the following definitions. The reader may wish to refer to Definition 2.2.1.

Definition 3.2.1 *Let L be a language over $\{0,1\}^*$. The **characteristic function** of L is the function f_L defined on all $x \in \{0,1\}^*$ such that $f_L(x) = 1$ if $x \in L$, and $f_L(x) = 0$ if $x \notin L$.*

Definition 3.2.2 *A language $L \subseteq \{0,1\}^*$ is* **decidable in sequential time** *$t(n)$ if and only if the characteristic function of L can be computed in sequential time $t(n)$.*

Definition 3.2.3 *A language $L \subseteq \{0,1\}^*$ is* **decidable in parallel time** *$t(n)$ with $p(n)$* **processors** *if and only if the characteristic function of L is computable in parallel time $t(n)$ and processors $p(n)$.*

A single sequential processor running in polynomial time can easily simulate a polynomial number of processors running in polynomial time, and conversely. So if we wanted, we could restrict our attention simply to PRAMs, as the following lemma indicates.

Lemma 3.2.4 *A language L is decidable in sequential time $n^{O(1)}$ if and only if L is decidable in parallel time $n^{O(1)}$ with processors $n^{O(1)}$.*

3.2.1   *P*, *NC*, *FP*, and *FNC*

We can now define the class of polynomial time sequential problems, P, and the class of feasible highly parallel problems, NC. (For the origin of the name NC, see Section 1.3.)

Definition 3.2.5 *The class* **P** *is the set of all languages L that are decidable in sequential time $n^{O(1)}$.*

Since deterministic complexity classes are closed under complement, $P = \text{co-}P$. (As an aside, notice that this implies the complement of every P-complete language is also P-complete.)

Definition 3.2.6 *The class* **NC** *is the set of all languages L that are decidable in parallel time $(\log n)^{O(1)}$ and processors $n^{O(1)}$.*

From Lemma 3.2.4, we know that $NC \subseteq P$. *The important question for parallel computation is whether this inclusion is proper.*

As we have seen, every decision problem of the form "Is $x \in L$?" can be expressed as a function problem of computing the characteristic function of L. Similarly, every function has an associated decision problem of the form "Is bit i of $f(x)$ a 1?" Thus, one could define the complexity of a function by the complexity of its associated language recognition question.

Although expressing complexity classes in terms of languages is convenient as noted previously, it is also useful to talk about the complexity of computing a function directly. We have seen that it is possible to convert easily between the two notions. Thus, we have the analogous function computation classes FP and FNC, which are sets of functions, not languages.

Definition 3.2.7 *The class* **FP** *is the set of all functions from* $\{0,1\}^*$ *to* $\{0,1\}^*$ *that are computable in sequential time* $n^{O(1)}$.

Definition 3.2.8 *The class* **FNC** *is the set of all functions from* $\{0,1\}^*$ *to* $\{0,1\}^*$ *that are computable in parallel time* $(\log n)^{O(1)}$ *and processors* $n^{O(1)}$.

These two classes are very stable in the sense that the composition of any two functions in the class remains in the class. This property ensures that when we use these classes later to define reducibilities we can easily establish transitivity.

Lemma 3.2.9 *The classes FP and FNC are closed under composition.*

Proof. The proof is left as an exercise for the reader. □

At this point we should remark that many authors use the symbol P (NC) to denote both P and FP (respectively, NC and FNC) relying on context to make the meaning clear.

3.2.2 The Classes NC^k and FNC^k

Under the uniform Boolean circuit family model, NC can be divided into subclasses that differ by a logarithmic factor in depth.

Definition 3.2.10 *For each integer* $k \geq 1$, *the class* **NC^k** *is the set of all languages L, such that L is recognized by a uniform Boolean circuit family* $\{\alpha_n\}$ *with* $\text{size}(\alpha_n) = n^{O(1)}$ *and* $\text{depth}(\alpha_n) = O((\log n)^k)$.

Observe that $NC = \bigcup_{k \geq 1} NC^k$. As two examples, we note that determining the ith bit in the multiplication of two n-bit numbers is in NC^1 and the problem of determining if the rank of a matrix is k is in NC^2.

In a similar manner FNC can be partitioned into the function classes FNC^k, $k \geq 1$. See Appendix D for the formal definition. So, for example, the problem of multiplying two n-bit numbers is in FNC^1. We note that analogous to Lemma 3.2.9, FNC^k is closed under composition.

3.2.3   Random NC

Many search problems have no known FNC algorithm, but they do
have randomized algorithms that find a solution with high probability, and in a feasible highly parallel way. For example, the problem
of computing a maximum matching (Problem B.9.7), and the problem of computing a depth-first search tree (Problem B.9.2). These
and other cases are mentioned in Appendix B.9.

To define RNC, the probabilistic version of NC, we first need
the notion of a *probabilistic circuit*.

Definition 3.2.11 *A* **probabilistic circuit** α *is a Boolean cir-
cuit with ordinary inputs* $x = \langle x_1, \ldots, x_n \rangle$, *random inputs* $z = \langle z_1, \ldots, z_r \rangle$, *and outputs* $y = \langle y_1, \ldots, y_m \rangle$.

For a given distribution of random inputs, the **probability** *that
on input* x, *the output of* α *equals* $b \in \{0,1\}^m$, *written* $P[\alpha(x) = b]$,
is defined to be the fraction of random input strings z *such that* α
outputs b *on input* $\langle x_1, \ldots, x_n, z_1, \ldots, z_r \rangle$.

We say α **computes** f **with error probability** ϵ *if*

$$P[\alpha(x) = f(x)] \geq 1 - \epsilon.$$

The notions of circuit family and uniformity carry over directly
to these types of circuits. The class RNC is defined as follows.

Definition 3.2.12 *Let all random inputs be obtained from a uniform distribution. For each integer* $k \geq 1$, *the class* **RNC^k** *is the
set of all languages* L, *such that* L *is recognized by a uniform probabilistic Boolean circuit family* $\{\alpha_n\}$ *with* $\text{size}(\alpha_n) = n^{O(1)}$ *and*
$\text{depth}(\alpha_n) = O((\log n)^k)$, *and having error probability at most* $1/4$.
The class **RNC** $= \bigcup_{k \geq 1} RNC^k$.

One can also define RNC in terms of randomized PRAMs.

The corresponding function classes, $FRNC^k$ and $FRNC$, are also
important. Definitions for them are provided in Appendix D.

3.3   Reducibility

In Section 3.1 we alluded to the notion of reducing one problem B
to another problem B' by expressing the solution to B in terms of
solutions to B'. When made precise, this concept of reducibility lets
us compare problems for relative difficulty and to characterize the
hardest problems in a complexity class.

3.3.1 Many-one Reducibility

There are two common forms of reducibility. The first is based on transforming an instance of one problem into a single instance of another; the transformation is called a *many-one reduction*. This is the usual kind of reducibility associated with *NP*-completeness results (Karp [193], Garey and Johnson [113]). It is called many-one because many distinct instances of the original problem B can be mapped to a single instance of the new problem B'.

Suppose that we have two languages L and L'. We want to determine if some string x is a member of L. Further suppose that we can transform x into a string y, using a function f, in such a way that y is a member of L' exactly when x is a member of L. That is, $x \in L$ if and only if $f(x) \in L'$. We have reduced L to L' in the sense that if we know how to test membership in L', then we can test membership in L. The function f is called a *reduction*. We use the notation $L \leq_m L'$ to denote that L is many-one reducible to L'.

If we actually know how to decide membership in L', then the complexity of testing $x \in L$ becomes the sum of the complexity of computing $f(x)$ and the complexity of testing whether $f(x) \in L'$. So we are of course interested in the complexity of the reduction, which in the case of many-one reductions is simply the complexity of computing f. We follow convention and denote such a resource bounded reduction by superscripting $\leq_m$ with the name of the *decision* problem complexity class associated with the complexity of the reducing function. In what follows we provide formal definitions for the ideas just presented.

Definition 3.3.1 *A language L is* **many-one reducible** *to a language L', written $L \leq_m L'$, if there is a function f such that $x \in L$ if and only if $f(x) \in L'$.*

We say that L is **P many-one reducible** *to L', written $L \leq_m^P L'$, if and only if the function f is in FP.*

For each $k \geq 1$, we say that L is **NC^k many-one reducible** *to L', written $L \leq_m^{NC^k} L'$, if and only if the function f is in FNC^k.*

We say that L is **NC many-one reducible** *to L', written $L \leq_m^{NC} L'$, if and only if the function f is in FNC.*

Since reductions are usually complicated, we would like to make repeated use of them. The following notion often allows us to do this.

Definition 3.3.2 *Suppose $\leq$ is a reducibility such that whenever $L \leq L'$ and $L' \leq L''$, then $L \leq L''$. We say that $\leq$ is* **transitive**.

Many-one reducibility is transitive. That is, if $x \in L$ if and only if $f(x) \in L'$, and $y \in L'$ if and only if $g(y) \in L''$, then $x \in L$ if and only if $g(f(x)) \in L''$, and so the language L is also reducible to L''. Furthermore, because FP, FNC^k, and FNC are closed under composition (Lemma 3.2.9 and remarks in Section 3.2.2) resource bounded reductions are also transitive.

Lemma 3.3.3 *The reducibilities $\leq_m$, $\leq_m^P$, $\leq_m^{NC^k}$ $(k \geq 1)$, and $\leq_m^{NC}$ are transitive.*

Proof. The proof is left as an exercise for the reader.   □

The next definition is useful for equating problems of the same complexity.

Definition 3.3.4 *Suppose that for some reducibility $\leq$ we have $L \leq L'$ and $L' \leq L$. Then we say that L and L' are* **equivalent** *under $\leq$.*

Often when reducing a language L to a language L', the exact complexity of L' is unknown. Although this gives us no absolute information about the computational complexity of L, it still provides useful information about the relative difficulties of the two languages. In particular, assuming the reduction is not too powerful, it implies that L is no more difficult to decide than L'. It is important to note that if the reduction is allowed too much power, it will mask the complexity of L'. As an extreme example, if polynomial time is allowed for the reduction, then any problem in P can be $\leq_m$ reduced to a trivial problem, such as the problem of deciding whether a given string x is a member of the set $\{1\}$. Note $\{1\}$ can be replaced by any set other than the $\emptyset$ or Σ^*.

Lemma 3.3.5

1. *If $L' \in P$ and $L \leq_m^P L'$, $L \leq_m^{NC^k} L'$, or $L \leq_m^{NC} L'$ then $L \in P$.*

2. *If $L' \in NC^k$ and $L \leq_m^{NC^k} L'$ then $L \in NC^k$.*

3. *If $L' \in NC$ and $L \leq_m^{NC} L'$ then $L \in NC$.*

Proof. The proof is left as an exercise for the reader.   □

As just defined, many-one reductions give us a way of comparing decision problems. The many-one notion can be extended to search problems so that search problem B is reduced to search problem B' by transforming the instance of B into an instance of B', solving B', and transforming the result into a solution for B. In practice, we often need to solve more than a single instance of B', and so such many-one search reductions are not nearly as useful as their generalization to Turing reductions, defined below.

3.3.2 Turing Reducibility

Turing reducibility is a generalization of many-one reducibility. Instead of performing a transformation on the input followed by asking just the single question "Is $f(x) \in L$?," we allow multiple questions, with new questions possibly being a function of the answers to previous questions. In this way, Turing reducibility corresponds to our usual notion of using subroutines to solve larger problems: to solve problem B we make many calls to a subroutine for solving problem B'.

Like many-one reducibility, Turing reducibility is often used to compare problems whose intrinsic difficulty is unknown. Consequently, the notion of complexity for Turing reductions must abstract out the cost of the subroutine to solve the problem, while at the same time accounting for the call in such a way that we get a result analogous to Lemma 3.3.5.

One way of achieving this isolation is to hide the solutions to problem B' behind an interface, called an *oracle*, and to only count the cost of placing questions and obtaining answers from the interface. For example, if we are reducing language L to L', the reduction is done on a machine that is provided with an oracle for answering membership questions to L'. Each oracle call is charged only unit cost. In this way the complexity of the reduction captures the difficulty of reducing L to L' independently of the true complexity of L'.

Oracles can be added to the PRAM model by slightly modifying the input/output conventions used for computations (Definition 2.2.1), and adding a new instruction.

A *B-oracle PRAM* for search problem B is a PRAM with an additional instruction, oracle(s), which behaves as follows: integer k is placed in shared memory cell C_s, and bits $x_1, \ldots, x_k$ encoding instance x of B are placed into shared memory cells $C_{s+1}, \ldots, C_{s+k}$. When the instruction oracle(s) is executed, an integer l is placed in shared memory cell C_s, and the bits $y_1, \ldots, y_l$ of answer y for instance

x are placed into shared memory cells $C_{s+1}, \ldots, C_{s+l}$. Different processors may make simultaneous oracle calls, and are responsible for preventing conflicts in shared memory access.

A Turing reduction is simply a computation by an oracle PRAM.

Definition 3.3.6 *A search problem B is* **Turing reducible** *to a search problem B', written $B \leq_T B'$, if and only if there is a B'-oracle PRAM that solves B.*

We say that B is **P Turing reducible** *to B', written $B \leq_T^P B'$, if and only if the B'-oracle PRAM on inputs of length n uses time $n^{O(1)}$ and processors $n^{O(1)}$.*

We say that B is **NC Turing reducible** *to B', written $B \leq_T^{NC} B'$, if and only if the B'-oracle PRAM on inputs of length n uses time $(\log n)^{O(1)}$ and processors $n^{O(1)}$.*

We discuss NC^k Turing reducibility in Section 3.4.1.

In the most general case, a search problem oracle returns any one of the possible solutions to instance x. Repeated calls for the same instance are not guaranteed to return the same answer. In the case that the search problem is functional, that is, there is a unique answer to every instance, then we can speak of one function f being Turing reducible to another function g. Finally, in the case of a decision problem, the oracle PRAM gives us a way of Turing reducing one language L to another L'.

If the oracle call was actually invoking a computation, then the cost of an oracle call should be a function of the length of the question and resulting answer. However, if we only require a result like that stated below in Lemma 3.3.9, it is sufficient to simply charge an oracle call the same as any other instruction. Since the setup of each bit of the oracle call requires one processor for one time unit, as does interpreting the bits of the result, the length of an oracle call is always less than the processor time product. Hence, on an input of length n, any feasible highly parallel reduction can only make oracle calls of length $n^{O(1)}$.

Lemma 3.3.7 *The reducibilities $\leq_T$, $\leq_T^P$, and $\leq_T^{NC}$ are transitive.*

Proof. The proof is left as an exercise for the reader.   □

Note these concepts, especially P Turing reducibility can be expressed in equivalent forms on other models, such as oracle Turing machines. It is also worth observing that many-one reducibility implies Turing reducibility.

Lemma 3.3.8

1. *If $L \leq_m L'$ then $L \leq_T L'$.*
2. *If $L \leq_m^P L'$ then $L \leq_T^P L'$.*
3. *If $L \leq_m^{NC} L'$ then $L \leq_T^{NC} L'$.*

Proof. Just supply an oracle for L', implement the reducing function f in the oracle PRAM, and ask one question to the oracle. □

We focus on *NC* reducibility because we are interested in transforming problems to one another quickly in parallel. *NC* reducibility lets us preserve complexity in the sense of the following lemma.

Lemma 3.3.9 *If $L \leq_T^{NC} L'$ and $L' \in NC$ ($L' \in P$), then $L \in NC$ (respectively, $L \in P$).*

Proof. Consider $L' \in NC$, and suppose that M' is a PRAM that decides L' in time $t'(n) = (\log n)^{O(1)}$ with $p'(n) = n^{O(1)}$ processors. Suppose that M is an L'-oracle PRAM that decides L. Furthermore, suppose that on an input of length n, M uses time $t(n) = (\log n)^{O(1)}$ with $p(n) = n^{O(1)}$ processors and makes oracle calls of length $l(n) = n^{O(1)}$. M makes at most $p(n)$ simultaneous oracle calls. If we replace each of these oracle calls by direct execution of M', the resulting machine uses at most $p(n) * p'(l(n)) = n^{O(1)}$ processors and takes time at most $t(n) * t'(l(n)) = (\log n)^{O(1)}$. Thus, L' is in NC. A similar argument works when NC is replaced by P. □

Lemmas 3.3.5 and 3.3.9 illustrate why choosing a reducibility *compatible* with the complexity classes that one is studying is important. This notion can be made precise.

Definition 3.3.10 *Let $\leq$ be a resource bounded reducibility, and let C be a complexity class. The reducibility $\leq$ is **compatible** with C if and only if for all problems B and B', when $B \leq B'$, and $B' \in C$ then $B \in C$.*

Lemma 3.3.11 *$\leq_T^{NC}$ reducibility is compatible with the classes P, NC, FP, and FNC.*

Proof. The proof is left as an exercise for the reader. □

For further details we refer the interested reader to the article by Johnson [177].

3.4   Other NC Compatible Reducibilities

When comparing problems in P and NC, any reduction compatible with NC will do. In the following we describe two more useful reductions.

3.4.1 NC^k Turing Reducibility

Suppose that we have two problems, B and B', with $B \leq_T^{NC} B'$. Suppose B' can be solved in $O((\log n)^2)$ time on a CREW-PRAM. Since the reducibility $\leq_T^{NC}$ is compatible with FNC, we know that the algorithm for B' can be used to implement a feasible highly parallel algorithm for B. But, unless we examine the details of the reduction from B to B', we cannot know the actual time complexity of the resulting algorithm.

If the reduction takes time $O(\log n)$, then we know that the algorithm for B has time $O((\log n)^3)$ at worst — at most $O(\log n)$ oracle calls, each of time $O((\log n)^2)$. So replacing the oracle call by the actual solution of B' increases the time to $O((\log n)^3)$ at worst.

Therefore, to obtain more precise time estimates, it is reasonable to consider a subclass of NC reducibility in which the time of the reduction is limited. Unfortunately, our definition of NC reducibility in Section 3.3 was stated in terms of PRAMs. Because of the logarithmic factor sloppiness between different versions of the PRAM model, if we are really interested in the fine details of reductions then we need a more precise model, such as Boolean circuit families.

Definition 3.4.1 *Let B be a search problem. A B-***oracle circuit family*** *is a Boolean circuit family $\{\alpha_n\}$ augmented with oracle gates for problem B. An* **oracle gate** *for B is a vertex with a sequence $\langle x_1, \ldots, x_k \rangle$ of input vertices and a sequence $\langle y_1, \ldots, y_l \rangle$ of output vertices. When given as input an encoding of an instance of problem B, the oracle gate outputs an encoding of a solution of B, provided that l bits is sufficient to contain the full encoding. For the purpose of defining the complexity of α_n, this oracle gate counts as depth $\lceil \log_2(k + l) \rceil$, and size $(k + l)$.*

Note that the output encoding of the oracle gate is usually designed so that it indicates whether the output encodes a complete or only partial result due to lack of sufficiently many output bits.

Oracle circuit families serve the same purpose as oracle PRAMs.

Definition 3.4.2 *For each $k \geq 1$, a search problem B is NC^k **Turing reducible** to a search problem B', written $B \leq_T^{NC^k} B'$, if and only if there is a uniform B'-oracle circuit family $\{\alpha_n\}$ that solves B, and has $\mathrm{depth}(\alpha_n) = O((\log n)^k)$ and $\mathrm{size}(\alpha_n) = n^{O(1)}$.*

Lemma 3.4.3 *Let B and B' be search problems. $B \leq_T^{NC} B'$ if and only if $B \leq_T^{NC^k} B'$ for some k.*

Proof. The proof is left as an exercise for the reader. □

Cook originally introduced the notion of NC^1 Turing reducibility for the purposes of studying subclasses of NC, such as those functions reducible to the problem of computing the determinant of an integer matrix [67]. NC^1 Turing reducibility has the advantage of preserving circuit depth — if $L \leq_T^{NC^1} L'$ and $L' \in NC^k$, then $L \in NC^k$. That is, $\leq_T^{NC^1}$ is compatible with NC^k for each $k \geq 1$.

NC^1 Turing reducibility can be used to establish the depth equivalence of problems, even though their precise complexities may be unknown. For example, Beame, Cook, and Hoover show that binary division, powering, and iterated product are all equivalent under $\leq_T^{NC^1}$ reducibility [26]. Thus, if one of these can be solved by an $O(\log n)$ depth uniform Boolean circuit family, then so can the other two. They fail to find a polynomial size $O(\log n)$ depth, logarithmic space uniform, family of circuits for any of the problems. However, by relaxing the notion of uniformity somewhat, they construct a P-uniform logarithmic depth circuit family for the iterated product. The NC^1 equivalence then places all three problems in small depth.

Note, any $\leq_m^{NC^1}$ reduction is also an $\leq_T^{NC^1}$ reduction. It is also worth noting that many NC reductions in the literature are in fact $\leq_m^{NC^1}$ reductions, and one could consider requiring only NC^1 reductions (either many-one or Turing) in order to ensure that depth is preserved across the reduction.

However, there is an advantage to sticking with NC reducibility. Firstly, one would always have to use circuits to describe the reductions because of the sloppiness between PRAM models. In addition, Ruzzo shows that for many different notions of uniformity, the class NC^k is stable for each $k \geq 2$, but there may be a difference for NC^1 [308]. One avoids this issue completely with NC reducibility and obtains a very stable notion of reduction.

3.4.2   Logarithmic Space Reducibility

The original P-completeness results were motivated by the question, still unresolved, of whether P equals polylogarithmic space (Cook [64], Jones and Laaser [181]). These results used logarithmic space reducibility as do many of the results currently appearing in the literature.

Definition 3.4.4 *A language L is* **logarithmic space reducible** *to a language L', denoted $L \leq_m^{log} L'$ if there exists a function f, computable in logarithmic space on a Turing machine, such that $x \in L$ if and only if $f(x) \in L'$.*

The reason for choosing logarithmic space reducibility is because such reductions are compatible with polynomial time, polylogarithmic space, or both combined. For example, if L is logarithmic space reducible to L', and if L' is in polynomial time, polylogarithmic space, or both simultaneously, then L is in the corresponding complexity class.

It should be noted that any logarithmic space reduction is also an NC many-one reduction (more precisely an NC^2 many-one reduction) as a consequence of the small space transitive closure simulation of Borodin [40].

3.5   Completeness

We introduced reductions to relate problems. Now we use them to relate a problem to an entire complexity class. The variants of many-one and Turing reductions given so far, which involve logarithmic space or NC, are compatible with NC; consequently, we can use the NC Turing reductions for any hardness results. In practice, we will state results using the weakest form of reducibility possible down to NC^1 many-one reducibility.

Suppose that we have two languages, L and L', with $L \leq_m^{NC} L'$. Lemma 3.3.5 tells us that if $L' \in NC$, then so is L, but it also tells us that if $L \notin NC$, then neither is L'. Thus, when attempting to understand the actual complexity of L and L', we can take two approaches: show that there is an NC membership test for L' by finding an NC upper bound, or show that no NC membership test for L is possible, say by proving a parallel polynomial time lower bound. Of course, we can make an even stronger statement about their complexity when we also have $L' \leq_m^{NC} L$. That is, L and L' are equivalent. In this case, an upper or lower bound for either one gives an upper or lower bound for the other.

Now consider the question of whether NC equals P. To distinguish these two classes, we need only find one problem in P that provably is not solvable in NC. Unfortunately, all attempts at finding such a problem have failed. However, the likely candidates for such problems have two interesting properties. The first is that they are all equivalent under NC Turing reductions. Consequently, a proof that any one is inherently sequential results in an entire class of inherently sequential problems. The second property is that every problem in P is NC Turing reducible to any of the candidate hard problems. This means that a feasible highly parallel algorithm for any one problem would imply NC equals P.

We call problems that capture the difficulty intrinsic to a class the *complete* problems for the class.

Definition 3.5.1 *A language L is* **P-hard** **under** NC **reducibility** *if $L' \leq_T^{NC} L$ for every $L' \in P$. A language L is* **P-complete** **under** NC **reducibility** *if $L \in P$ and L is P-hard.*

When we say a problem is P-hard, we are indicating that it is as difficult to solve as any other problem in P. Stating it is P-complete adds the additional information that the problem is in fact in P. Since all problems in P are decision problems, only a decision problem can be P-complete. But many search problems with polynomial time solutions also have the property that any language in P can be reduced to them. That is, they are P-hard. Since such problems cannot be P-complete, how should they be classified to indicate that they also capture the essential difficulty of polynomial time computations? Those search problems that are actually functions can be classified as FP-complete as follows.

Definition 3.5.2 *A function problem B is* **P-hard** **under** NC **reducibility** *if $L \leq_T^{NC} B$ for every $L \in P$. A function problem B is* **FP-complete** *if $B \in FP$ and B is P-hard.*

However, many search problems can only be stated as relations. For example, the problem of finding a spanning tree. Their solutions are not unique, so the problems are not in FP nor do such problems have their own named complexity class. We call such problems *quasi-P-complete.*

Definition 3.5.3 *A search problem B is* **P-hard** **under** NC **re-**
ducibility *if* $L \leq_T^{NC} B$ *for every* $L \in P$. *A search problem B is*
quasi-P-complete *if it has a polynomial time solution and is P-*
hard.

The key result allowing us to relate P-completeness to fast parallel computation is the following theorem.

Theorem 3.5.4 *If any P-complete problem is in NC then NC*
equals P.

Proof. The proof is left as an exercise for the reader.   □

There is considerable evidence, as the following chapters will illustrate, leading to the belief that NC and P are distinct classes.
Therefore, to say that a problem is P-complete is to say that it is
very unlikely to have an NC solution.

In Chapter 4 it is shown that the Circuit Value Problem (Definition 4.2.1) is P-complete. Thus, the question of whether every
feasible sequential problem has a highly parallel solution is equivalent to the following problem.

> *Given a polynomial size Boolean circuit, can its output*
> *be computed in polylogarithmic time using a polynomial*
> *number of processors?*

If it can, then NC equals P.

Chapter 4

Two Basic *P*-Complete Problems

We have now provided sufficient machinery to address the question posed in the introduction: Does every problem with a feasible sequential solution also have a highly parallel solution? We begin by asking the dual question.

Are there any inherently sequential problems?

We will try to develop some intuition for the answer to this question by closely examining two basic *P*-complete problems: the Generic Machine Simulation Problem and the Circuit Value Problem, both introduced below.

4.1 The Generic *P*-Complete Problem

The canonical device for performing sequential computations is the Turing machine, with its single processor and serial access to memory. Of course, the usual machines that we call sequential are not nearly so primitive, but fundamentally they all suffer from the same bottleneck created by having just one processor. So to say that a problem is inherently sequential is to say that solving it on a parallel machine is not substantially better than solving it on a Turing machine.

What could be more sequential than the problem of simulating a Turing machine computation? If we could just discover how to simulate efficiently, in parallel, every Turing machine that uses polynomial time, then every feasible sequential computation could be translated automatically into a highly parallel form. Thus, we are interested in the following problem. (See also Problem A.12.1 in Part II for related problems and remarks.)

Definition 4.1.1 *Generic Machine Simulation Problem (GMSP)*
Given: *A string x, a description $\overline{M}$ of a Turing machine M, and an integer t coded in unary. (To be precise, the input is the string $x\#\overline{M}\#^t$, where $\#$ is a delimiter character not otherwise present in the string.)*
Problem: *Does M accept x within t steps?*

Intuitively at least, it is easy to see that this problem is solvable in polynomial time sequentially — just interpret M's program step-by-step on input x until either M accepts or t steps have been simulated, whichever comes first. Such a step by step simulation of an arbitrary Turing machine by a fixed one is exactly the essence of the famous result that universal Turing machines exist. Given a reasonable encoding $\overline{M}$ of M, the simulation of it by the universal machine will take time polynomial in t and the lengths of x and $\overline{M}$, which in turn is polynomial in the length of the universal machine's input. (This is why we insist that t be encoded in *unary*.) See, for example, Hopcroft and Ullman [161, 162] for details of the universal machine's construction.

Reducing an arbitrary language L in P to the Generic Machine Simulation Problem is easy. Let M_L be a Turing machine recognizing L in polynomial time and let $p(n) = n^{O(1)}$ be an easy-to-compute upper bound on that running time. To accomplish the reduction, given a string x, simply generate the string $f(x) = x\#\overline{M_L}\#^{p(|x|)}$. Then $f(x)$ will be a "yes" instance of the Generic Machine Simulation Problem if and only if x is in L.

This transformation is easily performed by an NC^1 circuit (see Definition 3.2.10) as follows. First, note the string $\#\overline{M_L}\#$ is constant, independent of x, and that the string $1^{p(|x|)}$ is constant for any fixed $n = |x|$. Thus, for fixed n, the circuit that accomplishes the transformation for inputs x of length n simply outputs a copy of its input x followed by the *fixed* string $\#\overline{M_L}\#^{p(|x|)}$. This can be done by an n-input bounded fanin circuit α_n of small depth, in fact, one of constant depth. Basically, α_n consists of a sequence of n input gates, each of which computes the identity function, followed by a fixed sequence of constant gates computing the successive bits of $\#\overline{M_L}\#$, followed by $p(n)$ gates computing the constant "1." Each gate is also an output gate. Finally, note that the circuit family

$\{\alpha_n\}$ is highly uniform. The most difficult part of constructing α_n given n is to compute $p(n)$, which is easy since $p(n)$ can be chosen to have a very simple form, say $2^{k\lceil \log(n+1)\rceil}$ for some k being an integer power of 2. Note that $\lceil \log(n+1)\rceil$ is just the number of bits needed to express n in binary. Thus, the binary representation of $p(n)$ is a single one bit followed by some number of zero bits, where that number is determined by appending $\log k$ zeros to $\lceil \log(n+1)\rceil$. Hence, the uniformity computations are reduced to little more than counting and shifting.

In summary, we have shown the following theorem.

Theorem 4.1.2 *The Generic Machine Simulation Problem is P-complete under* $\leq_m^{NC^1}$ *reductions.*

4.2 The Circuit Value Problem

One obvious drawback of tackling the Generic Machine Simulation Problem directly is its generality. It is hard to see how one could take an arbitrary Turing machine program and, without any hints as to what problem it is solving, produce a highly parallel simulation. Instead, it might be useful to study a very simple problem that captures all the computational power of Turing machines and, in addition, has some obvious parallel aspects that could potentially be exploited.

As an analogy in the theory of *NP*-completeness, consider the Generic *Non*deterministic Machine Simulation Problem versus Satisfiability. Both are *NP*-complete, but the simplicity of the later problem has made it a valuable starting point for a wide variety of investigations. The *P*-complete problem analogous to Satisfiability is the *Circuit Value Problem* (CVP) proposed by Ladner [225]. (Also see Problem A.1.1 and related problems in Part II.)

Definition 4.2.1 *Circuit Value Problem (CVP)*
Given: *An encoding $\overline{\alpha}$ of a Boolean circuit α, inputs $x_1, \ldots, x_n$, and a designated output y.*
Problem: *Is output y of α TRUE on input $x_1, \ldots, x_n$?*

The formal statement of CVP requires a language for describing Boolean circuits. There are a variety of suitable choices. For definiteness, we will use the standard encoding, specified in Definition 2.3.4. It is worth noting that the formulation of CVP permits us to ask for the value of any gate of α, not just one of the outputs, by simply designating the gate as an output.

It is easy to see that the Circuit Value Problem is solvable sequentially in polynomial time. Simply make one pass through the circuit from inputs to outputs (that is, in topological order) evaluating each gate based on the values already computed for its immediate predecessors.

The fact that any polynomial time computation can be represented as a circuit evaluation problem is also easy to see, at least at an intuitive level. Ordinary digital computers are essentially built from Boolean logic circuits, and a polynomial time computation can "activate" at most a polynomial number of these gates. Therefore, a reduction of an arbitrary polynomial time computation to an instance of the Circuit Value Problem basically involves "unrolling" the machine's "wiring diagram" to produce the circuit activated by the computation. In outline, we have shown the following basic P-completeness result.

Theorem 4.2.2 (Ladner [225]) *The Circuit Value Problem is P-complete under $\leq_m^{NC^1}$ reductions.*

In the formal proof of this fact we will find it easier to simulate Turing machines by circuits, rather than more realistic digital computers. Even so, the proof is somewhat technical, and is deferred to Chapter 6.

Armed with the two basic P-complete problems introduced in this chapter, we can now answer the fundamental question raised in the introduction. We do not believe that every problem with a feasible sequential solution has a feasible highly parallel solution; specifically, we believe P-complete problems are inherently sequential. The explanation of our answer is the subject of the next chapter.

Chapter 5

Evidence That NC Does Not Equal P

5.1 Introduction

Why should we believe that NC does not equal P? One form of evidence is that many people have tried, but failed, to show them equal. More persuasive, perhaps, is the way they have failed, or rather, the character of the limited successes. Specifically, known approaches consistently leave a large gap between what we know how to solve by highly parallel algorithms, and general problems in P. In outline, the state of the art is as follows.

General simulations are not fast: The best known parallel simulations of general sequential models give very modest improvements, basically reducing sequential time T to parallel time $T/\log T$ or $\sqrt{T}$, depending on the parallel model. Furthermore, $2^{T^{\Omega(1)}}$ processors are needed to achieve even these modest improvements.

Fast simulations are not general: Rapid simulations of sequential models by highly parallel models are known only for rather weak sequential models.

Natural approaches provably fail: Certain natural approaches to highly parallel simulation are provably insufficient. Equivalently, in certain natural *structured* models of computation (Borodin [41]), one can prove that the analogs of NC and P are not equal, and indeed are separated by a nearly exponential gap, as suggested by the two points above.

In this chapter we will present this evidence in more detail. The nature of the available evidence renders this chapter, especially Section 5.4, somewhat more technical than the rest of Part I. The reader may wish to skim or skip it, at least on first reading.

5.2   General Simulations Are Not Fast

First, consider the Generic Machine Simulation Problem introduced in Section 4.1. Intuitively, why should we expect this problem to be hard to parallelize? Notice that we defined the problem in terms of Turing machines as a technical convenience; they are not in any way fundamental to the result. Theorem 4.1.2 remains true if we rephrase the Generic Machine Simulation Problem so that $\overline{M}$ becomes a *program* in FORTRAN, C, Pascal, Lisp, or any other reasonable programming language. The universal machine in the proof simply becomes an *interpreter* for that language. Thus, a highly parallel solution to the Generic Machine Simulation Problem would be precisely a programming language interpreter that is able to achieve highly parallel execution on completely *arbitrary* programs.

Is such a highly parallel interpreter likely? We believe it is not. In general, program code is remarkably opaque — our ability to mechanically deduce nontrivial properties of programs given just the text of the program is severely limited. Indeed, many such questions are undecidable, and many decidable ones are provably computationally infeasible. Feasible properties, such as those exploited by optimizing compilers, tend to be very syntactic, local, or relatively simplistic. In particular, compiler optimizations rarely make radical alterations to the set of intermediate values computed by a program, to the method by which they are computed, or even to the order in which they are computed. Such transformations would certainly be necessary to achieve a highly parallel Generic Simulation.

Additionally, experience to date has been that, while highly parallel algorithms are known for a large number of interesting problems in P, in many cases *all* such algorithms are strikingly different from good sequential algorithms for the same problem. The excellent survey by Karp and Ramachandran contains a number of examples of this nature [195]. In particular, automatic generation of these parallel algorithms from their sequential counterparts is far beyond the current state of the art in parallelizing compilers. Empirically, such compilers usually attain speedups of no more than a small constant factor, say 5 to 10, reaching perhaps a factor of 50 on rare occasions. While such achievements are impressive, and of undeniable practical importance, they fall far short of satisfying the demand for highly parallel algorithms to exploit the potentials of machines with hundreds or thousands of processors that are now becoming commercially available, let alone of answering the theoretical question we have posed.

The best methods known for speedup of general sequential computations give very limited speedup, and even then only at a very high cost. Paterson and Valiant have shown that for any bounded fanin Boolean circuit of size T, there exists an equivalent circuit of depth $O(T/\log T)$ (requiring size $2^{\Omega(T/\log T)}$) [282]. Dymond and Tompa present analogous results for Turing machines, showing that any Turing machine running in time T can be simulated by a uniform circuit of depth $O(T/\log T)$ (again, requiring size $2^{\Omega(T/\log T)}$) [102]. For bounded fanin parallel models, these are the best results known.

As noted in Chapter 2, unbounded fanin models are often faster than bounded fanin ones. As another example of this, Dymond and Tompa [102] also show that any Turing machine running in time T can be simulated by a CREW-PRAM running in time $O(\sqrt{T})$ (but again at the cost of an enormous number of processors — $2^{\omega(\sqrt{T})}$). The simulation involves precomputation in parallel of the (huge) table giving the ($\sqrt{T}$)-step transition function of the simulated Turing machine, after which it can be simulated rapidly by repeated table look-ups. Using a more complex table-building idea, Mak shows how to simulate a unit cost sequential random access machine (RAM) by a CREW-PRAM in time $O(\sqrt{T}\log T)$ (again, at the cost of an increase in the number of processors that is exponential in the time bound) [252]. See also Reif [299] for earlier, somewhat weaker results of this form, and Mak [251] and Parberry [281, Section 6.2] for related results.

In the case when the number of processors of the simulating parallel machine is *feasibly* bounded, little is known. In this case, the PRAM results of Dymond and Tompa, and of Reif can be modified to give constant factor speedups, but no stronger results are known.

5.3 Fast Simulations Are Not General

Another perspective on the difficulty of parallelizing the Generic Machine Simulation Problem can be obtained by looking at classes of algorithms for which automatic parallelization *is known to be possible*. In other words, for what restricted classes of (sequential) machines M is the problem known to be in NC? A handful of results of this flavor are known. We will describe four below. Three of the four examples have the following general characteristics (the remaining example is more specialized). Each class of machines allows running times that are at least polynomial, yet the computations in each class have certain special characteristics that have been exploited to allow highly parallel simulation. In each case the machine class is defined by simultaneously restricting two resources (for example, time and space). It is also true in each case that relaxing the constraint on one of the resources by a nearly exponential amount, from polylogarithmic to polynomial, gives a class that is known to equal P. Thus, we can conclude that NC equals P if and only if a nearly exponential increase in this resource adds no power to the model. Finally, in each case the *known* highly parallel simulation degrades to a polynomial time one, or worse, when applied to the relaxed variant.

It is difficult to give a simple intuitive characterization of the features making these machines amenable to parallelization, but the fact that different portions of their computations are only loosely coupled is perhaps a common thread. This is not a feature that is evident in the Generic Machine Simulation Problem. Table 5.1 summarizes the results discussed below.

For our first example, if M is a finite state machine, then the language it accepts is in NC^1. More generally, the output string produced by a one-way finite state transducer can be constructed in NC^1 by an application of the parallel prefix algorithm (Ladner and Fischer [226]; see also Blelloch [35, 36], Kruskal, Rudolph, and Snir [223], Ofman [273]). (This is the specialized example alluded to above; simple generalizations of finite state machines accept only languages in P, but not all such languages.)

For our second example, if M is a Turing machine that uses only logarithmic space, then the language it accepts is in NC^2 (Borodin [40]).

Both results have a similar intuitive justification — since M carries very little state information as it performs its computation, the first and second halves of its computation are only loosely coupled. More precisely, one can afford to simulate (recursively) the second half of the computation in parallel with the first, by trying in parallel *all* states that might be the state at the midpoint, and then select-

Model	Resource 1	Resource 2	Max R2 $\mathcal{C} \subseteq NC$	Min R2 $\mathcal{C} \supseteq P$
DTM	Time $= n^{O(1)}$	Space	$\log n$	$n^{O(1)}$
DTM	Time $= n^{O(1)}$	Reversals	$(\log n)^{O(1)}$	$n^{O(1)}$
D- or NauxPDA	$2^{\text{Space}} = n^{O(1)}$	log(Time)	$(\log n)^{O(1)}$	$n^{O(1)}$
Alternating TM	$2^{\text{Space}} = n^{O(1)}$	log(Treesize)	$(\log n)^{O(1)}$	$n^{O(1)}$
Uniform Circuit	Size $= n^{O(1)}$	Depth	$(\log n)^{O(1)}$	$n^{O(1)}$
PRAM	Procs $= n^{O(1)}$	Time	$(\log n)^{O(1)}$	$n^{O(1)}$

Let $\mathcal{C}$ be the class of languages accepted by machines of any type in the first column, with Resource 1 polynomially bounded, and some simultaneous bound on Resource 2.

"Max R2" gives the maximum consumption of Resource 2 for which $\mathcal{C} \subseteq NC$ is known.

"Min R2" gives the minimum consumption of Resource 2 for which $\mathcal{C} \supseteq P$ is known.

In all cases shown, $\mathcal{C} \subseteq P$, independent of Resource 2, so $\mathcal{C} \supseteq P$ implies $\mathcal{C} = P$. In all cases except the first row, with Resource 2 usage $(\log n)^{O(1)}$, $\mathcal{C} = NC$.

Table 5.1: The Gap Between Generic NC Simulations and P.

ing the correct second half after the state resulting from the first half is known. (A related idea underlies Savitch's Theorem [322].) A logarithmic space bounded Turing machine necessarily runs for only a polynomial number of steps (or else is in an infinite loop), so such machines only accept languages in P. Do they accept *all* languages in P? This is a long-standing open problem. Note, however, that many polynomial time algorithms use polynomial space as well, so this question has an affirmative answer only if every polynomial time, polynomial space algorithm can be converted to one using polynomial time but only logarithmic space.

For our third example, M can be an $O(\log n)$ space- and $2^{(\log n)^{O(1)}}$ time-bounded auxiliary pushdown automaton, or an $O(\log n)$ space- and $2^{(\log n)^{O(1)}}$ treesize-bounded alternating Turing machine (Ruzzo [307, 308]). We will not define these classes here; suffice it to say that both are generalizations of logarithmic space bounded Turing machines. As one example of the power of such machines, the polynomial time/treesize case, where we consider the exponents in both cases above to be $O(\log n)$, essentially corresponds to context-free language recognition. (Indeed, CFL parse trees were the major motivating example for the investigation of treesize bounds on alternating Turing machines. Connections between CFLs and pushdown automata are well known.) Containment of the bounded treesize classes in NC is basically a generalization of the method described above — since the machine's space bound is small, different subtrees are only loosely coupled, hence a large tree can be decomposed into a few trees of about half the size, each solved (recursively) in parallel, then recombined to solve the global problem. Tree contraction (Miller and Reif [259, 260, 261]) is a bottom-up method essentially equivalent to this top-down one. (See also Abrahamson *et al.* [1], Cole and Vishkin [57], Gazit, Miller, and Teng [114], He [151], Karp and Ramachandran [195], Kosaraju and Delcher [220], and Mayr [253]). The restricted storage access regimen of a pushdown automaton allows analogous efficient solutions. With the stated resource bounds, these classes characterize NC — that is, a language is in NC if and only if it is accepted by such a machine. Allowing their time/treesize bound to increase to $2^{n^{O(1)}}$ from $2^{(\log n)^{O(1)}}$ allows the machines to recognize any language in P (Chandra, Kozen, and Stockmeyer [49] and Cook [61]). Since the running time for the parallel algorithm sketched above is roughly the logarithm of the treesize, this algorithm would use polynomial time to simulate an alternating Turing machine with the larger treesize bound. Similar remarks apply to auxiliary pushdown automata. Thus, although this algorithm suffices to provide a highly parallel simulation of some feasible sequential computations, it clearly does not suffice for all of them. A nearly exponential gap remains between what can be simulated in NC and what would be required to simulate all of P.

As our fourth and final example, M can be a polynomial time and polylogarithmic *reversal bounded* Turing machine (Pippenger [285]). In a Turing machine computation a *reversal* occurs when any tape head first moves, or moves in the direction opposite to its last move. The key observation is that between reversals (a *phase*), the machine acts like a finite state transducer, and so by the first example above, each phase can be simulated quickly in parallel. Pippenger also shows a converse result — any polynomial processor, polylogarithmic time parallel algorithm can be simulated by a polynomial time, polylogarithmic reversal Turing machine, and thus the latter class exactly characterizes NC. The key observation in this direction of the simulation is that one parallel time step can be simulated with few ($O(\log n)$) reversals by using a sorting subroutine to gather operands of, and distribute results from, the (independent) operations performed in that step. Returning to the question of whether this class might equal P, note that general polynomial time Turing machines might make a *polynomial* number of reversals, rather than only polylogarithmic, and so are perhaps much more powerful. The notion of reversal has been generalized to other models including RAMs (Hong [157]), but the basic result remains unchanged — NC equals polylogarithmic reversals, P equals polynomial reversals, and hence NC equals P if and only if this nearly exponential increase in reversals adds no power.

In summary, in all known cases where a class of sequential machines accepts only languages in NC, the machines are very restricted. If a related class is known that accepts arbitrary languages in P, then the machines consume exponentially more of some resource to recognize such languages.

As an historical note, it was in recognition of Pippenger's surprising characterization of polynomial size, polylogarithmic depth uniform circuits [285] that Stephen A. Cook christened the class NC, for "Nick's Class." In return, Nicholas J. Pippenger dubbed the class of languages recognized by polynomial time, polylogarithmic space Turing machines, SC, for "Steve's Class," in recognition of Cook's surprising demonstration that deterministic context-free languages are in this class (Cook [65], von Braunmühl *et al.* [367]). Part of the motivation for interest in SC is an anomaly in Table 5.1. One might conjecture that the first row, (the polynomial time, logarithmic space case) should behave like the others, in that polynomial time and polylogarithmic space should provide yet another characterization for NC. Further support for this conjecture comes from the fact that Turing machine time and circuit size are polynomially related (Pippenger and Fischer [289], Savage [317]), as are Turing machine space and circuit depth (Borodin [40]); hence, it is natural to suspect that these two relations should hold simultaneously. However, Cook conjectures that this is not the case, and that directed *s-t* connectivity is an example of a problem in $NC - SC$ [65].

5.4   Natural Approaches Provably Fail

Another line of evidence supporting the conjecture that NC and P are different is the following. Certain approaches to highly parallel simulation of arbitrary polynomial time sequential computations have occurred naturally to many people who have studied the problem. To date, these approaches have been fruitless. In many of these cases, one can prove that the failure of the approach is intrinsic. To be more precise, one can formulate an abstract model that embodies the essence of the approach in a fairly general setting, and prove that in this abstract model, it is impossible to achieve a result strong enough to show that NC equals P.

Prime examples of this style of evidence concern "pebbling." By results of Borodin, any NC algorithm can be simulated using small (polylogarithmic) space, basically by doing a depth-first traversal of the circuit [40]. (The relationship between sequential space and parallel time is one aspect of the so-called Parallel Computation Thesis. See Section 1.3, Chandra and Stockmeyer [50], Goldschlager [126], Dymond and Cook [99, 100], and Parberry [280, 281].) Thus, if $P \subseteq NC$, then the Circuit Value Problem is solvable in small space. The naive algorithm for CVP that evaluates gates in topological order obviously uses a large amount of space, since it eventually stores the value of every gate. Some savings may be attained by discarding a gate's value after all its immediate successors have been evaluated, but the improvement is not asymptotically significant in the worst case. A natural approach to achieve greater space savings (at the expense of time) is to discard certain values even before all successors have been evaluated, and to recompute them when needed. Pebbling models this process.

Pebbling a circuit or other directed acyclic graph proceeds according to the following rules. A pebble placed on a gate represents the fact that the value of that gate is stored. A pebble may be removed from a gate at any time (corresponding to discarding the associated value and freeing its storage), or placed on an input at any time, but may not be placed on any other gate unless all of its immediate predecessors are pebbled (corresponding to (re-)evaluating the gate based on the stored values of its predecessors). The goal of the process is to pebble the circuit's output vertex. "Space" in the pebbling model is the maximum number of pebbles simultaneously present on the circuit, and "time" is the number of pebble placements. This seems to be a very natural model of algorithms for circuit evaluation. Indeed, although the model is restricted in that it cannot represent situations where *combinations* of gate values are stored in a single location, there are no known algorithms that exploit this potential behavior in any substantive way — essentially all known algorithms for CVP fit the pebbling model, or variants of it.

How few pebbles suffice to solve CVP? Clearly any n-vertex graph can be pebbled using n pebbles in time n, by following topological order. Paul, Tarjan, and Celoni have shown that there are n-vertex graphs that cannot be pebbled using fewer than $\Omega(n/\log n)$ pebbles [283]. Furthermore, Lengauer and Tarjan have extended the results to show that to pebble these graphs using $O(n/\log n)$ pebbles requires time $2^{n^{\Omega(1)}}$ [230]. Note that these are not just lower bounds on a specific algorithm. Instead, they show that *every* algorithm in the broad class of potential algorithms that follow the pebbling paradigm necessarily uses a large amount of space in the worst case. Thus, if pebbling algorithms were the only avenue for attaining small space solutions to CVP, we would have a proof that *NC* and *P* are distinct. Similar lower bounds are known for variants of the pebbling model, including black-and-white pebbling (Cook and Sethi [69]) and two-person pebbling (Dymond and Tompa [102]).

There is an extensive literature on pebbling. See the survey by Pippenger [286], and more recent papers by Pippenger [287, 288], Wilber [373], Venkateswaran [362], and Venkateswaran and Tompa [363] for other results and variants on the model.

5.5 Summary

In summary, the known speedups for arbitrary sequential models are modest, and/or come at the cost of an enormous number of processors. The sequential models for which we know highly parallel simulations seem on the face of it to be comparatively weak relatives of polynomial time Turing machines. Among the models discussed above, finite state machines provably cannot compute all polynomial time computable functions, and the other models require a nearly exponential increase in one resource before we can prove equivalence to P. Intuitively, this seems like a large gulf between NC and P. To date all approaches at bridging this gulf have failed, and broad classes of appealing natural approaches, like pebbling algorithms, provably must fail.

However, compelling though this evidence may be, it is ultimately inconclusive. It does not *prove* that a feasible highly parallel solution to the Generic Machine Simulation Problem is impossible. While we know, by the space hierarchy theorem [148], that $NC \neq PSPACE$, it is still possible, for example, that NC equals P, or NP, or even PH. It is safe to say, however, that any such result would be a significant breakthrough, with potentially dramatic practical implications.

Chapter 6

The Circuit Value Problem

In this chapter we return to the Circuit Value Problem, introduced in Section 4.2. First, we will give the formal proof of Theorem 4.2.2 that CVP is P-complete, which we only sketched previously. Then we will show that a number of useful variants and restricted versions of CVP are also P-complete.

6.1 The Circuit Value Problem Is P-Complete

Recall the definition of the Circuit Value Problem (Definition 4.2.1) in which given an encoding $\overline{\alpha}$ of a Boolean circuit α, a designated output y, and values for the inputs $x_1, \ldots, x_n$, we ask if output y of α is TRUE.

To show CVP is P-complete under $\leq_m^{NC^1}$ reducibility requires showing CVP is in P, and that each language L in P is $\leq_m^{NC^1}$ reducible to CVP. It is easy to see that given the encoding $\overline{\alpha}$ of a circuit and the values of its inputs, one can compute the value of each gate in a number of steps that is polynomial in the size of α. On a random access machine this can be done in linear time by considering the gates in topological order (which also can be computed in linear time; see Cormen, Leiserson, and Rivest [70], for example). On a deterministic Turing machine the process is a bit more clumsy but can still be done in polynomial time. Pippenger shows that even time $O(n \log n)$ suffices, where n is the length of the encoding of α [284]. Thus, we have the following lemma.

Lemma 6.1.1 *The Circuit Value Problem is in P.*

The more difficult step in proving that CVP is P-complete under $\leq_m^{NC^1}$ reducibility is showing there is a $\leq_m^{NC^1}$ reduction from each language in P to CVP. Ladner proved this by simulating Turing machines with circuits. The idea is as follows. First, recall that for each language L in P, there is a 1-tape Turing machine M that on input $x = x_1, \ldots, x_n$ halts in time $t(n) = n^{O(1)}$ with output equal to 1 if and only if x is in L. Note that, for each n, the machine M uses at most $t(n)$ space on its tape.

The entire computation of M is captured by the answers to the following questions. For $1 \leq i, j \leq t(n)$, at time i, what is the contents of tape cell j, is M's tape head positioned at cell j, and if so what is M's state? These are not easy questions to answer in isolation, but the answer to each is a simple function of the answers to the same questions for tape cells $j - 1$, j, and $j + 1$ at time $i - 1$. These functions are easily computed by a Boolean circuit of size $O(1)$, and hence the entire computation can be described by a Boolean circuit, β_n, of size $O(t^2(n))$ whose input is the input to M, and whose single output bit indicates whether or not M accepts the input. The key to the reduction will be to produce β_n in parallel efficiently.

The following lemma shows how this is done.

Lemma 6.1.2 (Ladner [225]) *If $L \in P$, then $L \leq_m^{NC^1} CVP$.*

Proof. As is customary, we assume M has its input in adjacent positions of the input tape with the tape head initially positioned over x_1. Without loss of generality, we can assume M never moves left of the initial position of its input head and halts with its head back at the initial position with the output bit written in the initial position. Consider an input to M of length n. Since M runs in time $t(n)$, its head can touch at most $t(n)+1$ tape cells. We will construct a circuit β_n that simulates M on the first $t(n) + 1$ tape cells.

Associated with each tape cell at each time step we have a *representation* r, consisting of two quantities — contents and state. The *contents* indicates the value stored in the tape cell. The *state* specifies whether the head of M is positioned over the cell, and if so, also specifies the internal state of M at that time. Suppose M has tape alphabet Σ and state set Q with $\Sigma \cap Q = \emptyset$. The representation for a given cell is encoded by $|\Sigma| + |Q| + 1$ bits r^a, $a \in \Sigma \cup Q \cup \{\neg\}$ in the obvious way: bit r^σ is TRUE for $\sigma \in \Sigma$ if and only if the contents

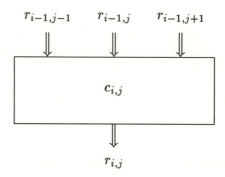

Figure 6.1.1: The $c_{i,j}$ Subcircuit.

is σ, and r^q is TRUE for $q \in Q$ if and only if the head is positioned over the cell and M's internal state is q. Bit $r^{\neg}$ is TRUE if and only if the head is not positioned over the cell.

The circuit simulating M will compute the representation $r_{i,j}$ of each cell j, $1 \leq j \leq t(n) + 1$, for each time i, $0 \leq i \leq t(n)$. It is also convenient to handle certain boundary conditions by introducing "dummy" cell representations for $r_{i,j}$ with $j = 0$ and $j = t(n)+2$ for all i, $0 \leq i \leq t(n)$. For $j = 0$ and $j = t(n) + 2$ and all i the representation $r_{i,j}$ is the same — the contents is the blank tape symbol b, and the head is not positioned there. That is, $r_{i,j}^{b}$ and $r_{i,j}^{\neg}$ are TRUE and all other bits of $r_{i,j}$ are FALSE. Similarly, the representations $r_{0,j}$ for $1 \leq j \leq t(n)+1$ are directly computed from the input — the contents of $r_{0,j}$ is the jth symbol of $x_1 \cdots x_n b^{t(n)+1-n}$, and the head is positioned over x_1 in M's initial state.

Representations of the remaining cells are computed by a $t(n) \times (t(n) + 1)$ array of identical subcircuits $c_{i,j}$, $1 \leq i \leq t(n)$, $1 \leq j \leq t(n) + 1$, connected in a regular way as follows. Subcircuit $c_{i,j}$ simulates the ith step of M on tape cell j, thus computing $r_{i,j}$. The inputs to $c_{i,j}$ are $r_{i-1,j+d}$ for $d \in \{-1, 0, 1\}$. Figure 6.1.1 depicts the $c_{i,j}$ subcircuit.

Each subcircuit $c_{i,j}$ performs as follows based on the transition function of M:

1. If $r_{i-1,j}$ indicates the head is positioned over the jth cell at the start of the ith step, then the contents portion of $r_{i,j}$ is dictated by M's transition function, based on the state and contents

portions of $r_{i-1,j}$. Otherwise, the contents portion of $r_{i,j}$ is the same as that of $r_{i-1,j}$.

For each $\sigma \in \Sigma$, let A_σ be the set of all pairs $q \in Q, \tau \in \Sigma$ for which M writes σ when in state q reading τ. Then $r_{i,j}^\sigma$ is computed as follows.

$$r_{i,j}^\sigma := \left(\bigvee_{(q,\tau) \in A_\sigma} (r_{i-1,j}^q \wedge r_{i-1,j}^\tau) \right) \vee (r_{i-1,j}^{\neg} \wedge r_{i-1,j}^\sigma).$$

2. The state portion of $r_{i,j}$ is computed similarly. If at the start of the ith step the head was positioned over the jth cell, and does not move as a result of the ith transition, then the state portion of $r_{i,j}$ will indicate that the head is present over the jth cell and indicate M's resulting internal state. Likewise, if the head was positioned over cell $j-1$ $(j+1)$ and moved right (respectively, left), then $c_{i,j}$ also computes the new state. In all other cases the state portion of $r_{i,j}$ will indicate that the head is not present.

Specifically, for each $q \in Q$, let B_q be the set of all triples $p \in Q, \tau \in \Sigma, d \in \{-1, 0, 1\}$ for which M when in state p reading τ enters state q and moves its head in direction d (where -1 means move left, $+1$ means move right, and 0 means sit still). Then $r_{i,j}^q$ is computed as follows.

$$r_{i,j}^q := \bigvee_{(p,\tau,d) \in B_q} (r_{i-1,j-d}^p \wedge r_{i-1,j-d}^\tau).$$

By convention, if state p is a halt state, its successor is defined to be state p regardless of the input symbol. This way we ensure that the machine is in a well-defined state at the end of the simulation, even if it halts earlier.

The head position component of the state, $r_{i,j}^{\neg}$, is computed as follows.

$$r_{i,j}^{\neg} := \left(\bigvee_{(p,\tau,d) \in C} (r_{i-1,j-d}^p \wedge r_{i-1,j-d}^\tau) \right) \vee \bigwedge_{d \in \{-1,0,1\}} r_{i-1,j-d}^{\neg},$$

where C is the set of all triples $p \in Q, \tau \in \Sigma, d \in \{-1, 0, 1\}$ for which M when in state p reading τ does *not* move its head in direction d.

The size of the circuit to compute the state change of one cell is $O(1)$, specifically $4|\Sigma||Q| + |\Sigma|$ fanin 2 AND's, one fanin 3 AND, plus $|\Sigma| + |Q| + 1$ OR's of fanin $O(1)$.

It is a straightforward induction on i to verify that the representations $r_{i,j}$ correctly encode the configuration of M after i steps.

The final step in the construction is to establish that β_n is NC computable. Since the circuit consists of many replicas of a single, fixed subcircuit $c_{1,1}$, the main tasks in constructing β_n are to compute the value of $t(n)$, to generate the correct number of copies of the basic subcircuit, with its constituent gates appropriately numbered so as to be unique, and to connect neighboring subcircuits appropriately. These tasks are easily accomplished by an NC algorithm, and indeed are NC^1 computable. We leave the details as an exercise.

Lastly, $x \in L$ if and only if a 1 is written into tape square 1 if and only if $r^1_{t(n),1}$ is TRUE. □

Combining Lemmas 6.1.1 and 6.1.2, we obtain Theorem 4.2.2.

Finally, we remark that the Circuit Value Problem remains P-complete if either the input or the circuit is fixed. Replacing n input bits by two (a 0 and a 1) with appropriate fanout, depending on the input, is straightforward. Alternatively, to see that the circuit can be fixed, replace the arbitrary machine M in the construction above by a polynomial time Turing machine solving the Generic Machine Simulation Problem (that is, a universal polynomial time Turing machine). This gives essentially a single circuit, fixed in all respects except for its size, whose evaluation is P-complete. Namely, the circuit consists of an $n \times (n+1)$ array of copies of the single, fixed subcircuit $c_{1,1}$ of size $O(1)$ arising in the construction above as particularized to the single universal machine. Any language in P can be reduced to evaluating this circuit for appropriately chosen input and appropriately chosen n.

An interesting question is to see just how simple CVP can be made while retaining P-completeness. For example, CVP for balanced binary trees of NOR gates of depth $\lceil \log_2 n \rceil$ is complete for NC^1. Perhaps CVP for an $n \times n$ grid of NOR's, each connected to the two nearest neighbors on the previous level is P-complete.

6.2 Restricted Versions of Circuit Value

The Circuit Value Problem plays the same role in P-completeness theory that Satisfiability (SAT) (Cook [62]) does in NP-completeness theory. Like SAT, CVP is the fundamental *P*-complete problem in the sense that it is most frequently used to show other problems are *P*-complete. Analogously to SAT, CVP has many variants that are also *P*-complete. In this section, we describe several, and prove them complete. Others are described in Section A.1. Restricted variants of a problem often simplify reductions, as in the case, for example, of the CNF-SAT and 3CNF-SAT variants of SAT in the theory of *NP*-completeness.

The following versions of CVP each have novel characteristics that can help simplify reductions to them. Additionally, their *P*-completeness proofs nicely illustrate a number of techniques frequently found in other reductions.

The CVP variants we will describe in this chapter are listed below. The formal specifications of the problems may be easily traced through the cross references provided.

Topologically Ordered CVP (TopCVP, Problem A.1.2) A *topological ordering* of a directed acyclic graph is a numbering of its vertices so that u is less than v for every (directed) edge (u, v). Any of the succeeding variants of CVP can be additionally restricted to have its circuit be topologically ordered, and furthermore to have the string encoding the circuit list the vertices in this order. One of the key properties of the Circuit Value Problem is that for any given circuit there is a simple sequential algorithm that given any input to the circuit evaluates individual gates of the circuit in a fixed order, evaluating each exactly once, and arriving at the circuit's designated output value in polynomial time. The virtue of a topologically ordered Circuit Value Problem is that this valuation order is transparently specified in the CVP instance.

NANDCVP (Problem A.1.5) This is the special case of the Circuit Value Problem where the circuit contains only NAND gates. Reductions are often simplified when only one type of gate needs to be simulated.

Monotone CVP (MCVP, Problem A.1.3) This is the restricted version of the Circuit Value Problem where the circuit contains only *monotone* gates, that is, AND's and OR's. This problem is useful in the common situation where negations are hard to simulate directly.

Alternating, Monotone CVP (AMCVP) This is a special case of the previous problem. A monotone circuit is *alternating* if on any path from an input to an output the gates on the path alternate between OR and AND gates. Additionally, we require that inputs connect only to OR gates, and that outputs be OR gates. Reductions often replace individual gates by certain small "gadgets." The alternating property reduces the number and kinds of interactions between gadgets that must be considered, which again often simplifies reductions.

Fanin 2, Fanout 2 AMCVP (AM2CVP, Problem A.1.4) This, again, is a restriction of the previous problem. In this case, all vertices in the circuit are restricted to have fanin and fanout two, with the obvious exception of the inputs and outputs, which by definition have fanin zero and fanout zero, respectively. Again, the potential advantage is that simpler gadgets can be used in a reduction, and there are fewer cases to consider in establishing its correctness.

Synchronous AM2CVP (SAM2CVP, Problem A.1.6) In a circuit, define the *level* of a vertex v, denoted level(v), to be zero for input vertices, and otherwise one more than the maximum level of a predecessor of (that is, input to) v. Equivalently, level(v) is the length of the longest path from an input to v. A circuit is *synchronous* if all inputs to a gate v come from vertices at level [level(v) $-$ 1]. Furthermore, we require that all output vertices be on one level, namely the highest. Thus, the vertices can be partitioned into layers, with all edges going from one layer to the next higher one, and all outputs on the last layer. *SAM2CVP* is the restriction of AM2CVP to synchronous circuits. Notice, in a circuit that is both alternating and synchronous, all gates on any given level must be of the same type. The fanin two and fanout two restrictions further imply that every level contains exactly the same number of vertices. Again, this structural regularity simplifies some reductions.

The construction given above in the proof of Lemma 6.1.2 yields a circuit with several of these properties. Specifically, the formulas we gave are all disjunctive normal form with two monotone literals per term except for one three-literal term. The circuit is therefore synchronous, alternating and monotone (but neither fanin nor fanout two). Rather than modify that construction, for pedagogical reasons we prefer to show the P-completeness of some of these variants by starting from the most general form of the Circuit Value Problem.

We will begin with topological ordering. The general problem of topologically ordering a directed acyclic graph, although in NC^2 (Cook [67]), is not known to be in NC^1. Nevertheless, Topologically Ordered CVP is still P-complete under $\leq_m^{NC^1}$ reductions.

Theorem 6.2.1 *The Circuit Value Problem when restricted to topologically ordered instances remains P-complete under $\leq_m^{NC^1}$ reductions.*

Proof. The construction used to prove CVP complete in the proof of Theorem 4.2.2 (see Lemma 6.1.2) can easily be modified to produce its circuit in topological order. Specifically, let C be the number of input vertices in the circuit. Number them $1, 2, \ldots, C$. Suppose that the basic subcircuit that is the template for $c_{i,j}$ has g gates, g a constant. Number these gates $1, 2, \ldots, g$ in topological order. Then, for $1 \leq i \leq t(n)$, $1 \leq j \leq t(n) + 1$, $1 \leq k \leq g$, give gate k in $c_{i,j}$ (that is, the kth gate in the $(i, j)^{th}$ instance of the template) the number

$$g * ((i - 1) * (t(n) + 1) + (j - 1)) + k + C.$$

This is a topological numbering and is easily computed in NC^1. $\square$

Two other useful gate numbering tricks are that gates need not be numbered consecutively starting from one, nor need they be listed in numerical order. An encoding lacking either or both of these properties can be converted (in NC^1) to one possessing both by first sorting the gate numbers, then replacing each number by its rank in the sorted list. Tricks such as these allow all the reductions presented later in this chapter to preserve the topological order (if any) of the input circuit. Thus, all the CVP variants considered in this chapter remain complete (under $\leq_m^{NC^1}$ reduction) when restricted to topologically ordered instances. Hence, we will generally not mention topological order subsequently.

Next, we consider the Monotone Circuit Value Problem (MCVP). As we already observed, the basic simulation of a Turing machine by a circuit in the proof of Theorem 4.2.2 is monotone. However, the general direct monotone reduction is interesting in its own right and we present it here.

We will also argue in more detail than elsewhere in this book that the reduction is in fact NC^1 computable, since the reduction is simple enough that it provides a convenient example of some techniques commonly used in this portion of P-completeness proofs.

Theorem 6.2.2 (Goldschlager [122]) *The Monotone Circuit Value Problem is P-complete under $\leq_m^{NC^1}$ reductions.*

Proof. We reduce a CVP instance α to a MCVP instance β by constructing "double railed" logic. That is, for every value v computed, we also compute $\neg v$. For each vertex v_k in the original circuit, construct a pair of vertices $u_k, \overline{u_k}$ in the new circuit. They will have the property that u_k is TRUE if and only if v_k is TRUE if and only if $\overline{u_k}$ is FALSE. If v_k is an input x_i, then u_k is also x_i and $\overline{u_k}$ is its negation $\neg x_i$. (Note that β has twice as many inputs as α; for each i, $\neg x_i$ is computed by the machine performing the reduction, and both x_i and $\neg x_i$ are provided as inputs to β. A monotone circuit, of course, cannot by itself compute $\neg x_i$ from x_i.) For an AND gate $v_k \leftarrow v_i \wedge v_j$ of the original circuit, construct the AND gate $u_k \leftarrow u_i \wedge u_j$ and the OR gate $\overline{u_k} \leftarrow \overline{u_i} \vee \overline{u_j}$. For an OR gate do the dual. Finally, add two new inputs having value 0 and 1, and for a NOT gate $v_k \leftarrow \neg v_i$ construct two gates $u_k \leftarrow \overline{u_i} \wedge 1$ and $\overline{u_k} \leftarrow u_i \vee 0$. It is easy to show by induction on vertex depth that v_k evaluates to TRUE in the original circuit if and only if u_k is TRUE and $\overline{u_k}$ is FALSE in the new circuit.

Next, we argue in some detail that the construction can be accomplished in NC^1.

We have not yet carefully specified how the circuit α is encoded. We assume the following reasonable formulation of the standard encoding scheme. An n-vertex circuit will be represented by $n * (2k + 2)$ bits, where $k = \lceil \log_2(n + 1) \rceil$. The string is viewed as n blocks, with $2k + 2$ bits per block, each block specifying one vertex, with the block number being used as the vertex number. The first two bits of each block indicate the type of the vertex (either input, OR, AND, or NOT), and the remaining $2k$ bits encode either the single input bit, or the vertex number(s) of the one or two vertices that are the predecessors of this vertex in the circuit.

As is often the case with such reductions, the key point is to devise a scheme for numbering vertices in the new circuit that allows its vertices and edges to be easily computed from vertices and edges in the circuit α. For this purpose, for each vertex v_i in α, we simply assign the numbers $2i + 2$ and $2i + 3$ to the two vertices u_i and $\overline{u_i}$ in β that are derived from v_i. The two new input vertices receiving values 0 and 1 (used for simulating NOT gates) are numbered 0 and

1, respectively.

Given this encoding, it is easy to see how, in NC^1, to transform the encoding of α to the encoding of β. Namely, compute $k' = \lceil \log_2(2n+3) \rceil$. Then simply build n replicas of a circuit of depth $O(\log n)$ with $2k+2$ input bits and $2(2k'+2)$ output bits that performs the obvious transformation on the block of bits describing one vertex of α to produce the two blocks of bits describing the two corresponding vertices in β. Note that the arithmetic necessary to recode vertex numbers (for example, $i \rightarrow (2i+3)$) is easily accomplished by a circuit of depth $O(\log n)$, especially considering that vertex numbers are themselves only $O(\log n)$ bits long. Remaining details are omitted.   □

We will not usually give proofs that our reductions are in fact NC^1 or NC computable. They are usually more tedious than the one presented above, but not conceptually more difficult. Known NC^1 algorithms[1] (see Karp and Ramachandran [195]) for a variety of basic operations such as arithmetic, sorting, ranking, and parallel prefix often prove useful.

Next, we show that CVP remains P-complete when restricted in all of the following ways: the circuit will be monotone, inputs will connect only to OR gates, outputs will be OR gates, along any paths from an input to an output the gates will strictly alternate between OR and AND gates, and all vertices will have indegree and outdegree exactly two, with the obvious exceptions that (by definition) the circuit's input vertices have indegree zero, and its outputs have outdegree zero. That is, we show that AM2CVP is P-complete. Of course, this implies that the less restricted AMCVP problem mentioned above is also P-complete.

Theorem 6.2.3 *The Alternating, Monotone Circuit Value Problem with fanin and fanout of gates restricted to two (AM2CVP) is P-complete under $\leq_m^{NC^1}$ reductions.*

Proof. We accomplish this, starting from a monotone circuit, by a series of five transformations, each of which assures one additional property without destroying any of the properties achieved by the previous steps. The transformations are as follows.

---

[1]The phrase NC^k *algorithm* means an algorithm with polynomial hardware and $(\log n)^k$ running time regardless of the type of problem it solves — decision, search, or other.

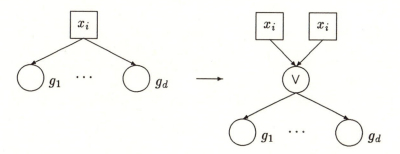

Figure 6.2.1: Connecting Inputs to OR Gates in Theorem 6.2.3, Step 1.

1. Replace each input vertex x_i of fanout d by an OR gate of fanin two and fanout d (connected to the same vertices $g_1, \ldots, g_d$ as x_i). This new OR gate will receive its inputs from two new input vertices, each with fanout one, each receiving as value a copy of x_i. See Figure 6.2.1. Thus, all inputs have fanout one and are connected only to OR gates.

2. For each fanout zero AND gate v, create a new OR vertex of fanin one, receiving its input from v. Thus, all output vertices are OR's.

   Replace any gate v with fanout d greater than two by a fanout tree consisting of v plus $d - 2$ new gates of fanin one. All $d - 1$ of these gates will have fanout two. The types of the new gates are arbitrary; for definiteness, say they are all OR's. Now all vertices have fanout at most two. See Figure 6.2.2.

3. Split any edge connecting two gates of the same type, inserting a fanin one, fanout one gate of the opposite type. Thus, types will strictly alternate along all paths.

4. For all OR gates v of fanin one, create a new input vertex receiving the value 0, and connect it to the fanin two replacement for v. For all AND gates v of fanin one, create three new vertices. Two of them will be input vertices receiving the value 1. They will be connected to the third, a fanin two, fanout one OR gate that is in turn connected to the fanin two replacement for v. Thus, all gates have fanin exactly two. Note that we took care to preserve the properties introduced in steps 1 and 3.

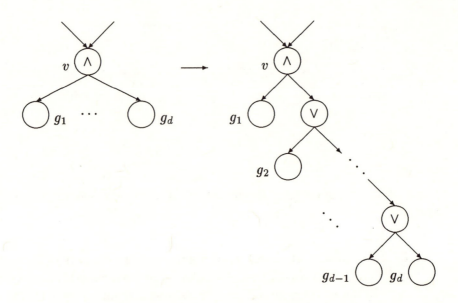

Figure 6.2.2: Fanout Tree in Theorem 6.2.3, Step 2.

5. Replicate the circuit, excluding its input vertices, with both replicas fed from the one set of inputs. More precisely, let α be the circuit at the beginning of this step. Form a new circuit β as follows. In addition to the original gates and edges, for all gates (but not input vertices) v in α, add to β a copy v' of v. For every edge (u,v) in α, if u is an input vertex, also add the edge (u,v'); otherwise, add the edge (u',v'). Next, for every AND vertex v of outdegree one, create a new OR vertex v'' of outdegree zero and indegree two, with inputs from v and v'. For every OR vertex v of outdegree one, create four new vertices v'', v_0, v_1, and v_2. Gate v'' will be a fanin two, fanout two AND gate receiving its inputs from v and v'. Vertex v_0 will be a new input vertex receiving value 0. Gates v_1 and v_2 are OR gates of outdegree zero and indegree two, each connected to v_0 and v''. Thus, all gates (except outputs) have fanout two. See Figure 6.2.3.

The resulting circuit has all of the desired properties.   □

It is well known that NAND is a complete basis for the set of Boolean functions. Thus, reduction of an arbitrary instance of the Circuit Value Problem to an instance of NANDCVP is easy. There

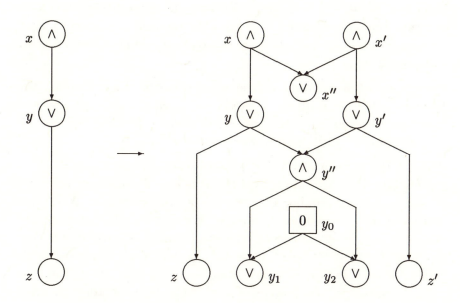

Figure 6.2.3: Replication in Theorem 6.2.3, Step 5.

is an even more straightforward reduction from AM2CVP to NAND-CVP.

Theorem 6.2.4 *The NAND Circuit Value Problem is P-complete under $\leq_m^{NC^1}$ reductions.*

Proof. Reduce AM2CVP to NANDCVP by complementing all inputs, and relabeling all gates as NAND gates. Correctness follows from DeMorgan's Laws.[2]   □

    Finally, we examine the synchronous version of the Circuit Value Problem.

    A natural approach to transforming a circuit into a synchronous one would be to identify and "fix" each edge that violates the synchronous restriction, that is an edge (u, v) such that $\text{level}(v) - \text{level}(u)$ is greater than 1. The offending edge could be fixed by inserting $\text{level}(v) - \text{level}(u) - 1$ new vertices along it. This approach is workable, but not as simple as we would like. In particular, the *level* function depends on knowledge of the *global* structure of the graph. Further, level numbers are not known to be NC^1 computable, (although they are NC^2 computable), which would preclude an NC^1

---

[2] $x \vee y = \neg(\neg x \wedge \neg y)$ and $x \wedge y = \neg(\neg x \vee \neg y)$.

reduction using this approach. Instead, as is often the case with
P-completeness reductions, we are able to take an approach that
achieves our goal (synchrony) by globally applying a simple local
transformation.

Theorem 6.2.5 (Greenlaw, Hoover, and Ruzzo, THIS WORK) *The
Synchronous, Alternating, Monotone Circuit Value Problem with
fanin and fanout of gates restricted to two (SAM2CVP) is P-
complete under $\leq_m^{NC^1}$ reductions.*

Proof.   We show AM2CVP $\leq_m^{NC^1}$ SAM2CVP. Since AM2CVP is
P-complete, it follows that SAM2CVP is also P-complete.

Let n be the number of gates in the instance α of AM2CVP
and let m be the number of inputs. We make $\lceil n/2 \rceil$ copies of the
vertices (both input vertices and gate vertices) of this circuit. For
$0 \leq i \leq \lceil n/2 \rceil - 1$, the ith copy will be organized into two levels.
The first level in the ith copy, which will be level $2i$ in the new
circuit, consists of the (copies of the) input vertices, together with
the (copies of the) AND gates, and is called an AND *level*. On level 0,
all vertices will be input vertices; on level $2i$, where i is greater than
0, all vertices will be AND gates. The second level in the ith copy,
which will be level $2i + 1$ in the new circuit, consists of the (copies of
the) OR gates, and is called the OR *level*. All gates on all OR levels
will be OR gates. Thus, in odd (even) numbered levels all gates are
OR (respectively, AND) gates, with the obvious exception of the input
level. All edges will connect adjacent levels, so the synchronous and
alternating properties easily follow.

In an instance of AM2CVP, since the OR's have fanin exactly two,
all being from AND or input vertices of fanout exactly two, it must be
true that the number of OR gates equals the number of inputs plus
the number of AND gates. Thus, each level in the new circuit will
have exactly $(n + m)/2$ vertices. By similar reasoning, the number
of output vertices is equal to the number of input vertices, m. We
will need this fact shortly.

We describe below how to connect the $\lceil n/2 \rceil$ copies to make a
new circuit equivalent to α.

For a given vertex v, label the copies of it v_i, $0 \leq i \leq \lceil n/2 \rceil - 1$.
The edges *into* OR gates in α are preserved within each copy. That
is, if (u, v) is an edge in α, with v being an OR gate, then there are
edges (u_i, v_i) for all $0 \leq i \leq \lceil n/2 \rceil - 1$. The edges *out* of OR gates in
α go from one copy into the corresponding vertex in the next copy.
That is, if (u, v) is an edge in α, with u being an OR gate, then there

are edges (u_i, v_{i+1}) for all $0 \leq i \leq \lceil n/2 \rceil - 2$.

The input vertices, which are the vertices on level zero, are assigned values as follows. Those that are copies of input vertices in α are given the same input values as in α. Those that are copies of AND gates in α are given input 0, arbitrarily. The copies of output vertices (recall, they are all OR gates) on the last level are the circuit's correct outputs, as we will argue shortly. Copies of input and output vertices on all other levels must be handled specially. We need to deliver each of α's input bits to the copy of the corresponding input vertex on the ith AND level for all $1 \leq i \leq \lceil n/2 \rceil - 1$. Also, the copies of the output vertices on each OR level other than the last must be connected to something, to satisfy the synchrony restriction. Recall that the number of inputs and outputs are both m. Pair them arbitrarily. Then it suffices to add $2m$ replicas of the gadget shown in Figure 6.2.4 (Luc Longpré, Personal Communication, 1986). This gadget can deliver a copy of its input bit to each even numbered level greater than zero, while providing a sink for the useless output from the paired output vertex on the previous odd numbered level.

This completes the construction. It should be clear that the circuit satisfies the restrictions of synchrony, alternation, fanin, and fanout. Correctness is established by induction using the following assertion. Let v be a vertex whose level in α is $\text{level}(v) = i$. Then in β all copies v_k of v with $k \geq \lfloor i/2 \rfloor$ compute the same value as v does in α. Since the depth of α is at most n, and is odd, we have $\lceil n/2 \rceil - 1 \geq \lfloor \text{depth}(\alpha)/2 \rfloor$ and so all output gates have the correct value.

Again we omit the straightforward argument showing that the reduction can be performed in NC^1. □

We will close the chapter with a few technical remarks. The reductions performed in Theorems 6.2.2, 6.2.3, and 6.2.4 increased the size of the original circuit by only a constant factor. However, the reduction in Theorem 6.2.5 produces a circuit of size $O(n^2)$ from one of size n. We remark that the later reduction also provides an alternative proof of Theorem 6.2.1, which showed that CVP is $\leq_m^{NC^1}$ reducible to Topologically Ordered CVP, even though topological numbering of a directed acyclic graph is not known to be NC^1 computable. The price one pays for this seems to be the quadratic increase in size.

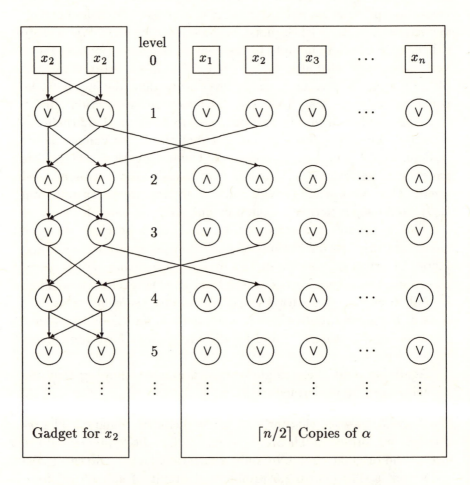

Figure 6.2.4: Input Propagation Gadget in Theorem 6.2.5.

Chapter 7

Greedy Algorithms

We consider the selection of two basketball teams at a neighborhood playground to illustrate the greedy method. Usually the top two players are designated captains. All other players line up while the captains alternate choosing one player at a time. Usually, the players are picked using a greedy strategy. That is, the captains choose the best unclaimed player. The system of selection of choosing the best, most obvious, or most convenient remaining candidate is called the *greedy method*. Greedy algorithms often lead to easily implemented efficient sequential solutions to problems. Unfortunately, it also seems to be that sequential greedy algorithms frequently lead to solutions that are *inherently sequential* — the solutions produced by these algorithms cannot be duplicated rapidly in parallel, unless NC equals P. In the following subsections we will examine this phenomenon.

7.1   Lexicographic Greedy Algorithms

We illustrate some of the important aspects of greedy algorithms using one that constructs a maximal independent set in a graph. An *independent set* is a set of vertices of a graph that are pairwise nonadjacent. A *maximum* independent set is such a set of largest cardinality. It is well known that finding maximum independent sets is *NP*-hard. An independent set is *maximal* if no other vertex can be added while maintaining the independent set property. In contrast to the maxim*um* case, finding maxim*al* independent sets is very easy. Figure 7.1.1 depicts a simple polynomial time sequential algorithm computing a maximal independent set. The algorithm

---

Greedy Maximal Independent Set Algorithm
Input: An undirected graph $G = (V, E)$ with the vertices
numbered $1, \ldots, |V|$.
Output: The lexicographically first maximal independent set
of G.
begin
    $I \leftarrow \emptyset$;
    for $j \leftarrow 1$ to $|V|$ do
        if vertex j is not connected to any vertex in I
           then $I \leftarrow I \cup \{j\}$;
end.

Figure 7.1.1: A Greedy Maximal Independent Set Algorithm.

is a greedy algorithm: it processes the vertices in numerical order, always attempting to add the lowest numbered vertex that has not yet been tried.

The sequential algorithm in Figure 7.1.1, having processed vertices $1, \ldots, j-1$, can easily decide whether to include vertex j. However, notice that its decision about j potentially depends on its decisions about *all* earlier vertices — j will be included in the maximal independent set if and only if all j' less than j and adjacent to it were excluded. Thus, the algorithm seems highly sequential. Based on this intuition, Valiant conjectured that this algorithm would be difficult to parallelize [356]. Cook showed that the following natural decision problem derived from it is P-complete [67], which we take to be strong evidence in support of Valiant's conjecture. (Actually, Valiant and Cook considered the dual problem of finding a maximal clique, Problem A.2.2.)

In general, a graph may have many maximal independent sets. The algorithm in Figure 7.1.1, being deterministic, finds one unique maximal independent set among the many candidates. The solution it finds is dictated by the way the vertices are numbered — and it finds the "first" solution in the following sense.

Take any maximal independent set $I = \{v_1, \ldots, v_{|I|}\}$, and suppose that $v_1 < v_2 < \cdots < v_{|I|}$. Now list the elements in ascending order by vertex number, $v_1, v_2, \ldots, v_{|I|}$ and call this sequence the *signature* of I. Then any two maximal independent sets I and I' can be *lexicographically ordered* by their signatures. That is, $I < I'$ if and only if the signature of I is less than the signature of I' when they are compared as strings.

The algorithm in Figure 7.1.1 finds the lexicographically first maximal independent set. Below we define a natural decision problem based on maximal independent sets. (See also Problem A.2.1 in Part II for related problems and remarks.)

Definition 7.1.1 *Lexicographically First Maximal Independent Set Problem (LFMIS)*
Given: *An undirected graph $G = (V, E)$ with an ordering on the vertices and a designated vertex v.*
Problem: *Is vertex v in the lexicographically first maximal independent set of G?*

Theorem 7.1.2 (Cook [67]) *The Lexicographically First Maximal Independent Set Problem is P-complete under $\leq_m^{NC^1}$ reductions.*

Proof. Membership in P follows from the algorithm in Figure 7.1.1.

Completeness follows by reducing the NOR Circuit Value Problem (NORCVP) to LFMIS by modifying a construction due to Anderson (Richard J. Anderson, Personal Communication, 1987). Without loss of generality, we assume the instance α of NORCVP has its gates numbered (starting from 1) in topological order with inputs numbered first and outputs last. Suppose y is the designated output gate in the instance of NORCVP. We construct from α an instance of LFMIS, namely an undirected graph G. The graph G will be exactly the same as the graph underlying the circuit α, except that we add a new vertex, numbered 0, that is adjacent to all 0-inputs of α. It is easy to verify by induction that a vertex i in G is included in the lexicographically first maximal independent set if and only if either i equals 0 (the new vertex), or gate i in α has value TRUE. A choice of v equal to y completes the reduction.

The proof that the reduction can be performed in NC^1 is left to the reader. □

We show in Chapter 10 that the simpler problem of computing just the size of the lexicographically first maximal independent set is also difficult.

There are many other decision problems based on greedy algorithms that are known to be P-complete. Several examples are

Lexicographically First Depth-first Search (Problem A.3.3), Lexicographically First $\Delta + 1$ Vertex Coloring (Problem A.2.6), and First
Fit Decreasing Bin Packing (Problem A.4.7). These examples fit
within the common framework of the next section.

7.2   Generic Greedy Algorithms

Many problems can be formulated as independence systems, and
consequently can be solved by greedy methods. An *independence
system* is a pair $I = (E, \mathcal{F})$, where E is an ordered set of *elements*
$\{e_1, \ldots, e_n\}$, and $\mathcal{F}$ is a collection of subsets of E, each called an
independent set. We require that the independent sets have the
property that $\emptyset \in \mathcal{F}$, and that independence is *hereditary*, that is if
X is in $\mathcal{F}$ then all subsets of X are also in $\mathcal{F}$. The computational
problem of interest is to compute the lexicographically first maximal
independent set in $\mathcal{F}$. More precisely, we must compute the greedy
set $G = \{e_{j_1}, \ldots, e_{j_k}\}$ for I, where

- $1 = j_0 \leq j_1 < j_2 < \cdots < j_k < j_{k+1} = n + 1$,
- for each $0 \leq i \leq k$, the set $G_i = \{e_{j_1}, \ldots, e_{j_i}\}$ is independent
  (with $G_0 = \emptyset$), and
- for all $j_i < l < j_{i+1}$, $G_i \cup \{e_l\}$ is *not* independent.

For example, for any graph G, if E_G is the set of vertices of
G, and $\mathcal{F}_G$ is the set of subsets of E_G whose members are pairwise
nonadjacent in G, then $I_G = (E_G, \mathcal{F}_G)$ is an independence system.
Furthermore, the lexicographically first maximal independent set in
I_G is precisely the lexicographically first maximal independent set
in G. Thus, the LFMIS problem for graphs is a special case of
the Lexicographically First Maximal Independent Set Problem for
independence systems.

How difficult is this more general problem on independence systems? *Sequentially* it is very simple — a straightforward modification of the greedy LFMIS algorithm in Figure 7.1.1 solves the
problem easily. This is true even in the abstract setting where $\mathcal{F}$ is
not given explicitly but rather as an oracle A for membership in $\mathcal{F}$
(an *independence oracle*). That is, we do not have an explicit listing
of $\mathcal{F}$ (it can be quite large), nor may we assume anything about the
underlying structure of $\mathcal{F}$ (e.g., we may not assume that $\mathcal{F}$ is $\mathcal{F}_G$
for some graph G). Instead, oracle A simply lets us test whether a
given subset X of E is in $\mathcal{F}$.

Although easy to solve sequentially, this problem is provably not parallelizable. Karp, Upfal, and Wigderson show that any deterministic parallel decision tree algorithm for finding a maximal independent set, given an independence oracle, must take time at least $\Omega(n/\log p)$ where p is the number of processors [197]. Even a randomized algorithm requires $\Omega(n/\log(np))$ [197].

Are there natural restrictions of the general problem that are highly parallelizable? One important class of restrictions is where the set E of the independence system is the vertex set of a graph G, and the set X, a subset of E, is included in $\mathcal{F}$ just in case the vertex induced subgraph determined by X has some special property. For example, take the independence system I_G corresponding to the LFMIS problem in the case where the vertex induced subgraph contains no edges. Are these special cases parallelizable? We know that they cannot all be parallelizable, unless P equals NC, because LFMIS is P-complete. Surprisingly, as shown by the following result of Miyano, essentially *all* other special cases of this form are also P-complete [265]. We first present the terminology necessary for explaining his result.

A *graph property* π is simply a predicate on graphs. A property π is *nontrivial* on a given graph family D if there are infinitely many graphs in D satisfying π and at least one graph violating π. A property is *hereditary* (*on induced subgraphs*) if whenever a graph G satisfies π, so do all vertex induced subgraphs. Some examples of nontrivial hereditary properties are planarity, acyclicity, and edgelessness. The *LFMS(π) problem* is to compute the lexicographically first maximal vertex induced subgraph satisfying π. For example, when π is the edgelessness property, the LFMS(π) problem is just the LFMIS problem. Note that the simple greedy algorithm shows the LFMS(π) problem is in *FP* for any polynomial time computable hereditary property π. Miyano has shown that this problem is highly sequential for *any* graph property π, no matter how simple, provided only that π is nontrivial and hereditary.

Theorem 7.2.1 (Miyano [265]) *Let π be a polynomial time testable property that is nontrivial on graphs (respectively, on bipartite graphs and on planar graphs) and is hereditary on vertex induced subgraphs. Then LFMS(π), the lexicographically first maximal subgraph problem for property π, (respectively restricted to bipartite graphs, restricted to planar graphs) is complete for FP.*

**Parallel Greedy Matroid Maximal Independent Set
Algorithm Using a Rank Oracle**
Input: A matroid $I = (E, \mathcal{F})$ with elements $E = \{e_1, \ldots, e_n\}$,
and with $\mathcal{F}$ given via a rank oracle.
Output: The lexicographically first maximal independent set
of I.
begin
    $r_0 \leftarrow 0$; $G \leftarrow \emptyset$;
    for $j \leftarrow 1, \ldots, n$ do in parallel
        $r_j \leftarrow rank\{e_1, \ldots, e_j\}$;
        if $r_{j-1} < r_j$ then include e_j in G;
end.

Figure 7.2.1: Parallel Greedy Algorithm Using a Rank Oracle.

The foregoing results suggest that greedy algorithms are always difficult or impossible to parallelize. This is too pessimistic a view. With further restrictions on the independence system, or relaxed requirements on the solution, it is sometimes possible to obtain highly parallel algorithms. The idea is that if order among elements is unimportant, do not make it part of the problem specification. Examples are discussed below.

The study of independence systems above was motivated in part by the greedy algorithm for matroids. *Matroids* are independence systems with the additional property that all maximal independent sets have the same cardinality (Lawler [227]). Thus all maximal independents sets are maximum independent sets and the greedy algorithm obtains the optimal solution. Construction of minimum weight spanning trees is a classic application of matroid theory. For this application, the elements of the independence system are the edges of a graph, and a set of edges is called independent if it is acyclic. That is, if it is a forest. Cook gives a fast parallel greedy algorithm for matroids given a *rank oracle*, a function $rank\{e_1, \ldots, e_j\}$ giving the size of some (hence any) maximal independent set among $\{e_1, \ldots, e_j\}$ [67]. See Figure 7.2.1.

Notice that this algorithm computes the lexicographically first maximal independent set. Cook applies the algorithm to show that finding the minimum weight spanning tree for a graph is in *NC*. This is accomplished by sorting the edges in the graph according to their weight and then directly applying the algorithm. The value $rank\{e_1, \ldots, e_j\}$ is simply n minus the number of connected components in the n-vertex subgraph induced by $\{e_1, \ldots, e_j\}$, an *NC* computable function.

In the general case, where the independence system is not necessarily a matroid, finding a maximum independent set using a rank oracle is still difficult. Karp, Upfal, and Wigderson show that any deterministic parallel decision tree algorithm for maximum independent set with a rank oracle requires time $\Omega(n/\log(np))$ [197]. But when randomization is allowed, a feasible highly parallel algorithm exists that takes time $O((\log n)^2)$ on n processors. This is a clear example of the power of randomization in parallel computation. For more on this subject, the reader is referred to the survey article by Rajasekaran and Reif [294].

The second example shows that even in cases where the problem solved by a greedy algorithm is *P*-complete, it may be possible to obtain a highly parallel solution to a related problem. Specifically, although finding the lexicographically first maximal independent set in a graph is *P*-complete, there is an *NC* algorithm to find *some* maximal independent set (Luby [246]). For a summary of the history about the development of results regarding the independent set problem see Karp and Ramachandran [195].

As another example fitting into this group, consider the first fit decreasing algorithm for bin packing. There is a well known greedy heuristic that is guaranteed to find a packing within 11/9 of optimal — first fit decreasing. Anderson, Mayr, and Warmuth show that it is *P*-complete to construct the same packing as the first fit decreasing algorithm (Problem A.4.7), but that there is an *NC* algorithm giving another packing that is also within 11/9 of optimal [17]. Other examples of problems for which the greedy solution is *P*-complete but naturally related problems are known to be in *NC* or *RNC* include Depth-first Search (see Problems A.3.3 and B.9.2), $\Delta + 1$ Vertex Coloring (see Problem A.2.6), and Maximal Path (see Problems A.3.1 and B.9.4).

Chapter 8

P-Complete Algorithms

8.1   Introduction

Our focus up to this point has been primarily on problems — either decision, search, or function. In this chapter we shift directions and apply *P*-completeness theory to the study of algorithms. The theory when extended properly will allow us to make statements about whether or not certain sequential algorithms will parallelize well.

The phrase "inherently sequential algorithm" is one that appears frequently in the research literature. The general intent of the phrase is obvious. However, if pressed for details one might come up with several different possible formal meanings. In this chapter we describe one approach that gives the phrase a precise interpretation.

The work on *P-complete algorithms* began with Anderson [12] and was continued by Greenlaw [133, 135]. Much of the discussion contained in this chapter is taken from these references.

That a problem is *P*-complete is evidence it is unlikely to have small space sequential solutions, or unlikely to have fast parallel solutions using a polynomial amount of hardware. Of course, being *P*-complete also means that the problem does have a polynomial time algorithm. For many *P*-complete decision problems, this algorithm appears explicitly or implicitly in the statement of the problem. For example, asking whether a vertex is in the lexicographically first maximal clique is essentially asking whether the vertex is in the maximal clique found by the obvious greedy algorithm — the same greedy algorithm that shows the problem is in *P*. This specification of a particular polynomial time algorithm in addition to the non-algorithmic properties desired of a solution occurs in most of the search problems in Section A.3, many of the problems of a greedy or lexicographically first nature, and numerous graph problems in Section A.2. These P-completeness results say more about the difficulty of parallelizing the associated sequential algorithm than they do about the intrinsic difficulty of the decision problem.

In many cases the particular sequential algorithm does not seem to adapt well to parallelism. Yet it may be the case that a modified version of the problem that avoids mentioning a sequential algorithm does have a highly parallel solution. For example, consider the Bin Packing Problem. In Problem A.4.7 Anderson, Mayr, and Warmuth show that computing the first fit decreasing bin packing is P-complete [17]. But they also show that there is an NC algorithm for producing an alternative bin packing that achieves the same performance as first fit. Its problem description specifies only a performance bound, not an associated algorithm.

Sometimes the associated sequential algorithm can be efficiently parallelized. In Problem A.3.5 a variant of breadth-first search that is implemented on a stack is P-complete, whereas an alternative implementation based on queues can be parallelized to run in NC (Greenlaw [135]).

Thus, there are two ways in which we can interpret the fact that a problem is P-complete. First, if the statement of the problem makes no mention of an associated sequential algorithm, then it is reasonable to say that the problem itself is inherently sequential. Second, if the statement of the problem involves an associated sequential algorithm, then it is more appropriate to say that it is the algorithm that is inherently sequential.

The second situation indicates that we need a more sophisticated way to compare the relative parallel complexities of sequential algorithms than just making a statement about the decision problems underlying the algorithms. Anderson took the first step towards this by proposing the following definition of a P-complete algorithm.

Definition 8.1.1 (Anderson [12]) *An **algorithm** A **for a search problem** is P-**complete** if the problem of computing the solution found by A is P-complete.*

Suppose one were given a graph G and wanted to compute a spanning tree of G. One algorithm for computing a spanning tree could be P-complete, whereas another algorithm might find a different spanning tree and run in NC. It is conceivable that the two algorithms could in fact find the same tree yet have different parallel complexities.

Anderson observed that a shortcoming of his definition is its failure to directly tie in with the internal computations of algorithms [12]. He suggests including a trace of the algorithm as part of the result it computes as a way to incorporate the internal computations. Greenlaw then proposed a model whose focus is directly on algorithms [133]. In the next section we summarize the description of the model.

8.2   Inherently Sequential Algorithms

A model to satisfy the issues raised above needs to incorporate enough detail to permit classification of algorithms with respect to their parallel complexities. As Anderson pointed out, the intermediate values that algorithms compute can be used to distinguish their parallel complexities. Thus, the model should be capable of capturing a trace of the algorithm. The base model chosen in [133] to do this was the random access machine (RAM). The idea is to assign a value to each step of an algorithm. Then by examining the sequence of values an algorithm generates on a given input, one can classify the algorithm's parallel complexity.

We begin with some preliminaries and terminology taken from Greenlaw [133]. A *RAM algorithm* is a RAM program whose statements are numbered sequentially. Corresponding to each RAM algorithm statement, there is an associated value. The value associated with each statement is simply the valuation of the left hand side of the statement. The instruction is assumed to have already been executed. Sample values for a couple instructions are shown in Table 8.1. A full table is given in [133]. An explanation of the notation used is presented below. The notation is based on that given in Aho, Hopcroft, and Ullman [7].

In the table $c(i)$ denotes the contents of register i. As is customary register 0 of the RAM serves as the accumulator. This is the register where all computation is performed. $v(a)$ denotes the value of operand a as follows:

$$v(=i) = i, \quad v(i) = c(i), \quad v(*i) = c(c(i)).$$

Two values are associated with indirect addressing instructions. The second value determines which cell was read or written. Corresponding to each step of a RAM algorithm executed, there is an associated value generated. Each statement generates as many values as the number of times it is executed.

Instruction	Associated Value
LOAD a	$v(c(0))$
STORE $*i$	$v(c(i)); v(c(c(i)))$
ADD a	$v(c(0))$
WRITE a	$v(a)$
HALT	—

Table 8.1: Sample RAM Instructions and Their Associated Value(s).

The following definition illustrates how a function is associated with a particular RAM algorithm.

Definition 8.2.1 *Given any RAM algorithm A over an alphabet Σ with statements numbered sequentially starting from 1, the* **RAM flow function** $f_A : \Sigma^* \times \mathbb{N} \to (\mathbb{N} \times \mathbb{N})^*$ *corresponding to A is defined to be*

$$f_A(x_1 \cdots x_n, t) = v_1, v_2, \ldots, v_t$$

where the v_i's represent the ordered pairs consisting of statement numbers and value(s) pairs associated with the execution of t statements of A on input $x_1 \cdots x_n$.

Let $x = x_1 \cdots x_n$. For all algorithms halting on all inputs, define $f_A(x)$ as $f_A(x, T(n))$, where $T(n)$ denotes the maximum running time of algorithm A on inputs of length n. The length of the flow function for algorithm A on input x, denoted $|f_A(x)|$, is related to the running time of A. In Definition 8.2.1 statement numbers of A and the values generated by each statement are represented by integers using any reasonable encoding scheme. Thus, if the logarithmic cost model is assumed, $|f_A(x)|$ is no more than three times the running time of A on x.

The flow function plays an important role in classifying an algorithm with respect to its parallel complexity as illustrated by the following definition.

Definition 8.2.2 *Let A be a RAM algorithm with flow function f_A.* *A* **RAM algorithm** *A* **is** **inherently** **sequential** *if the language* $L_A = \{x \# i \# j \mid \text{bit } i \text{ of } f_A(x) = j\}$ *associated with its flow function is P-complete.*

For an algorithm to be considered inherently sequential, the flow function must be at least as difficult to compute as a *P*-complete problem. Furthermore, under this definition, Theorem 8.2.3 shows that any polynomial time algorithm computing the solution to a *P*-complete problem is indeed inherently sequential.

Theorem 8.2.3 *If polynomial time RAM algorithm A decides a P-complete language L, then A is inherently sequential.*

Proof. The proof is left as an exercise for the reader.   □

8.3   Applications of the Model

A few results illustrating the use of the model are presented in this section. The first example involves biconnectivity. It is easy to see that the ordered depth-first search algorithm, which is the standard depth-first search algorithm that is based on fixed ordered adjacency lists, is inherently sequential in the sense defined above. To prove it apply Theorem 8.2.3 and the result in Problem A.3.3. From this observation, it follows that an algorithm for biconnected components based on the ordered depth-first search algorithm is inherently sequential. This is in contrast to the fact that there is a well known parallel algorithm for computing the biconnected components of a graph that runs in time $O(\log n)$ time using n^2 processors on a CRCW-PRAM (Tarjan and Vishkin [350, 351]). The two algorithms described above have the same output but one is inherently sequential and the other is in *NC*. The role of the model in this case is that it highlights the individual steps of the algorithms. This allows us to compare their parallel complexities in a meaningful way.

There are some search problems for which one algorithm may find a solution to the problem in *NC*, whereas another approach might be inherently sequential. Usually, the solutions computed by the algorithms are different. Such problems are interesting since it is usually not important which specific solution is found. Thus, finding an alternative to an inherently sequential algorithm can be very useful. An example of such a problem involves maximal paths. The problem of computing a lexicographically first maximal path is *P*-complete (Anderson and Mayr [16]). It follows directly from Theorem 8.2.3 and this result that the greedy algorithm to compute such a path is inherently sequential. It is known that a different approach can be taken to obtain a maximal path in *RNC*. See Problem B.9.4 for additional details and references.

We present one final example involving Gaussian elimination and simply note that there are numerous other examples. If Gaussian elimination with partial pivoting is used to solve a system of equations, the process will be inherently sequential since this problem is *P*-complete (Vavasis [361]). By using another approach, a solution to the system can be found in *NC*. Once again this illustrates the idea that the intermediate values an algorithm computes and not just its final answer are important in determining the algorithm's parallel complexity. See Problem A.8.4, Gaussian Elimination with Partial Pivoting.

Results such as these strongly suggest that inherently sequential algorithms will not be amenable to automatic parallelization by compilers even though the problems they solve may in fact have *NC* solutions. This is due to the fact that compilers are not sophisticated enough to discover the alternative parallel approach. Proving that an algorithm is inherently sequential is perhaps a first step toward showing that a problem is not likely to be parallelizable, or at least toward showing a different algorithmic approach needs to be found for the problem. An example of a problem for which this approach was taken is Fill Slots (Problem A.8.25).

Chapter 9

Two Other Notions of *P*-Completeness

9.1 Strong *P*-Completeness

The usual conventions of algorithm analysis express the complexity of finding a solution in terms of the length of the problem input. This will generally make the complexity sensitive to the encoding scheme used to describe problem instances. As an extreme example, the complexity of factoring a positive integer encoded in binary is quite different from that of factoring a number encoded in unary, or encoded as a product of prime factors. Realistic complexity analysis assumes that the encoding conventions for a problem are reasonable, that is, they do not make it trivial to do something for which there is evidence of difficulty (see Section 3.2).

This sensitivity to encodings is particularly significant for *number problems*. In such problems, the numerical values of the parameters of a problem instance are much larger than the size of the problem description. For example, a description of size $O(n^3)$ can represent a network of n vertices and n^2 edges, with edge capacities of size $O(2^n)$. Thus, the flows in the network described by problem instance I can be exponentially larger than the size of I. The following definition captures this concept.

Definition 9.1.1 *For any instance I of a problem, let $\mathbf{Max}(I)$ denote the maximum magnitude of all numbers in I. For any encoding scheme for the problem, let $|I|$ denote the length of the encoding of the instance. A problem is a **number problem** if and only if there* exists an encoding scheme for the problem such that there does not exist a polynomial p such that for any instance I, $\text{Max}(I) \le p(|I|)$.

A typical characteristic of a number problem is that when binary encodings of parameters in an instance I are replaced with unary encodings, the size of the encoding increases exponentially. Often, the unary encoded version is large enough to permit the problem to be solved efficiently in terms of the input length.

Definition 9.1.2 *An algorithm (with its associated encoding scheme) that solves a problem is called a* **pseudo-NC** *algorithm if and only if there is a two variable polynomial p and a single variable polynomial q such that every instance I of the problem can be solved in parallel time $p(\log(|I|), \log(\text{Max}(I)))$, and processors $q(|I|)$.*

The key feature of a pseudo-NC algorithm is that its execution time is sensitive to the size of the numbers in the problem instance. For example, Helmbold and Mayr show that General List Scheduling, Problem A.4.8, has a pseudo-NC algorithm [154].

One can also have a notion similar to pseudo-NC expressed in terms of the size of the numbers in the output, which can be applied to problems where the run time of the sequential algorithm is polynomial in the size of the result. For example, if one knows that the lexicographically first maximal independent set of a graph has size at most $(\log n)^k$ then there is an NC^{k+1} algorithm that will find it — simply run the obvious greedy algorithm in parallel (see Figure 7.1.1) for $(\log n)^k$ steps (at a cost of $O(\log n)$ per step). Similarly, if the maximum flow in a network is at most $(\log n)^k$ then the standard augmenting path algorithm converges in at most $(\log n)^k$ iterations. At $(\log n)^2$ cost per iteration, such a bounded flow can be determined in NC^{k+2}.

If a problem is not a number problem, then under all encodings, all numbers in any instance I are polynomially bounded in terms of $|I|$, and so can be efficiently encoded in unary. This means that any pseudo-NC algorithm for the problem is also an NC algorithm. Thus, the following observation is in direct analogy with the case for NP-completeness theory.

Observation 9.1.3 *If a problem is P-complete and it is not a number problem, then the problem cannot be solved by a pseudo-NC algorithm, unless NC equals P.*

The P-completeness proof for a decision problem may involve a reduction in which the numbers generated have magnitudes that are exponential in the original problem size. If such large numbers are unlikely to occur in the common problem instances, one can argue the particular proof of P-completeness is rather weak evidence that the problem is hard in practice. A reduction using only small numbers would provide a more convincing argument that even the common cases of the problem are difficult.

In fact, the restriction to small numbers for some problems makes their solutions easier in parallel. For example, General List Scheduling (Problem A.4.8) is P-complete, but when the job times are restricted to small integers, Helmbold and Mayr give an NC algorithm for the problem [154].

These considerations give rise to the notion of *strong P-completeness* (Anderson [12]) analogous to that of strong NP-completeness (Garey and Johnson [113]).

Definition 9.1.4 *A decision problem is **P-complete in the strong sense** (alternatively, **strongly P-complete**) if and only if the problem is P-complete, and there exists a polynomial p such that the problem remains P-complete even when restricted to instances I that satisfy* $\mathrm{Max}(I) \leq p(|I|)$.

The remarks presented in Section 3.3.2 pertaining to the type of reducibility employed also apply here.

An example of a strongly P-complete problem is Linear Inequalities (Problem A.4.1) — a variation on Linear Programming (Problem A.4.3). Linear Inequalities remains P-complete even when the coefficients are restricted to being ± 1 (Stephen A. Cook, Personal Communication, 1982). Other problems that are strongly P-complete are Gaussian Elimination with Partial Pivoting (Problem A.8.4) and First Fit Decreasing Bin Packing (Problem A.4.7). It is not known if Maximum Flow (Problem A.4.4) is strongly P-complete.

Problems that do not involve numbers are automatically strongly P-complete. For example, the Circuit Value Problem is strongly P-complete. Thus, the notion of strong P-completeness is useful for differentiating only among number problems.

Observation 9.1.5 *If a decision problem is P-complete in the strong sense, then the problem cannot be solved by a pseudo-NC algorithm, unless NC equals P.*

9.2   Strict *P*-Completeness

This section describes very recent material. We have tried to cover the main results regarding strict *P*-completeness theory but have omitted numerous technical details from our presentation.

Let L be a language that can be solved sequentially in time $t(n)$. We say that L has *parallel speedup* $s(n)$ if and only if there is a parallel algorithm (on any reasonable model) for L that takes time $t(n)/s(n)$ for some function $s(n)$. We say that L has *polynomial speedup* if L has parallel speedup $s(n)$ and there exists an $\epsilon > 0$ such that $s(n) = \Omega(n^\epsilon)$.

The existence of *P*-complete problems means that it is unlikely that every problem with sequential time $t(n)$ will have a parallel speedup of $t(n)/(\log n)^k$ for some constant k. But even if such a dramatic speedup is impossible, any polynomial speedup could be useful. For example, a parallel speedup of $\sqrt{t(n)}$ using a feasible number of processors is a dramatic improvement for any problem in practice.

Kruskal, Rudolph, and Snir [223], and Vitter and Simons [366] observed that limited polynomial speedup was possible for a number of problems. For example, the second set of authors considered and exhibited speedups for non-sparse versions of the Circuit Value Problem, Depth-first Search, Path Systems, and Unification. See Problems A.1.3, A.3.3, A.6.8, and A.6.9 for additional remarks. The first set of authors introduced the class *SP*, defined on page 253, of semi-efficient parallel time algorithms that have polynomial speedup.

Is some polynomial speedup possible for every problem in *P*? Condon introduced the notion of *strict P-complete* to identify those problems that exhibit some parallel speedup, and for which any further improvement in performance would imply that *all* problems in *P* possessed polynomial speedup [58]. If one believes that there are problems in *P* that do not have polynomial speedup, then strict *P*-complete problems have polynomial lower bounds on their parallel performance.

The definition of strict *P*-complete is somewhat technical, and requires the following notions. First, since the problems we are considering do not have speedups sufficient to produce *NC* solutions, we can smooth out differences between parallel models of computation by dropping any powers of $\log n$ and preserving only the dominant polynomial terms of running times. This is expressed with the "soft

Oh" notation, $\tilde{O}$, defined below.

Definition 9.2.1 *Let f and g be two functions whose domains are the natural numbers and whose ranges are the positive real numbers. $g(n) = \tilde{O}(f(n))$ (or more precisely, $g(n) \in \tilde{O}(f(n))$) if and only if there exist constants $c > 0$, $k > 0$, and $n_0 \in \mathbb{N}$ such that $g(n) \leq c(\log n)^k f(n)$ for all natural numbers $n \geq n_0$.*

Secondly, the reductions we use require the following properties. A reduction f is *honest* if and only if there exist constants c and k such that for all x, $|f(x)| \geq c|x|^{1/k}$. A function f is *eventually nondecreasing* if and only if there exists an n_0, such that for all $m \geq n \geq n_0$, we have $f(m) \geq f(n)$. Every eventually nondecreasing polynomial function has the following useful upper and lower bound property (see (Condon [58]) for a proof).

Lemma 9.2.2 *Let t be an eventually nondecreasing function such that $t(n) = \Omega(n)$ and $t(n) = n^{O(1)}$. For all $\delta > 0$ there is a rational number σ and a natural number n_0 such that*

1. $t(n) \leq n^\sigma$ for $n \geq n_0$, and

2. $n^\sigma = O(t(n)n^\delta)$.

The key idea of strict P-completeness is to find problems that are not only P-complete, but that have the additional property that they simulate P in a way that preserves polynomial speedup. That is, if a problem is strict P-complete then any further polynomial speedup in performance for its parallel solution implies that all problems in P have polynomial speedup. Since most any Turing machine program has polynomial speedup on a PRAM (or a RAM for that matter), for the notion of strict P-complete to be useful the model in which sequential time is stated must be comparable to the single processor instance of the model in which parallel time is stated. For this reason, the sequential time complexity of strict P-complete problems is stated in terms of RAM algorithms.

The definition below captures the following idea. Suppose that there is an NC many-one reduction f of language L' to language L. This means that any NC solution to L results in an NC solution to L'. But it also means that *any* parallel solution, say of time $T(n)$ for L results in a parallel solution for L'. What is the resulting parallel time for L'? Testing if $x \in L'$ requires performing the reduction and then testing if $f(x) \in L$. The testing takes time $T(|f(x)|)$. Because $|f(x)|$ could be quite large, it is possible that the parallel time for L'

obtained via reduction f is worse than the sequential time of L'.

What is the worst parallel running time for L such that solving L' in parallel via the reduction is no worse than solving L' sequentially? For example, suppose that L was in parallel time $T(n)$, and that reduction f had $|f(x)| = |x|^4$. Then L' would be in parallel time $T'(n) = T(n^4)$. If L' was in sequential time $t'(n) = n^2$ then $T(n)$ must be at most $O(\sqrt{n})$ in order for the parallel time $T'(n)$ of L' to be no worse than the sequential time $t'(n)$.

Definition 9.2.3 *A language L is* **at most** $T(n)$-**P-complete** *if and only if for every language $L' \in P$, for every sequential RAM running time $t'(n)$ for L' with $t'(n) = \Omega(n)$ and $t'(n)$ eventually nondecreasing, and for every $\epsilon > 0$ there exists an honest many-one NC reduction f from L' to L such that for all x,*

$$T(|f(x)|) = O(t'(|x|) \, |x|^\epsilon).$$

The definition contains a number of technical considerations, of which the most important is $|x|^\epsilon$ to mask any polylogarithmic factors in $T(n)$.

To say that language L with sequential running time $t'(n)$ is at most $T(n)$-P-complete says that the parallel time for a language L' reducible to L is $\tilde{O}(t'(n))$ so long as L is in parallel time $\tilde{O}(T(n))$. When L has a known parallel running time, we have the following result.

Definition 9.2.4 *A language L is* **strict** $T(n)$-**P-complete** *if and only if it is at most $T(n)$-P-complete and L has parallel running time $\tilde{O}(T(n))$.*

The fundamental strict P-complete problem is that of solving a square version of SAM2CVP (Problem A.1.6).

Definition 9.2.5 *Square Circuit Value Problem (SquareCVP)*
Given: *An encoding $\overline{\alpha}$ of a synchronous, alternating, monotone, fanin 2, fanout 2 Boolean circuit α; inputs $x_1, \ldots, x_n$; and a designated output y. The circuit has the additional restriction that it is* **square**. *That is, the number of gates at every level equals* depth(α).
Problem: *Is output y of α TRUE on input $x_1, \ldots, x_n$?*

Condon shows that square circuits can efficiently simulate RAM computations as stated in the theorem below [58]. The theorem requires the technical notion of time constructibility. A function $t(n)$ is *time constructible* in *NC* if and only if the value of $t(n)$ can be computed in *NC*.

Theorem 9.2.6 *Any RAM that runs in time $t(n) = \Omega(n)$ can be simulated by a family of square circuits of depth $\tilde{O}(t(n))$. Furthermore, for any specific RAM and input, if $t(n)$ is time constructible in NC then the corresponding circuit can be constructed in NC.*

The careful reader will notice the reasons for the various technical considerations in the definition of strict P-complete.

Theorem 9.2.7 *The Square Circuit Value Problem is strict $\sqrt{n}$-P-complete.*

Proof. It is easy to see that a size n square circuit can be evaluated in parallel time (and processors) $\tilde{O}(\sqrt{n})$.

Let L' be a language in P and let $t'(n) = \Omega(n)$ be a sequential running time for L', with t' eventually nondecreasing. Let M' be a RAM that accepts any x in L' in time $t'(|x|)$. Let $T(n) = \sqrt{n}$ for all n.

For any $\epsilon > 0$ we need to show that there is an honest many-one NC reduction f from L' to SquareCVP, such that $T(|f(x)|) = O(t'(|x|)\,|x|^\epsilon)$. From Lemma 9.2.2, with $\delta = \epsilon/2$, there is a rational number σ and a natural number n_0 such that

$$t'(n) \leq n^\sigma \text{ for } n \geq n_0, \tag{9.1}$$

and

$$n^\sigma = O(t'(n)n^{\epsilon/2}). \tag{9.2}$$

Since n^σ is computable in NC, and $t'(n) = \Omega(n)$ implies $n^\sigma = \Omega(n)$, we can apply Theorem 9.2.6 to machine M' running on input x, and obtain a square circuit of depth $\tilde{O}(|x|^\sigma)$. For inputs x with $|x| \geq n_0$, this circuit correctly decides membership of $x \in L'$.

Let f be the function that, given x, produces the corresponding square circuit. $|f(x)|$ is order the size of this circuit, and so $|f(x)| = \tilde{O}(|x|^{2\sigma}) = O(|x|^{2\sigma+\epsilon})$. By Equation 9.1 and the lower bound on $t'(n)$, we get that for some c, $|f(x)| \geq c|x|$ and so f is honest. By Equation 9.2 we get $|f(x)| = O(t'(|x|)^2\,|x|^{2\epsilon})$.

Thus, $T(|f(x)|) = O(t'(|x|)\,|x|^\epsilon)$ as required.   □

The only other known example of a strict P-complete problem is the Finite Horizon Markov Decision Process (FHMDP, Problem A.8.1). On the assumption that the finite horizon time T satisfies $T = \Theta(m)$, where m is the number of states, Condon shows that FHDMP is strict $n^{1/3}$-P-complete [58].

Problems that are not known to be strict P-complete, but that are at most $\sqrt{n}$-P-complete are the Synchronous, Alternating, Monotone Circuit Value Problem with fanin and fanout two restrictions (Problem A.1.6), Lexicographically First Maximal Independent Set (Problem A.2.1), Lexicographically First Depth-first Search Ordering (Problem A.3.3), Stack Breadth-first Search (Problem A.3.5), First Fit Decreasing Bin Packing (Problem A.4.7), and Unification (Problem A.6.9) [58].

The Lexicographically First Maximal Clique (Problem A.2.2) is an example of a problem for which there is an $\tilde{O}(\sqrt{n})$ parallel algorithm, but the problem is only known to be at most $n^{1/4}$-P-complete [58].

Chapter 10

Approximating
P-Complete Problems

10.1   Introduction

Suppose that finding the solution to a problem is *P*-complete. It is natural to ask if it is any easier to obtain an approximate solution. For decision problems this might mean considering the corresponding *combinatorial optimization problem*. That is, a problem in which we try to minimize or maximize a given quantity. As one might expect from the theory of *NP*-completeness, the answer is both yes (for example in the case of Bin Packing, Problem A.4.7) and no (for example in the case of the Lexicographically First Maximal Independent Set Size Problem, see Lemma 10.2.2.).

There are several motivations for developing good *NC* approximation algorithms. First, in all likelihood *P*-complete problems cannot be solved fast in parallel. Therefore, it may be useful to approximate them quickly in parallel. Second, problems that are *P*-complete but that can be approximated well seem to be special boundary cases. Perhaps by examining these types of problems more closely we can improve our understanding of parallelism. Third, it is important to build a theoretical foundation for studying and classifying additional approximation problems. Finally, it may be possible to speed up sequential approximation algorithms, of *NP*-complete problems, using fast parallel approximations.

Our goal in this section is to develop the basic theory of parallel approximation algorithms. We begin by showing that certain *P*-complete problems are not amenable to *NC* approximation algorithms. Later we present examples of P-complete problems that can be approximated well in parallel.

10.2   Approximating LFMIS Is Hard

We start by considering the Lexicographically First Maximal Independent Set Problem, introduced in Definition 7.1.1, and proven P-complete in Problem A.2.1. As defined, LFMIS it is not directly amenable to approximation. We can phrase the problem in terms of computing the *size* of the independent set.

Definition 10.2.1 *Lexicographically First Maximal Independent Set Size (LFMISsize)*
Given: *An undirected graph $G = (V, E)$ with an ordering on the vertices and an integer k.*
Problem: *Is the size of the lexicographically first maximal independent set of G less than or equal to k?*

The following lemma shows that computing just the size of the lexicographically first maximal independent set is P-complete.

Lemma 10.2.2 (Greenlaw, Hoover, and Ruzzo, THIS WORK) *The Lexicographically First Maximal Independent Set Size Problem is P-complete under $\leq_m^{NC^1}$ reductions.*

Proof. We reduce LFMIS to LFMISsize. Let (G, v) be an instance of LFMIS. Assume G has vertices numbered $1, \ldots, n$. Form a new graph G' by adding to G a set of $n + 1$ new vertices $W = \{n + 1, \ldots, 2n + 1\}$, each adjacent only to v. Output the pair (G', n). Let the size of the lexicographically first maximal independent set in G (G') be s (s', respectively). Then, s' will be either s or $s + n + 1$, with the former holding if and only if v is in the lexicographically first maximal independent set of G. Thus, v is in the lexicographically first maximal independent set of G if and only if s' is less than or equal to n. It is evident that the reduction is NC^1 computable. $\square$

Given this result it is natural to ask, "Is there an NC algorithm for approximating the size of the LFMIS?"

Consider an approximation algorithm that given a graph G having a LFMIS of size S_o, computes an estimate S_e of S_o. One might hope to approximate S_o by an estimate S_e that is at worst a polynomial over or under estimate of S_o. That is, $\epsilon S_o^{1/k} \leq S_e \leq S_o^l / \delta$

for appropriate constants ϵ, k, l, and δ. Note that one could imagine requiring the approximation algorithm to also deliver a solution that achieved the estimate. Of course, this makes sense only if one is underestimating a maximization problem — while one could produce a lexicographically first independent set that is smaller that the maximal, finding one that is larger is impossible. Even in this very general setting, no such approximation algorithm is possible for LFMISsize, unless *NC* equals *P*.

Theorem 10.2.3 (Greenlaw, Hoover, and Ruzzo, THIS WORK) *Let S_o be the size of the lexicographically first maximal independent set of a graph $G = (V, E)$. Then, unless NC equals P, for all $\epsilon, \delta > 0$ and $k, l \geq 1$, there is no NC approximation algorithm that will compute an estimate S_e of S_o such that*

$$\epsilon S_o^{1/k} \leq S_e \leq S_o^l / \delta.$$

Proof. We modify the construction given in the proof of Lemma 10.2.2. There an independent set W was added to G producing a new graph G'. In G' the lexicographically first maximal independent set, I', is smaller than or equal to $|V|$ if and only if the lexicographically first maximal independent set I of G contains a designated vertex v; otherwise, $|I'|$ is greater than $|W|$. Independent set W was chosen so that $|W|$ is greater than $|G|$, thereby producing a separation that can be used to determine the answer to the LFMIS instance (G, v).

We do the same here except using a larger W. For given $\epsilon, \delta > 0$ and $k, l \geq 1$, construct W so that it has integer size greater than $|G|^{lk} / (\epsilon \delta)^k$. Next add W to G as in Lemma 10.2.2 to form G'. Note, the size of W is only polynomially larger than the size of G.

Let $S_o = |I'|$. Let S_e be any integer obeying the bounds given in the statement of the theorem. If $v \in I$, then S_o is less than or equal to $|G|$, and so $S_e \leq S_o^l / \delta \leq |G|^l / \delta$. On the other hand, if $v \notin I$, then S_o is greater than $|W|$, and so $S_e \geq \epsilon S_o^{1/k} > \epsilon |W|^{1/k} > |G|^l / \delta$. Thus, $v \in I$ if S_e is less than or equal to $|G|^l / \delta$, and $v \notin I$ if S_e is greater than $|G|^l / \delta$. Consequently, approximating S_o is *P*-hard.   □

Reductions like the one above can frequently be scaled in such a way to defeat any polynomial time approximation algorithm. Additional problems for which there are no *NC* approximation algorithms, whose *P*-completeness proofs are based on a scaling process, are Unit Resolution (Problem A.6.1), Generability (Problem

A.6.7), Path Systems (Problem A.6.8), and the Circuit Value Problem (Serna [326], Serna and Spirakis [328]).

Other problems exhibit a threshold type behavior. Consider a maximization problem where we need to compute the maximum possible size of a quantity. There are problems for which existence of an NC algorithm that approximates the maximum to within a factor of $1/2$ or better implies NC equals P, whereas for any factor less than $1/2$, NC algorithms exist for solving these problems. Examples of problems possessing this behavior are High Degree Subgraph (see Problem A.2.7) and High Connectivity Subgraph (see Problem A.2.8).

These kinds of algorithms give rise to approximation schemes that generate a class of algorithms, each one in NC. Again we can make an analogy to the case for NP-completeness.

10.3 Approximation Schemes

Suppose that one is given a combinatorial optimization problem in which one must maximize or minimize some quantity. For example, deliver a flow that is maximum, or a schedule that is of minimum length. An approximation scheme takes an instance of the optimization problem and delivers a candidate solution that is near optimal. To measure the performance of the optimization scheme, one takes the ratio of the performance of the candidate solution to the optimal one. We formalize this notion below by adapting the definitions of Garey and Johnson [113] to our framework.

Definition 10.3.1 *Suppose that some approximation algorithm A on instance I of a minimization (maximization) problem delivers a candidate solution with value $A(I)$. Let* **Opt(I)** *denote the value of the optimal solution. Then the* **performance ratio** *of A on I is given by $R_A(I) = A(I)/\mathrm{Opt}(I)$ (respectively, $R_A(I) = \mathrm{Opt}(I)/A(I)$). The* **absolute performance ratio** *for approximation algorithm A is given by*

$$R_A = \text{infimum } \{r \geq 1 \mid R_A(I) \leq r \text{ for all instances } I\}.$$

Definition 10.3.2 *Let Π be a problem. An algorithm A with inputs $\epsilon > 0$ and $I \in \Pi$ is an* **approximation scheme for** Π *if and only if it delivers a candidate solution on instance $I \in \Pi$ with performance ratio $R_{A_\epsilon}(I) \leq 1 + \epsilon$. Algorithm A is an NC* **approximation**

scheme *if and only if for each fixed $\epsilon > 0$ A runs in parallel time $(\log(|I|))^{O(1)}$ and processors $|I|^{O(1)}$.*

Note, in the definition both ϵ and I are inputs to algorithm A, and in general the time and processor bounds for A depend on both the value of ϵ and the size of instance I. In an NC approximation scheme, the parameter ϵ is fixed, so that the resource requirements depend only on $|I|$. An NC approximation scheme could be exponential in $1/\epsilon$. If it behaves nicely in $1/\epsilon$ then we have a fully NC approximation scheme.

Definition 10.3.3 *Let Π be a problem. An algorithm A with inputs $\epsilon > 0$ and $I \in \Pi$ is a **fully NC approximation scheme** for Π if and only if there is a two variable polynomial p and a two variable polynomial q such that a candidate solution $A(I)$ to instance I with $R_A(I) \leq 1 + \epsilon$ can be computed in parallel time $p(\log(|I|), \log(1/\epsilon))$ and processors $q(|I|, \log(1/\epsilon))$.*

An example of a problem with a fully NC approximation scheme is Bin Packing, Problem A.4.7. Anderson, Mayr, and Warmuth observe that a sequential approximation algorithm that achieves a packing to within a factor of $1 + \epsilon$ for any $\epsilon > 0$ can be converted into an NC algorithm [17]. See also Mayr [254]. Another example is the $0 - 1$ Knapsack Problem. Mayr shows that given any $\epsilon > 0$, a solution with profit at least $1 - \epsilon$ can be found in $O(\log n(\log n + \log 1/\epsilon))$ time using n^3/ϵ^2 processors on an EREW-PRAM [254]. Mayr also shows that the *Makespan Problem* and a *List Scheduling Problem* have fully NC approximation schemes [254].

Theorem 10.3.4 *Let Π be an integer-valued combinatorial optimization problem. If there exists a two variable polynomial p such that all instances I of Π satisfy*

$$\text{Opt}(I) < p(|I|, \text{Max}(I)),$$

then the existence of a fully NC approximation scheme for Π implies the existence of a pseudo-NC algorithm for Π.

Proof. The proof is similar to that of Theorem 6.8 of Garey and Johnson [113]. We translate their proof into our setting below.

Suppose A is a fully NC approximation scheme for Π and suppose, without loss of generality, that Π is a maximization problem. Let p_A and q_A be the two polynomials corresponding to A. Consider a choice of

$$\epsilon = 1/p(|I|, \text{Max}(I)).$$

A computes a candidate solution $A(I)$ for instance I in parallel time

$$p_A(\log(|I|), \log(1/\epsilon)) = p_A(\log(|I|), \log(p(|I|, \mathrm{Max}(I))))$$

which is
$$p_1(\log(|I|), \log(\mathrm{Max}(I)))$$

for an appropriate polynomial p_1. A uses processors

$$q_A(|I|, \log(1/\epsilon)) = q_A(|I|, \log(p(|I|, \mathrm{Max}(I))))$$

which is $q_1(|I|)$ for an appropriate polynomial q_1 since $\log(\mathrm{Max}(I)) \leq |I|$. Since $R_A(I) \leq 1 + \epsilon$, it follows that

$$\mathrm{Opt}(I) \leq (1 + \epsilon)A(I).$$

Therefore,
$$\mathrm{Opt}(I) - A(I) \leq \epsilon A(I).$$

Since $\epsilon A(I) \leq \epsilon \mathrm{Opt}(I)$ and by the original assumption $\mathrm{Opt}(I) < 1/\epsilon$, we get
$$\mathrm{Opt}(I) - A(I) \leq \epsilon A(I) \leq \epsilon \mathrm{Opt}(I) < 1.$$

Since Π is integer-valued, this implies $\mathrm{Opt}(I) = A(I)$.

Combining this with the existence of the polynomials p_1 and q_1, we see a pseudo-NC algorithm exists for Π. Its steps are to compute ϵ quickly in parallel and then run A_ϵ on input I. □

The corollary stated below follows from Theorem 10.3.4 and Observation 9.1.3.

Corollary 10.3.5 *Suppose that an integer-valued combinatorial optimization problem satisfies the hypothesis of Theorem 10.3.4. If the problem is strongly P-complete, then it cannot be solved by a fully NC approximation scheme, unless NC equals P.*

Chapter 11

Closing Remarks

The previous chapters have laid out the history, foundations, and mechanics of the theory of P-completeness. We have shown that this theory plays roughly the same role in the parallel complexity domain as NP-completeness does in the sequential domain. Having devoted much effort to establishing the notion of feasible highly parallel algorithms and arguing that P-completeness captures the notions of inherently sequential problems and algorithms, it is now appropriate to temper our case a bit with some additional observations.

For some problems depending on the relevant input size, it may not be worth the effort to search for a feasible highly parallel algorithm assuming for example that you already have a $\sqrt{n}$ time parallel algorithm. The following table shows the relationship between square roots and logarithms for various input sizes. Of course, for small input sizes the constants on the running times also play a major role.

k	n
1	4
2	65536
3	$6.2 * 10^8$
4	$1.3 * 10^{13}$
5	$4.9 * 10^{17}$

Table 11.1: Values of k and n Such That $\sqrt{n} \geq (\log n)^k$.

Although it is extremely risky to predict hardware trends, it seems safe to say that massively parallel computers containing billions of processors are not "just around the corner" and although potentially feasible, machines with millions of processors are not soon to become commodity personal computers. Thus, highly parallel algorithms will not be feasible if the processor requirements for an input of size n are much greater than n^2, and probably more like $n \log n$.

Even if you have sufficient numbers of processors for problems that interest you, your algorithm may succumb to the tyranny of asymptotics. For example, a parallel algorithm that uses $\sqrt{n}$ time is probably preferable to one that uses $(\log n)^4$ time, at least for values of n less than 10^{13}. As Table 11.1 illustrates, the only really practical polylogarithmic parallel time algorithms are $O((\log n)^2)$. Perhaps the limit to feasible highly parallel algorithms are those that run in $(\log n)^2$ time and use $O(n^2)$ processors.

However, the search for an *NC* algorithm often leads to new insights into how a problem can be effectively parallelized. That is, a problem frequently is found to exhibit unexpected parallelism when the limits of its parallelism are pushed. Thus, the development of feasible highly parallel algorithms can be viewed as a useful first step toward practical parallel algorithm development. It forces one to consider different methods for splitting up and recombining solutions to subproblems and to consider alternative approaches to merely parallelizing existing sequential algorithms.

So on balance, the theory of *P*-completeness is an extremely rich and important one in terms of the foundations of parallel computation. Like any theory, it needs to be applied and interpreted correctly. Only as parallel computers become more widely available will we see how widely the theory is applied in practice. The theory has already helped to greatly increase our understanding of parallel computing, guide algorithm designers, and suggest new approaches to problem solving. Evidence for this follows in Appendices A and B where we systematically categorize many of the known results. We believe that the utility of the field will continue to grow rapidly as it is at present.

In fact, the field has grown so rapidly in recent years that it has been difficult for us to keep our problem lists up to date (and finish this book). We would appreciate readers supplying us with references and copies of papers for works we inadvertently omitted, and copies of their new research papers on the subject as they become available.

Finally, the NC versus P question seems to be a very difficult open problem. It appears that new mathematical proof techniques will be required to solve it.

• • •

Having shown that the bandersnatch design problem is P-complete, you begin your search for a sublinear time parallel algorithm, secure in the knowledge of your continuing employment.

Part II:
A Compendium of
Problems

Introduction

The second part of this book is divided into two main appendices. The intention is to provide a comprehensive list of P-complete problems and to provide an up to date list of open problems. Our other goal is to provide lists of problems in the classes CC and RNC.

Appendix A contains a list of about 140 P-complete problems. With variations on the problems counted, there are probably closer to 500 entries in the list. The problems are classified into a dozen different subject areas. The grouping is not precise but we have tried to put related problems into the same category. The problems are ordered so that most of them are defined before they are used in reductions. If this was not possible, because of the way the categories were defined and ordered, then a cross-reference to the problem's definition is given. We often include cross-references to similar problems.

Appendix B contains a list of about 30 open problems — problems not known to be in NC or P-complete. These problems are split into seven different subject areas. Appendix B also lists about 15 problems in the classes CC and RNC.

Appendix C describes notation used throughout the book.

Appendix D groups together complexity class definitions.

Appendix A

P-Complete Problems

This appendix contains a compendium of *P*-complete problems. For each entry we give a description of the problem and its input, provide references to source papers showing the problem is *P*-complete, give a hint illustrating the main idea of the completeness reduction, and mention related versions of the problem. Often the remarks include a variation of the problem that is known to be in *NC*. For many problems other variations that are also *P*-complete are described.

Problems marked by (*) are *P*-hard but are not known to be in *P*. Most of the problems marked by (*) are in *FP*. We make the distinctions here between decision problems and search problems. (Note, sometimes we use the word *computation problem* synonymously with search problem.) Other problems are in *P*, although we usually omit the proofs demonstrating this. Such proofs can usually be found in the accompanying references to the problems.

Many of the problems given here were originally shown to be *P*-complete with respect to logarithmic space reductions. Any logarithmic space computation is immediately in NC^2 by Borodin's simulation [40]. Thus, any problem logarithmic space complete for *P* is also $\leq_m^{NC^2}$ complete for *P*. In most cases the same reduction can be done in NC^1, that is, the problem is $\leq_m^{NC^1}$ complete for *P*. We have noted some exceptions to this below, but have not been exhaustive.

A word of caution is in order regarding our proof hints. The hints vary greatly in the amount of detail they provide. An "expert" will be able to construct many of the *P*-completeness proofs directly from our hints. In fact, for many problems we completely spellout the reduction involved. For other problems it may not be possible to deduce the entire reduction from our hint. For some very complex reductions, we have often decided not to reproduce the entire reduction here. Rather in such cases the reader should refer back to the original paper or to one of the other references provided. Lastly, a similar hint on two different problems might involve one simple reduction and another extremely complex one.

The problems are divided into the following categories.

A.1	circuit complexity
A.2	graph theory
A.3	searching graphs
A.4	combinatorial optimization and flow
A.5	local optimality
A.6	logic
A.7	formal languages
A.8	algebraic
A.9	geometry
A.10	real analysis
A.11	games
A.12	miscellaneous

A complete list of all the *P*-complete and open problems can be found in the Problem List on page 285. In addition, the index has entries for each problem by name as well as by its acronym.

A.1 Circuit Complexity

The Circuit Value Problem (CVP) plays the same role in *P*-completeness theory that the Satisfiability Problem does in *NP*-completeness theory. In this section we present many variants of CVP that are *P*-complete, and are particularly useful for proving other problems are *P*-complete. See Chapter 6 for more details regarding CVP and Chapter 2 for an introduction to Boolean circuits.

A.1.1 Circuit Value Problem (CVP)

Given: An encoding $\overline{\alpha}$ of a Boolean circuit α, inputs $x_1, \ldots, x_n$, and designated output y.
Problem: Is output y of α TRUE on input $x_1, \ldots, x_n$?
Reference: Ladner [225].
Hint: A proof is given in Chapter 6.
Remarks: For the two input basis of Boolean functions, it is known that CVP is *P*-complete except when the basis consists solely of OR, consists solely of AND, or consists of any or all of the following: XOR, EQUIVALENCE, and NOT (Goldschlager and Parberry [127], Parberry [281]).

A.1.2 Topologically Ordered Circuit Value Problem (TopCVP)

Given: An encoding $\overline{\alpha}$ of a Boolean circuit α, inputs $x_1, \ldots, x_n$, and designated output y with the additional assumption that the vertices in the circuit are numbered and listed in topological order.
Problem: Is output y of α TRUE on input $x_1, \ldots, x_n$?
Reference: Folklore.
Hint: A proof is given in Theorem 6.2.1. Also, see the remarks following the proof of Theorem 6.2.5.
Remarks: All of the reductions in Chapter 6 and this section preserve topological ordering, so the restrictions of all of these variants of the Circuit Value Problem to topologically ordered instances remain *P*-complete.

A.1.3 Monotone Circuit Value Problem (MCVP)

Given: An encoding $\overline{\alpha}$ of a Boolean circuit α, inputs $x_1, \ldots, x_n$, and designated output y with the additional assumption that α is *monotone*. That is, it is constructed solely of AND and OR gates.
Problem: Is output y of α TRUE on input $x_1, \ldots, x_n$?
Reference: Goldschlager [122].
Hint: Reduce the Circuit Value Problem to MCVP. A proof is given in Section 6.2. Vitter and Simons give a $\sqrt{n}$ time parallel algorithm for the non-sparse version of the problem [366].

A.1.4 Alternating Monotone Fanin 2, Fanout 2 CVP (AM2CVP)

Given: An encoding $\overline{\alpha}$ of a monotone Boolean circuit α, inputs $x_1, \ldots, x_n$, and designated output y. On any path from an input to an output the gates are required to *alternate* between OR and AND gates. Inputs are required to be connected only to OR gates, and outputs must come directly from OR gates. The circuit is restricted to have fanout exactly two for inputs and internal gates, and to have a distinguished OR gate as output.
Problem: Is output y of α TRUE on input $x_1, \ldots, x_n$?
Reference: Folklore.
Hint: A proof is given in Section 6.2.
Remarks: Goldschlager, Shaw, and Staples gave a *P*-completeness proof for Monotone, Fanout 2 CVP [128].

A.1.5 NAND Circuit Value Problem (NANDCVP)

Given: An encoding $\overline{\alpha}$ of a Boolean circuit α, inputs $x_1, \ldots, x_n$, and designated output y. Circuit α is constructed only of NAND gates and is restricted to have fanout two for inputs and NAND gates.
Problem: Is output y of α TRUE on input $x_1, \ldots, x_n$?
Reference: Folklore.
Hint: The reduction is from AM2CVP to NANDCVP. A proof is given in Section 6.2.
Remarks: Any *complete* basis of gates suffices, by the obvious simulation of NAND gates in the other basis. For example, NOR gates form a complete basis. NORCVP is defined analogously to NAND-CVP. See Post for a characterization of complete bases [292]. See the

remarks for Problem A.1.1 for other bases, not necessarily complete, for which the associated Circuit Value Problem is still complete.

A.1.6 Synchronous Alternating Monotone Fanout 2 CVP (SAM2CVP)

Given: An encoding $\overline{\alpha}$ of a monotone Boolean circuit α, inputs $x_1, \ldots, x_n$, and designated output y. In addition to the restrictions of Problem A.1.4, this version requires the circuit to be *synchronous*. That is, each level in the circuit can receive its inputs only from gates on the preceding level.
Problem: Is output y of α TRUE on input $x_1, \ldots, x_n$?
Reference: Greenlaw, Hoover, and Ruzzo, THIS WORK.
Hint: A proof is given in Section 6.2. The reduction is from AM2CVP, Problem A.1.4.

A.1.7 Planar Circuit Value Problem (PCVP)

Given: An encoding $\overline{\alpha}$ of a planar Boolean circuit α, inputs $x_1, \ldots, x_n$, and designated output y. A *planar* circuit is one whose graph can be drawn in the plane with no edges crossing.
Problem: Is output y of α TRUE on input $x_1, \ldots, x_n$?
Reference: Goldschlager [122].
Hint: Reduce Circuit Value, Problem A.1.1, to PCVP. Lay out the circuit and use cross-over circuits to replace crossing lines with a planar subcircuit. A planar XOR circuit can be built from two each of AND, OR, and NOT gates; a planar cross-over circuit can be built from three planar XOR circuits.

A m gate CVP instance is embedded in a $m \times m$ grid as follows. Gate i will be in cell (i, i), with its value sent along a wire in the ith row both to the left and to the right. Gate i's inputs are delivered to it through two wires in the ith column, with data flowing down the wires from above and up from below. Let gate i's inputs be the outputs of gates j and k, and suppose j happens to be less than i. In cell (j, i), which happens to be above (i, i) at the point where j's horizontal (rightgoing) output wire crosses i's first (respectively, vertical, downgoing) input wire, insert a two input, two output planar subcircuit that discards the value entering from above and passes the value entering from the left both to the right and down. The input to i from k is treated similarly, with the obvious changes of orientation if k is greater than i. At all other wire crossings, insert a copy of the planar cross-over circuit. Note that given i and j, the wiring of cell (i, j) is easily determined based on whether $i < j$, $i = j$, or i is an input to j, and so on. Hence, the reduction can be performed in NC^1 (even if the original circuit is not topologically sorted).

Remarks: It is easy to see that monotone planar cross-over networks do not exist, so the reduction above cannot be done in the monotone case. In fact, the monotone version of PCVP is in $LOGCFL \subseteq NC^2$ when all inputs appear on one face of the planar embedding (Dymond and Cook [99, 100], Goldschlager [124], Mayr [253]). The more general problem where inputs may appear anywhere is also in NC (Delcher and Kosaraju [87], Kosaraju [219]). A complete characterization of all bases from which it is possible to construct planar cross-over circuits is given in McColl [256].

A.1.8   Arithmetic Circuit Value Problem (*) (ArithCVP)

Given: An encoding $\overline{\alpha}$ of an *arithmetic circuit* α with dyadic operations $+$, $-$, and $*$, together with inputs $x_1, \ldots, x_n$ from a ring.

Problem: Does α on input $x_1, \ldots, x_n$ output 1?

Reference: (H. Venkateswaran, Personal Communication, 1983).

Hint: Reduce NANDCVP to ArithCVP as follows: TRUE $\rightarrow$ 1, FALSE $\rightarrow$ 0, and $\neg(u \wedge v) \rightarrow 1 - u * v$, where 0 denotes the additive identity and 1 denotes the multiplicative identity of the ring.

Remarks: The problem is not necessarily in FP for infinite rings like $\mathbb{Z}$ or $\mathbb{Q}$, since intermediate values need not be of polynomial length. It will be in FP for any finite ring, and remains P-hard in any ring. It is also P-hard to decide whether all gates in an arithmetic circuit over $\mathbb{Z}$ have "small" values, say values of a magnitude $2^{n^{O(1)}}$. Cucker and Torrecillas look at related problems [73]. The problem is in NC for circuits of degree $2^{(\log n)^{O(1)}}$, where the *degree* of a vertex is one for inputs, and $d_1 + d_2$ $(\max(d_1, d_2))$ when the vertex is a product (respectively, sum) of the values computed by two vertices of degree d_1 and d_2 (Miller, Ramachandran, and Kaltofen [258], Valiant *et al.* [358]).

A.1.9 Min-plus Circuit Value Problem (MinPlusCVP)

Given: An encoding $\overline{\alpha}$ of a $(\min, +)$ circuit α and rational inputs $x_1, \ldots, x_n$.

Problem: Does α on input $x_1, \ldots, x_n$ output a nonzero value?

Reference: (H. Venkateswaran, Personal Communication, 1983).

Hint: Reduce Monotone Circuit Value, Problem A.1.3, to Min-PlusCVP as follows: TRUE $\to$ 1, FALSE $\to$ 0, $u \wedge v \to \min(u, v)$, and $u \vee v \to \min(1, u + v)$.

Remarks: The above reduction works in any ordered semi-group with additive identity 0 and an element 1 such that $1 + 1 \geq 1 > 0$. If there is a nonzero element 1 such that $1 + 1 = 0$ (e.g. in $\mathbf{Z}_2$), then reduce NANDCVP via $\neg(u \wedge v) \to 1 + \min(u, v)$. In a *well-ordered* semigroup where 0 is the minimum element, one or the other of these cases holds. If the semigroup is infinite, the problem may not be in P.

A.1.10 ϵ-Circuit Depth Ones (*) (ϵCDO)

Given: An encoding $\overline{\alpha}$ of a Boolean circuit α, plus inputs $x_1, \ldots, x_n$, and a number $\epsilon \in (0, 1]$. Let d denote the maximum depth that a TRUE value propagates to in α on the given input.

Problem: Find an integer d' such that $d \geq d' \geq \epsilon d$.

Reference: Kirousis and Spirakis [215].

Hint: This problem is stated as a computation problem. Thus, it is technically not in P. The reduction showing the problem is P-hard is from MCVP, Problem A.1.3. Given α it is easy to construct a deeper circuit such that if we could approximate the depth of ones in the new circuit, we could determine the output of α.

Remarks: The extension to α can be constructed to preserve properties such as monotonicity, fan-out, alternation, and planarity (Kirousis and Spirakis [215], Serna [327]).

A.1.11 ϵ-Circuit TRUE Gates (*) (ϵCTG)

Given: An encoding $\overline{\alpha}$ of a Boolean circuit α, plus inputs $x_1, \ldots, x_n$, and a number $\epsilon \in (0, 1]$. Let t denote the number of gates in α that evaluate to TRUE.

Problem: Find an integer d such that $\lfloor \epsilon t \rfloor \leq d < t$.

Reference: Serna [326, 327].

Hint: This problem is stated as a computation problem. Thus, it is technically not in P. The reduction showing the problem P-hard is from CVP [327]. Given α it is easy to construct a larger circuit such that if we could approximate the output of the new circuit, we could determine the output of α.

Remarks: The extension to α can be constructed to preserve properties such as monotonicity, fan-out, alternation, and planarity [327].

A.1.12 Inverting An NC° Permutation (*) (InvNC0Perm)

Given: An n-input, n-output NC^0, see definition page 250, circuit computing a bijective function $f : \{0,1\}^n \to \{0,1\}^n$ and $y \in \{0,1\}^n$.
Problem: Is the last bit of $f^{-1}(y)$ equal to 1?
Reference: Håstad [149, Section 2.5], [150].
Hint: The reduction is from CVP, Problem A.1.1. This problem is called straight-line program in [150]. Let α be an instance of CVP, where $x_1, \ldots, x_n$ denote the inputs and $b_{n+1}, \ldots, b_m$ denote the gates. Gate b_m is the output gate. The notation $b_k(i_1, i_2)$ represents the value of gate b_k and indicates that gate b_k receives its inputs from the outputs of gates i_1 and i_2, where i_1 and i_2 are less than k. From the circuit α, a permutation g is constructed from $\{0,1\}^m$ to $\{0,1\}^m$. Let $z_1, \ldots, z_m$ (collectively z) denote input bits for g and $g_1, \ldots, g_m$ output bits. g is defined as follows:

1. $g_k(z) = z_k$, for $k = 1, \ldots, n$, and

2. $g_k(z) = z_k \oplus b_k(z_{i_k}, z_{j_k})$ for $k = n+1, \ldots, m$.

It is not hard to see that the mth bit of $g^{-1}(x_1, \ldots, x_n, 0, \ldots, 0)$ is the value of gate b_m in α.

Remarks: The problem is not known to be in P in general, although the family of permutations used to show P-hardness is polynomial time invertible. See Boppana and Lagarias [39] for some additional remarks about one-way functions.

A.1.13 Circuit Evaluation over Monoids (CEM)

Given: A *finite monoid* $(M, \oplus, 1)$ containing a nonsolvable group, where M is a finite set, $\oplus$ is an associative binary operation on the elements of M, and 1 acts as an identity element; an encoding $\overline{\alpha}$ of a circuit α, whose gates are of type $\oplus$, inputs $x_1, \ldots, x_n \in M$, and designated output y.

Problem: Does α evaluate to y on input $x_1, \ldots, x_n$?

Reference: Beaudry, McKenzie, and Péladeau [28].

Hint: The reduction is from Circuit Value, Problem A.1.1.

Remarks: If M is solvable the same problem is in DET, the class of problems NC^1 Turing reducible to computing integer determinants, see page 248. Also see Problems A.1.8 and A.1.9.

A.2   Graph Theory

A.2.1   Lexicographically First Maximal Independent Set (LFMIS)

Given: An undirected graph $G = (V, E)$ with an ordering on the vertices and a designated vertex v.

Problem: Is vertex v in the lexicographically first maximal independent set of G?

Reference: Cook [67].

Hint: A proof is given in Section 7.1.

Remarks: This is an instance of the Lexicographically First Maximal Subgraph for π, Problem A.2.16. LFMIS is P-complete for bipartite or planar graphs restricted to degree at most three Miyano [265]. Karp observed that the completeness of LFMIS implies that determining the ith vertex chosen by any deterministic sequential algorithm for either LFMIS or LFMC, Problem A.2.2, is also complete [194]. Computing or approximating the size of the lexicographically first maximal independent set is also P-complete; see Section 10. Luby gave the first NC algorithm for finding a maximal independent set [198], subsequently improved by Luby [246], by Alon, Babai, and Itai [10], and by Goldberg and Spencer [121]. These algorithms do not compute the *lexicographically first* maximal independent set. Using a general result involving *inference systems*, Miyano shows that when G is a forest LFMIS can be solved on a CREW-PRAM in $O(\log |V|)$ time using a polynomial number of processors [263].

A.2.2   Lexicographically First Maximal Clique (LFMC)

Given: An undirected graph $G = (V, E)$ with an ordering on the vertices and a designated vertex v.

Problem: Is vertex v in the lexicographically first maximal clique of G?

Reference: Cook [67].

Hint: Finding a maximal clique is equivalent to finding a maximal independent set in the complement graph of G, see Problem A.2.1. Stewart shows that *Ordered Greedy Clique* and *Ordered Remaining*

Clique are both *P*-complete [343]. These two decision problems are based on heuristic greedy algorithms for computing cliques.

A.2.3 Alternating Graph Accessibility Problem (AGAP)

Given: A directed graph $G = (V, E)$, a partition $V = A \cup B$ of the vertices, and designated vertices s and t.

Problem: Is $apath(s, t)$ TRUE?, where $apath$ is defined as follows. Vertices in A are "universal," those in B are "existential." Such a graph is called an *alternating* graph or an AND/OR graph. The predicate $apath(x, y)$ holds if and only if

1. $x = y$, or

2. x is existential and there is a $z \in V$ with $(x, z) \in E$ and $apath(z, y)$, or

3. x is universal and for all $z \in V$ with $(x, z) \in E$, $apath(z, y)$ holds.

Reference: Chandra, Kozen, and Stockmeyer [49], Immerman [168, 169].

Hint: Reduce AM2CVP, Problem A.1.4, to AGAP. Create two existential vertices 0 and 1. Put edge $(x_i, 0)$ into E if input x_i is 0, and edge $(x_i, 1)$ into E if input x_i is 1. AND gates are universal vertices and OR gates are existential vertices. Inputs to a gate correspond to children in the alternating graph. For output gate z of the circuit, $apath(z, 1)$ holds if and only if the output z is 1.

Remarks: The original proof simulated an alternating Turing machine (ATM) directly to show that AGAP was complete for ATM logarithmic space [168]. Since $ALOG = P$ [49], this showed AGAP was *P*-complete too. When this problem is generalized to hierarchical graphs it remains in P, provided the graph is "breadth-first ordered;" see Lengauer and Wagner [231]. The proof sketched above also shows that the problem remains *P*-complete when the partition (A, B) induces a bipartite graph. When restricted to only existential vertices, the problem is equivalent to the *Directed Graph Accessibility Problem*, variously called "GAP" and "STCON," and shown by Savitch to be complete for $NLOG$ [322]. Peterson (Gary Peterson, Personal Communication, 1980's) shows that the undirected version of AGAP is also *P*-complete. When restricted to undirected graphs with only existential vertices, this problem is equivalent to the *Undirected Graph Accessibility Problem*, called "UGAP" or "USTCON," which is known to be complete for the special case of nondeterministic logarithmic space known as symmetric logarithmic space or *SLOG* (Lewis and Papadimitriou [233]). Yasuura shows a generalization of AGAP is *P*-complete via a reduction to Path Systems, Problem A.6.8 [374]. He considers the graph reachability problem on directed *hypergraphs*, graphs whose edges consist of a subset of vertices and a single vertex.

A.2.4   Hierarchical Graph Accessibility Problem (HGAP)

Given: A hierarchical graph $G = (V, E)$, and two designated vertices s and t. A *hierarchical graph* $\Gamma = (G_1, \ldots, G_k)$ consists of k subcells G_i, $1 \leq i \leq k$. Each *subcell* is a graph that contains three types of vertices called pins, inner vertices, and nonterminals. The *pins* are the vertices through which the subcell can be connected to from the outside. The *inner vertices* cannot be connected to from the outside. The *nonterminals* stand for previously defined subcells. A nonterminal inside G_i has a name and a type. The *name* is a unique number or string. The *type* is a number from $1, \ldots, i-1$. A nonterminal v of type j stands for a copy of subcell G_j. The neighbors of v are in an one-to-one correspondence with the pins of G_j via a mapping that is specified as part of Γ.

Problem: Is there a path between s and t in the expansion graph of G? An *expansion graph* is a hierarchical graph expanded. The graph is *expanded* by expanding cell G_k recursively. To expand subcell G_i expand its subcells $G_1, \ldots, G_{i-1}$ recursively and replace each nonterminal of v of type j with a copy of the expansion of subcell G_j.

Reference: Lengauer and Wagner [231].

Hint: The reduction is from Alternating Graph Accessibility, Problem A.2.3.

Remarks: Hierarchical versions of the following problems are also *P*-complete: graph accessibility in undirected graphs, determining whether a directed graph contains a cycle, and determining whether a given graph is bipartite [231]. There are several other very restricted versions of hierarchical graph problems that are *P*-complete. See [231] for details.

A.2.5 Restricted Chromatic Alternating Graph Accessibility Problem (RCAGAP)

Given: An alternating graph $G = (V, E)$, two natural numbers k and m (where $k \leq m \leq \log |V|$), a coloring $c : E \to \{1, \ldots, m\}$, and two vertices s and t. Note that the coloring is an unrestricted assignment of colors to the edges. It may assign the same color to several edges incident to a common vertex. See Problem A.2.3 for the definition of an alternating graph.

Problem: Are there k different colors $i_1, \ldots, i_k \in \{1, \ldots, m\}$ such that $apath(s, t)$ holds in the subgraph of G induced by the edges with colors $i_1, \ldots, i_k$? See Problem A.2.3 for the definition of *apath*.

Reference: Lengauer and Wagner [231].

Hint: There is a trivial reduction from Alternating Graph Accessibility, Problem A.2.3. Membership of RCAGAP in P follows from membership of AGAP in P, since there are at most $2^k \leq |V|$ possible sets of colors to try.

Remarks: The problem remains P-complete if the vertices are restricted to being breadth-first ordered [231]. When generalized to hierarchical graphs, the problem becomes NP-complete [231].

A.2.6 Lexicographically First $\Delta + 1$ Vertex Coloring (LFDVC)

Given: An undirected graph $G = (V, E)$ with Δ equal to the maximum degree of any vertex in V, an ordering $v_1, \ldots, v_n$ on the vertices of V, a designated color c, and a vertex v.

Problem: Is vertex v colored with color c in the lexicographically least coloring of the vertices of G? A *coloring* is an assignment of colors to the vertices such that no adjacent vertices receive the same color. The coloring uses at most $\Delta + 1$ colors. If c_i is the color of v_i, where $c_i \in \{1, \ldots, \Delta + 1\}$, then each coloring corresponds to a $(\Delta + 1)$-ary number, and the least coloring is well-defined.

Reference: (Michael Luby, Personal Communication, 1984), Luby [246].

Hint: Computing the lexicographically least coloring is easily done in polynomial time by examining each vertex in order and coloring it with the smallest available color. To show completeness, reduce NANDCVP, Problem A.1.5, to LFDVC. The coloring will correspond to evaluating the circuit in topological order. Let $v_1, \ldots, v_n$ be the gates of a circuit α and assume the gates are numbered in topological order. Each gate in the circuit will be represented by four vertices in G, with the order on the vertices induced from the order of the gates. Consider a NAND gate, $v_i \leftarrow \neg(v_j, v_k)$. Introduce three new vertices v_i', v_j', and v_k'; where v_j' and v_k' appear after v_j, and v_k and v_i' appear after all these, but before v_i, in the topological ordering. The gate is then represented by the edges (v_j, v_j'), (v_k, v_k'), (v_j', v_i'), (v_k', v_i'), and (v_i', v_i). One final fix is necessary. To keep the degree down to three, a fanout tree may be required on the output of each gate. The resulting graph can be colored with only three colors in the order $\{T, F, X\}$ (even though four might be necessary for a different ordering).

Remarks: The problem of $\Delta - 1$ coloring is NP-complete (Garey and Johnson [113]). For graphs that are not an odd cycle or complete, a Δ coloring can be found in polynomial time (Brook's Theorem, see Brooks [47] or, for example, Bondy and Murty [37]). However, this is not necessarily the lexicographically first coloring. $\Delta + 1$ vertex coloring is NC^1 reducible to finding a maximal independent set (Michael Luby, Personal Communication, 1984), but the maximal independent set algorithm (Karp and Wigderson [198]) does not produce the lexicographically first maximal independent set. It is possible to color a graph with Δ colors in NC, although again the coloring produced is not the lexicographically first (Hajnal and Szemerédi [146], Karchmer and Naor [187], Karloff [189]). Chlebus *et al.* show that for *tree structured* graphs LFDVC can be solved in NC [55]. There are also NC algorithms for five coloring planar graphs (Boyar and Karloff [45], Naor [272]). Karloff and Shmoys give NC algorithms for edge coloring problems [191]. In particular, they show that multigraphs can be edge colored with $3\lceil \Delta/2 \rceil$ colors on a COMMON CRCW-PRAM using $O((\log(\Delta|V|))^3)$ time and $\Delta|V|$ processors. For the same model and multigraphs with Δ equal to three, they use four colors, and $O(\log|V|)$ time and $|V| + |E|$ processors. Again on the same model for simple graphs using $\Delta + 1$ colors, Karloff and Shmoys obtain a $\Delta^{O(1)}(\log|V|)^{O(1)}$ time, $|V|^{O(1)}$ processor algorithm. This results in an NC algorithm for polylogarithmic Δ. See also Problem B.9.3.

A.2.7   High Degree Subgraph (HDS)

Given: An undirected graph $G = (V, E)$ and an integer k.
Problem: Does G contain a vertex induced subgraph with minimum degree at least k?

Reference: Anderson and Mayr [14].

Hint: Reduce AM2CVP, Problem A.1.4, to HDS. The proof illustrated here is for k equals three, although it can be generalized to any fixed k greater than or equal to three. A TRUE input k_1 connected to gate i is represented by a gadget with five vertices k_1, v_1, v_2, v_3, and k_1'. The edges in the gadget are (v_1, k_1), (v_1, k_1'), (v_1, v_2), (v_2, k_1'), (v_2, v_3), (v_3, k_1), and (v_3, k_1'). k_1' is connected to a vertex in the gadget for gate i as described below. A FALSE input is represented by a single vertex. An AND gate i with inputs l_1 and l_2, and outputs l_1' and l_2' is represented by a fourteen vertex gadget. The gadget is composed of two of the gadgets used to represent TRUE inputs and an additional four vertices. l_1' and l_2' label the vertices corresponding to k_1' in the TRUE input gadget. w_1 and w_2 label the positions corresponding to k_1 in their respective copy of the TRUE input gadget. The four additional vertices are labeled l_1, l_2, w_3, and w_4. l_1, l_2, and w_3 are connected into a three clique. w_4 is connected to w_1, w_2, and w_3. Inputs to gate i are connected to l_1 and l_2, and the outputs l_1' and l_2' are connected to the appropriate input positions of other gates. The representation of an OR gate is very similar to the AND gadget; omitting w_3 and connecting l_1 and l_2 directly to w_4. Finally, there is a binary tree that has as its leaves the vertices corresponding to the k_1's of the TRUE inputs and has the vertex corresponding to the output vertex of the circuit as its root. The computation of a HDS of degree three proceeds on this new graph so that HDS is nonempty if and only if the output of the circuit is TRUE.

Remarks: Although not stated as a lexicographically first problem, the HDS in a graph is unique. Hence, this is another instance of the Lexicographically First Maximal Subgraph for π, Problem A.2.16. There is an *NC* algorithm computing a HDS for k equals two. Let $K(G)$ denote the largest k such that there is an induced subgraph of G with minimum degree k. For fixed $0 \leq c \leq 1$, consider finding an approximation d such that $K(G) \geq d \geq cK(G)$. For any c less than $1/2$ there is an *NC* algorithm for finding d, and for any c greater than $1/2$ the problem of finding d is *P*-complete [14]. The complementary *Low Degree Subgraph Problem*, see Problem B.1.5, has also been studied and for several natural decision problems it is *NP*-complete (Greenlaw [134]). Decision problems based on ordered vertex removal relating to subgraph computations are also *P*-complete [134]. A special case of HDS is the Color Index Problem (Vishwanathan and Sridhar [365]): given an undirected graph $G = (V, E)$, is the color index of G less than or equal to four? The *color index* is the maximum over all subgraphs H, of G, of the minimum degree of H. Asking if the color index is less than or equal to four is complementary to asking if there are any high degree subgraphs of order five. The original reduction for Color Index is from Ordered Low Degree Vertex Removal, Problem A.2.11. See remarks for Problem A.2.6.

A.2.8   High Connectivity Subgraph (HCS)

Given: An undirected graph $G = (V, E)$ and an integer k.
Problem: Does G contain a vertex induced subgraph of vertex (edge) connectivity at least k?
Reference: Kirousis, Serna, and Spirakis [214], Serna [326].
Hint: The reduction is from Monotone Circuit Value, Problem A.1.3, and is similar to that used to prove Problem A.2.7, the High Degree Subgraph Problem, is P-complete.
Remarks: Approximation algorithms for this problem exhibit a threshold type behavior. Below a certain value on the *absolute performance ratio* the problem remains P-complete for fixed k, and above that ratio there are NC approximation algorithms for the problem (Serna and Spirakis [328]). Specifically, let o be the maximum size of a k-vertex connected induced subgraph of G. Then for $0 \leq c \leq 1/4$ it is possible to find, in NC, a vertex induced subgraph of size greater than or equal to co, but for $1/4 < c \leq 1$ this is not possible, unless NC equals P. For edge connectivity, the threshold is c equal to $1/2$. Khuller and Schieber present an algorithm for an ARBITRARY CRCW-PRAM that given an undirected graph G and an integer k tests whether G is k-vertex connected [209]. If G is not k-vertex connected, they obtain a set of at most $k-1$ vertices whose removal disconnects G. Their algorithm runs in $O(k^2 \log n)$ time and uses $k(n + k^2)C(n, m)$ processors, where $C(n, m)$ is the number of ARBITRARY CRCW-PRAM processors required to compute the connected components of an n-vertex, m-edge graph in logarithmic time. For polylogarithmic k, this is an NC algorithm.

A.2.9   Reliable Connectivity for Failures of Incoming Edges (RCIN)

Given: A directed acyclic graph $G = (V, E)$, and two distinguished vertices s and t. Additionally, a function f that assigns a nonnegative integer to every vertex $v \in V$ such that $f(v)$ is less than or equal to the indegree of v. A choice of *failed edges* for a vertex v is denoted $F(v)$. It consists of a set of incoming edges to v of cardinality less than or equal to $f(v)$.

Problem: Is there a directed path between s and t consisting of edges that are not in $\bigcup_{v \in V} F(v)$?

Reference: Kavadias, Kirousis, and Spirakis [205].

Hint: The reduction is from Monotone Circuit Value, Problem A.1.3. The idea is to consider the circuit as a directed acyclic graph. Inputs are represented by vertices and all edges are directed towards the output gate, which will be t. A vertex s is introduced that is connected to all TRUE inputs. f has value 0 for all vertices except those corresponding to AND gates for which it has value 1. The output of the circuit instance is TRUE if and only if s remains connected to t for any set of failure edges.

Remarks: The general problem in which the input graph is not required to be a directed acyclic graph is co-NP-complete [205]. Kavadias, Kirousis, and Spirakis point out that the apparent reduction in complexity of RCIN is not due to the restriction to directed acyclic graphs but because of allowing only failures of in-edges [205]. They also show that approximating RCIN is P-complete. They define another problem called *Feasible Connectivity* in which every vertex causes at least $f(v)$ edges to fail. The question then is whether there exists at least one failure pattern in which there is a s to t path. This problem is in NC [205]. Kirousis and Spirakis define another problem called ϵ*Reliably Long Path* [215]. In this problem exactly one of the arcs leading into a vertex fails; the goal is to compute the maximum number k such that the directed acyclic graph has a path from the source vertex of length at least k with probability one. They show that this problem is P-complete [215].

A.2.10 Ordered High Degree Vertex Removal (OHDVR)

Given: An undirected graph $G = (V, E)$ with a numbering on the vertices in V, and two designated vertices u and v.

Problem: Is there an elimination order on V, $v_1, \ldots, v_n$, satisfying the properties that u is eliminated before v and for $1 \leq i \leq n$, v_i is the lowest numbered vertex of maximum degree in the $(i-1)$-st remaining subgraph of G? An *elimination order* is a sequence of vertices ordered as they and their corresponding edges are to be deleted from the graph.

Reference: Greenlaw [134].

Hint: The reduction is from NANDCVP, Problem A.1.5, with fanin and fanout restrictions to two. The circuit is transformed directly into a graph. The vertices in the graph are ordered so that gates evaluating to FALSE in the circuit are deleted first in the instance of OHDVR. A special vertex of degree four is added and its removal order is compared with that of the vertex corresponding to the output gate of the circuit.

A.2.11   Ordered Low Degree Vertex Removal (OLDVR)

Given: An undirected graph $G = (V, E)$ with a numbering on the vertices in V, and two designated vertices u and v.

Problem: Is there an *elimination order* on V, $v_1, \ldots, v_n$, satisfying the properties that u is eliminated before v and for $1 \leq i \leq n$, v_i is the lowest numbered vertex of minimum degree in the $(i-1)$-st remaining subgraph of G?

Reference: Vishwanathan and Sridhar [365], Greenlaw [134].

Hint: This is the complementary problem to Problem A.2.10.

Remarks: The problem defined in [365] is more restricted than the one presented here. Their graphs are also required to have the property that u appears before v in some minimum elimination sequence if and only if u appears before v in all minimum degree elimination sequences.

A.2.12   Ordered Vertices Remaining (OVR)

Given: An undirected graph $G = (V, E)$ with a numbering on the vertices in V, a designated vertex u, and an integer k.

Problem: Is there an *elimination order* on V, $v_1, \ldots, v_n$, satisfying the properties that $u = v_j$ for some $j < (n - k)$ and for $1 \leq i \leq n$, v_i is the lowest numbered vertex of maximum degree in the $(i-1)$-st remaining subgraph of G?

Reference: Greenlaw [134].

Hint: The reduction is from Ordered High Degree Vertex Removal, Problem A.2.10.

Remarks: The *Ordered Low Degree Subgraph Membership Problem* is also P-complete [134]. The problem here is to determine whether a designated vertex is in a remaining subgraph when all vertices in that remaining subgraph have small degree.

A.2.13 Neighborhood Removal (NR)

Given: An undirected graph $G = (V, E)$ with a numbering on the vertices in V, and two designated vertices u and v.

Problem: Is vertex u removed before vertex v when the neighborhood removal algorithm is run on G? The *neighborhood removal algorithm* processes maximum degree vertices in the remaining subgraph of G that have the lowest vertex numbers. It iterates through such vertices, deleting them as well as their neighborhoods from the remaining subgraph.

Reference: Greenlaw [133].

Hint: The reduction is from Ordered High Degree Vertex Removal, Problem A.2.10.

Remarks: The neighborhood removal algorithm (or a slight variant of it) is used as a subroutine in Wigderson's heuristic algorithm for the *Graph Coloring Problem* [372] and also in a heuristic algorithm for the *Minimum Vertex Cover Problem* (Lingas [240]). In light of the fact that NR is *P*-complete, it is unlikely that heuristic algorithms using the neighborhood removal algorithm as a subroutine will parallelize well.

A.2.14 Greedy Dominating Set (GDS)

Given: An undirected graph $G = (V, E)$ with a numbering on the vertices in V and a designated vertex u.

Problem: Is vertex u in the dominating set formed by the execution of the greedy dominating set algorithm? A *dominating set V'* is a subset of V such that for all $v \in V - V'$ there exists a vertex $w \in V'$ such that $\{v, w\} \in E$. w is said to *cover v*. The *greedy dominating set algorithm* builds up a dominating set by placing the least numbered vertex that covers the most vertices in the dominating set. This procedure is repeated until all vertices are covered.

Reference: Stewart [342].

Hint: The reduction is from Ordered High Degree Vertex Removal, Problem A.2.10.

Remarks: This greedy heuristic is used to find "small" dominating sets. It is well known that the general version of the problem called *Dominating Set* is *NP*-complete (Garey and Johnson [113]).

A.2.15   Nearest Neighbor Traveling Salesman Heuristic (NNTSH)

Given: A finite set $C = \{C_1, \ldots, C_n\}$ of cities, and a distance matrix D with entries (d_{ij}) that are positive integers $(1 \leq i, j \leq n)$, and two distinguished vertices s and l.

Problem: Does the nearest neighbor tour starting at s visit l as the last vertex before completing the tour at s? The *nearest neighbor tour* is a greedy heuristic that always chooses the nearest unvisited vertex as the next vertex on the tour.

Reference: Kindervater, Lenstra, and Shmoys [212].

Hint: Reduce NNTSH to NANDCVP, Problem A.1.5. Without loss of generality, assume the gates are numbered in topological order. Gate k with inputs i_1 and i_2, and outputs o_1 and o_2 is replaced by the gadget described below. The gadget has vertices A, i_1, i'_1, i_2, i'_2, o'_1, o_1, o_2, o'_2, and B. Let the triple (x, y, z) mean the distance between x and y is d. The triples in the gadget are $(A, B, 3k + 2)$, $(A, i_1, 3k)$, $(A, i_2, 3k + 1)$, $(i_1, i'_1, 0)$, $(i_2, i'_2, 0)$, $(i'_1, o'_1, 3k + 1)$, $(i'_2, o'_1, 3k)$, $(o'_1, o_1, 0)$, $(o_1, o_2, 3k)$, $(o_2, o'_2, 0)$, and $(o'_2, B, 3k)$. Vertex B of gate k is connected to vertex A of gate $k+1$. The distances between vertices that have been left unspecified are assumed to be very large. The edges between "i" vertices and those between "o" vertices represent inputs and outputs respectively. An edge included (not included) in the tour represents a TRUE (respectively, FALSE) value. TRUE circuit inputs are "chained" together and the tour begins at the first TRUE input. By inserting a new vertex C before vertex B in the last gadget, and connecting B and C to the first TRUE input in the input chain, the tour constructed by the NNTSH is such that B (C) is visited last if and only if the circuit evaluates to TRUE (respectively, FALSE).

Remarks: The *nearest merger*, *nearest insertion*, *cheapest insertion*, and *farthest insertion* heuristics are all *P*-complete [212]. The *double minimum spanning tree* and *nearest addition* heuristics are in *NC* [212]. See also Problem A.5.9.

A.2.16   Lexicographically First Maximal Subgraph for π (LFMS(π))

Given: An undirected graph $G = (V, E)$ with an ordering on V, a designated vertex v, and a *polynomial time testable*, nontrivial, hereditary property π. A property is *nontrivial* if there are infinitely many graphs that satisfy the property and at least one graph that does not. A property π is *hereditary* on induced subgraphs if whenever G satisfies π, so do all vertex induced subgraphs.

Problem: Is v in the lexicographically first maximal subgraph H of G that satisfies π?

Reference: Miyano [263, 265].

Hint: Given a property π that is nontrivial and hereditary, Ramsey's theorem implies that either π is satisfied by all cliques or by all independent sets of vertices. This observation combined with the facts that the Lexicographically First Maximal Clique, Problem A.2.2, and the Lexicographically First Maximal Independent Set, Problem A.2.1, are P-complete are used to show LFMS(π) is P-complete.

Remarks: The following are examples of properties that meet the criteria stated in the problem: bipartite, chordal, clique, comparability graph, edge graph, forest, independent set, outerplanar, and planar. Not all problems involving a lexicographically first solution are P-complete. For example, the Lexicographically First Topological Order Problem is complete for $NLOG$ (Shoudai [331]) and the Lexicographic Low Degree Subgraph Membership Problem is NP-complete (Greenlaw [134]). For additional remarks relating to this problem see Chapter 7 and also Miyano [263, 266].

A.2.17 Minimum Feedback Vertex Set (MFVS)

Given: A directed graph $G = (V, E)$ that is cyclically reducible (defined below) and a designated vertex v.

Problem: Is v contained in the minimum feedback set of G that is computed by the algorithm given by Wang, Lloyd, and Soffa [371]?

Reference: Bovet, De Agostino, and Petreschi [44].

Hint: We review some terminology from [371]. A vertex z of G is *deadlocked* if there is a directed path in G from z to a vertex y that lies on a directed cycle. The *associated graph of vertex x with respect to G, $A(G, x)$,* consists of vertex x and all vertices of G that are not deadlocked if x is removed from G. A directed graph is *cyclically reducible* if and only if there exists a sequence of vertices $(y_1, \ldots, y_k)$ such that each of the graphs $A(G_{i-1}, y_i)$ is cyclic, where $G_0 = G$ and $G_i = G_{i-1} - A(G_i, y_i)$, for $1 \leq i \leq k$.

A set is called a *feedback vertex set* if it contains at least one vertex from every cycle (Karp [193]). It is *minimum* if no other feedback vertex set has fewer elements. Wang, Lloyd, and Soffa gave a polynomial time algorithm for computing feedback sets in cyclically reducible graphs [371]. Thus, MFVS is in P. The reduction is from Monotone Circuit Value, Problem A.1.3. Let $(g_1, \ldots, g_k)$ denote an instance α of MCVP including inputs, where g_k is the output gate. From α a graph G is constructed as follows:

1. associate vertices g'_i and g''_i with each g_i,

2. for each input g_i, if g_i is TRUE (FALSE) add a loop edge to g'_i (respectively, g''_i),

3. for each AND gate g with inputs i and j add edges (g', i''), (i'', j''), (j'', g'), (g'', i'), (i', g''), (g'', j'), and (j', g'') to G,

4. for each OR gate g with inputs i and j add edges (g'', i'), (i', j'), (j', g''), (g', i''), (i'', g'), (g', j''), and (j'', g') to G,

5. add edges (g'_k, g''_k) and (g''_k, g'_k).

It is easy to see that G is cyclically reducible. Set v equal to g'_k to complete the reduction.

Remarks: The question of whether a general graph has a feedback vertex set of size k is *NP*-complete (Karp [193]). Bovet, De Agostino, and Petreschi give an algorithm for finding a minimum feedback set in cyclically reducible graphs that requires $O(k(\log n)^2)$ time and $O(n^4)$ processors on a CREW-PRAM, where k denotes the size of the minimum feedback set. Greenlaw proved that a related problem, the *Lexicographically First Maximal Acyclic Subgraph Problem*, is *P*-complete [136, 137]. Ramachandran proved that finding a *minimum weight feedback vertex set* in a reducible flow graph with arbitrary weights is *P*-complete [296, 297]. She also proved the following four problems are *NC* equivalent: finding a minimum feedback arc set in an unweighted reducible flow graph, finding a minimum weight feedback arc set in a reducible flow graph with unary weights on the arcs, finding a minimum weight feedback vertex set in a reducible flow graph with unary weights on the vertices, and finding a minimum cut in a flow network with unary capacities [296, 297].

A.2.18 Edge Maximal Acyclic Subgraph (EMAS)

Given: A directed graph $G = (V, E)$ with an ordering on the edges and a designated edge e.

Problem: Is e contained in the edge maximal acyclic subgraph?

Reference: Greenlaw [136].

Hint: The *edge maximal acyclic subgraph* is defined to be the subgraph computed by an algorithm that builds up the acyclic subgraph by processing edges in order. It adds an edge to the subgraph if its inclusion does not introduce a cycle. The reduction is from NORCVP, see Problem A.1.5. A gadget is designed that replaces each gate in the circuit. A gadget for gate g with inputs i_1 and i_2, and outputs o_1 and o_2 has three vertices $g(\text{top})$, $g(\text{mid})$, and $g(\text{bot})$. The edges in the gadget are $(g(\text{top}),i_1(\text{mid}))$, $(g(\text{top}),i_2(\text{mid}))$, $(g(\text{mid}),i_1(\text{bot}))$, $(g(\text{mid}),i_2(\text{bot}))$, $(g(\text{bot}),o_2(\text{top}))$, $(g(\text{top}),g(\text{mid}))$, $(g(\text{mid}),g(\text{bot}))$, $(g(\text{bot}),o_1(\text{top}))$, and $(g(\text{bot}),g(\text{top}))$. The first five edges are upwarding pointing edges and are ordered first. The last four edges are ordered within the gadget as listed. TRUE input i to gate g is represented by a vertex with an edge to $g(\text{top})$. FALSE input i to gate g is represented by two vertices forming a cycle with $g(\text{top})$. The edges are ordered so that the edge leading into $g(\text{top})$ is not put in the set the algorithm constructs. The edges of the output gate are "grounded." One of the edges leaving $g_{out}(\text{bot})$ is used as the designated edge e.

Remarks: The decision problem "Is the edge maximal subgraph of size k?" is also *P*-complete [136]. The *Feedback Arc Set Problem* (Karp [193]) is an equivalent formulation of the *Maximum Acyclic Subgraph Problem*. Approximation algorithms for this problem are important because there are very few classes of graphs for which the problem is known to be in *P* (Berger and Shor [32]). These versions are both *NP*-complete (Garey and Johnson [113]). Greenlaw proves decision problems based on several other natural approximation algorithms for this problem are *P*-complete [136, 137]. There are other reasonable approximation algorithms that are in *NC*, see [136, 137]. Berger presented an *NC* approximation algorithm that, assuming the input graph does not contain two-cycles, generates a subgraph containing more than half the arcs [31]. Ramachandran, Ramachandran proved that finding a *minimum weight feedback arc set* in a reducible flow graph with arbitrary weights on the arcs is *P*-complete [296, 297]. Also see Problem A.2.17.

A.2.19   General Graph Closure (GGC)

Given: An undirected graph $G = (V, E)$, a subset $E' \subseteq V \times V$ with $E' \cap E = \emptyset$, and a designated edge $e = (u, v) \in E'$.

Problem: Is e in the *general closure* $\mathcal{G}(G, E')$ of G? That is, the graph obtained from G by repeatedly joining nonadjacent pairs of vertices u and v whose degree sum is at least $|V|$ and such that $(u, v) \in E'$. The edges in E' are called *admissible edges*.

Reference: Khuller [208].

Hint: An $O(n^3)$ algorithm solving the problem is given in [208]. The reduction is from Monotone Circuit Value, Problem A.1.3. The idea is to replace gates in the circuit by gadgets. We will describe only the gadgets for inputs and AND gates. The gadgets for OR gates are similar. A TRUE (FALSE) value is associated with the output vertex of a gadget if its degree has increased by the addition of an admissible edge (respectively, remained the same). The gadget is constructed so that values do not propagate back up through the circuit. N will denote the total number of vertices contained in all the gadgets. An additional N vertices are added and connected so as to double the degrees of the vertices in the construction of the graph containing gadgets. The total degree of the graph constructed is $2N$. A TRUE input is represented by two vertices with an admissible edge between them and the degree of each vertex is N. A FALSE input is represented similarly except on the output side the vertex has degree $N - 1$. The gadget representing an AND gate α_k consists of thirteen vertices. We describe the upper left part first. It consists of five vertices. We will call the vertices 1, 2, 3, 4, and 5. Vertex 1 has a connection from one of α_k's inputs. Vertices 1 and 5 have degree $N - 1$ and vertices 2, 3, and 4 have degree N. The admissible edges are $(1, 2), (1, 3), (1, 4), (2, 5), (3, 5)$, and $(4, 5)$. The upper right part of the gadget is similar with vertices $6-10$ playing the roles of $1-5$. Vertices 5 and 10 are connected to vertex 11 via admissible edges. Vertex 11 has degree $N - 2$. Vertex 11 is connected to the outputs of the gadget. These are vertices 12 and 13. They both are of degree N. The gadgets are connected in the obvious manner. The circuit evaluates to TRUE if and only if the admissible edge $(11, 13)$ of the gadget corresponding to the output gate is added to G.

Remarks: The complexity of the *General Graph Closure Problem* in which $E' = V \times V - E$ is open, see Problem B.1.4.

A.2.20   Generating Random Matchings (GRM)

Given: A bipartite graph $G = (V_1, V_2, E)$ with $|V_1| = |V_2| = n$ and a designated edge $\{u, v\}$. Let $M_n(G)$ denote the set of perfect matchings in G and $M_{n-1}(G)$ denote the set of near perfect matchings, that is, matchings of size $n - 1$. Broder [46] and Jerrum and

Sinclair [173] give probabilistic algorithms for generating elements in $M_n(G) \cup M_{n-1}(G)$. We call these algorithms *Broder's algorithm* and *Jerrum and Sinclair's algorithm*.

Problem: (1) Is $\{u, v\}$ in the matching generated by Broder's algorithm?

Problem: (2) Is $\{u, v\}$ in the matching generated by Jerrum and Sinclair's algorithm?

Reference: Teng [352].

Hint: Both of these problems are P-complete [352]. The reductions are from Lexicographically First Maximal Independent Set, Problem A.2.1.

Remarks: These algorithms are important for approximating the *permanent*. Also, see Problems B.9.7 and B.9.8 for some related open problems.

A.2.21 Lexicographically First Maximal k-cycle Free Edge Induced Subgraph (LFEdge)

Given: An undirected graph $G = (V, E)$ with an ordering on the edges in E and a designated edge $e \in E$.

Problem: Is e in the lexicographically first maximal k-cycle free edge induced subgraph of G? The *lexicographically first maximal k-cycle free edge induced subgraph of G* is the graph formed by processing each edge in E in order and adding it to the subgraph being built if it does not form a cycle of size k.

Reference: Miyano [264, 265].

Hint: The reductions (for different values of k) are from several variants of Circuit Value, Problem A.1.1.

Remarks: Miyano proves the problem is P-complete for several different fixed values of k. For $k = 3, 4, 5, 6$, or greater than or equal to 7 and G of maximum degree 6, 4, 4, 3, or 3, respectively, the problem is P-complete. For G a planar graph, and $k = 4, 5, 6$, or greater than or equal to 7 and G of maximum degree 5, 4, 4, or 3, respectively, the problem is P-complete. For G a general graph, and $k = 3$ or 4 and G of maximum degree 4 or 3, respectively, the problem is in NC^2 [264, 265]. See Problems A.2.17 and A.2.18 for results with a similar flavor. It is also interesting to contrast the results for the edge induced subgraph problem with those for the vertex induced subgraph problem, see Problem A.2.16. Also see Problem B.1.8 for related open questions. Lastly, note that for $k = 1$ this problem becomes Lexicographically First Maximal Matching, Problem B.8.2; it is in CC.

A.3   Searching Graphs

A.3.1   Lexicographically First Maximal Path (LFMP)

Given: An undirected graph $G = (V, E)$ with a numbering on the vertices, and two designated vertices s and t.

Problem: Is vertex t on the lexicographically first maximal path in G beginning at s? A *maximal path* is a path that cannot be extended because any attempt at extending it will result in an encounter with a vertex that is already on the path. The *lexicographically first maximal path* is the maximal path that would appear first in the "alphabetical" listing of all paths from s, where the alphabetizing is done with respect to the vertex numbers.

Reference: Anderson and Mayr [16].

Hint: The reduction is from a version of CVP consisting of NOT and OR gates, see Problem A.1.1. The key idea is the construction of a subgraph called a *latch*. A latch consists of six vertices connected in a rectangular fashion. The latches are hooked together and labeled in a clever manner. A latch that has been traversed (not traversed) in the construction of the lexicographically first maximal path indicates a TRUE (respectively, FALSE) value for the corresponding gate. Vertex t is a special vertex in a latch corresponding to the output gate.

Remarks: LFMP remains P-complete when restricted to planar graphs with maximum degree three. If the maximum degree of any vertex in G is at most Δ, there is an algorithm that can find a maximal path in $O(\Delta(\log n)^3)$ time using n^2 processors [16]. There is also an NC algorithm for finding a maximal path in planar graphs [16]. The complexity of the general problem of finding a maximal path is open [16], although Anderson shows it to be in RNC [13]. See Problem B.9.4.

A.3.2   Maximal Vertex Disjoint Paths (PATHS)

Given: An undirected graph $G = (V, E)$, a subset U of V, an integer k, and a designated vertex v.

Problem: Is vertex v on the kth path found when constructing paths greedily from vertices in U? The paths are formed by taking lexicographically first paths from vertices in U. The set is maximal in the sense that no more paths joining vertices in U can be added.

Reference: Anderson [12].

Hint: The reduction is from a restricted version of CVP [12]. The result holds for layered directed acyclic graphs, and thus, the complexity of the problem is not due to the construction of the lexicographically first paths, see Problem A.3.1.

Remarks: The construction of maximal sets of vertex disjoint paths is important for developing fast, parallel, randomized algorithms for depth-first search (Aggarwal and Anderson [5], Aggarwal, Anderson, and Kao [6]). See Problems B.9.2 and B.9.5.

A.3.3 Lexicographically First Depth-first Search Ordering (LFDFS)

Given: An undirected graph $G = (V, E)$ with fixed ordered adjacency lists, and two designated vertices u and v.

Problem: Is vertex u visited before vertex v in the depth-first search of G induced by the order of the adjacency lists?

Reference: Reif [300].

Hint: Follows easily from Problem A.3.1, since the leftmost path in the lexicographically first depth-first search tree is the lexicographically first maximal path (Anderson [12]). Reif gives a direct reduction from NORCVP, see Problem A.1.5, to LFDFS, taking advantage of the fixed order by which the adjacency lists are examined [300]. We present the directed case from which the undirected case is easily derived. Without loss of generality, assume gates are numbered in topological order. The gadget described below replaces NOR gate i having inputs i_1 and i_2, and outputs to gates j_1 and j_2. The gadget has eight vertices $enter(i)$, $in(i, i_1)$, $in(i, i_2)$, $s(i)$, $out(i, 1)$, $out(i, 2)$, $t(i)$, and $exit(i)$. Let the triple (x, y, z) denote a directed edge (x, y) with y appearing z^{th} on x's adjacency list. The gadget has triples

- $(enter(i), in(i, i_1), 1)$, $(in(i, i_1), in(i, i_2), 2)$, $(in(i, i_2), s(i), 2)$,
- $(s(i), out(i, 1), 1)$, $(out(i, 1), s(i), 1)$, $(out(i, 1), in(j_1, i), 2)$,
- $(out(i, 2), out(i, 1), 1)$, $(out(i, 2), in(j_2, i), 2)$, $(t(i), out(i, 2), 1)$,
- $(enter(i), t(i), 2)$, $(t(i), exit(i), 2)$, $(s(i), exit(i), 2)$, and
- $(exit(i), enter(i + 1), 1)$.

Additionally, $(in(j_1, i), out(i, 2), 1)$ and $(in(j_2, i), t(i), 1)$ are triples connected to the gadget. TRUE inputs are "chained" together. The lexicographic first DFS of the graph constructed visits vertex $s(n)$, where n corresponds to the output gate, before (after) $t(n)$ if and only if the circuit evaluates to TRUE (respectively, FALSE).

Remarks: The directed case can be reduced to the undirected case easily. The reduction is dependent on the adjacency lists fixing the order in which the adjacent vertices are examined. The problem remains open if this constraint is relaxed. For example, the problem remains open for graphs presented with all adjacency lists sorted in order of increasing vertex number. The problem remains P-complete if the input graph is given with a fixed vertex numbering and the search order is based on this numbering rather than the fixed ordered adjacency lists ([12], Greenlaw [133]). Anderson showed that computing just the first branch of the lexicographically first DFS tree, called the lexicographically first maximal path, is P-complete [12], see Problem A.3.1. Computing the LFDFS tree in planar graphs is P-complete as well [12]. However, *Planar Directed Depth-first Search* is in NC (Kao [186]). The depth-first search tree constructed in [186] is not the lexicographically first. Hagerup shows that a depth-first search tree can be constructed in a planar graph on a PRIORITY CRCW-PRAM using $O(\log n)$ time and n^3 processors [145]. In RNC, it is possible to find *some* depth-first vertex numbering and the depth-first spanning tree corresponding to it; see Problem B.9.2. Computing a depth-first vertex numbering for planar graphs is in NC (He and Yesha [152], Smith [334]). Computing the lexicographically first depth-first numbering for directed acyclic graphs is in NC (de la Torre and Kruskal [85, 86], Greenlaw [135], Zhang [379]). Determining whether a directed spanning tree of a general graph has a valid DFS numbering is in NC (Schevon and Vitter [325]). Vitter and Simons give a $\sqrt{n}$ time parallel algorithm for the non-sparse version of the problem [366]. Computing a LFDFS in a *tree structured* or *outerplanar* graph is in NC (Chlebus *et al.* [55]).

A.3.4 Breadth-depth Search (BDS)

Given: An undirected graph $G = (V, E)$ with a numbering on the vertices, and two designated vertices u and v.

Problem: Is vertex u visited before vertex v in the breadth-depth first search of G induced by the vertex numbering? A *breadth-depth first search* (Horowitz and Sahni [163]) starts at a vertex s and visits all children of s pushing them on a stack as the search proceeds.

After all of s's children have been visited, the search continues with the vertex on the top of the stack playing the role of s.

Reference: Greenlaw [139].

Hint: The proof sketched below is from (Richard J. Anderson, Personal Communication, 1988). Reduce LFDFS, Problem A.3.3, to BDS. Insert a new vertex between every pair of connected vertices in the original graph. Suppose in the original graph corresponding to the circuit that vertex u_i has neighbors $v_1, \ldots, v_k$ and that these vertices are listed in the order they would be selected in from u_i. Let $c_1, \ldots, c_k$ be the vertices inserted by the reduction between (u_i and v_1), $\ldots$, (u_i and v_k), respectively. The c_i's are assigned numbers so that in increasing order they are listed as $c_k, \ldots, c_1$. The vertex numbers assigned to these vertices are specified to "reverse" the breadth-depth search in the new levels. In this way the depth-first search order of the original graph can be maintained. Vertex u is visited before vertex v in an instance of LFDFS if and only if the vertex corresponding to u is visited before the vertex corresponding to v in the constructed instance of BDS.

Remarks: A reduction from NORCVP is presented in [133] for both undirected and directed graphs. Several other reductions for the problem are described in detail in [139].

A.3.5 Stack Breadth-first Search (SBFS)

Given: An undirected graph $G = (V, E)$ with a numbering on the vertices, and two designated vertices u and v.

Problem: Is vertex u visited before vertex v in the stack breadth-first search of G induced by the vertex numbering? A *stack breadth-first search* is a breadth-first search that is implemented using a stack. The vertices most recently visited on a new level are searched from first at the next level.

Reference: Greenlaw [133, 135].

Hint: The reduction is from SAM2CVP, Problem A.1.6, to SBFS. Sort the input vertices and assign FALSE inputs lower numbers than TRUE inputs. In increasing order let $f_1, \ldots, f_k, t_1, \ldots, t_m$ denote the ordering induced by this numbering. A new vertex e_1 is introduced and given a number between f_k and t_1. For each gate a vertex is introduced and its connections in the circuit are maintained in the graph being constructed. A start vertex s is added and connected to all inputs. Additionally, a new chain of vertices starting from s is added. The vertices in this chain are $s, e_1, e_2, \ldots, e_d$, where d denotes the depth of the circuit. The search order specified by stack breadth-first search is such that vertex e_l for l odd (even) corresponding to an OR (respectively, AND) level in the instance of SAM2CVP is visited before vertex v if and only if the gate corresponding to vertex v evaluates to FALSE (respectively, TRUE) in the circuit.

Remarks: The *Lexicographic Breadth-first Search Problem*, which has a natural implementation on a queue, is defined as follows: given a graph G with fixed ordered adjacency lists, is vertex u visited before vertex v in the breadth-first search of G induced by the order of the adjacency lists? This problem is in NC (de la Torre and Kruskal [85, 86], Greenlaw [133]).

A.3.6   Alternating Breadth-first Search (ABFS)

Given: An undirected graph $G = (V, E)$ with E partitioned into two sets M and U, a designated vertex v, and a designated start vertex s.

Problem: Does vertex v get visited along an edge from the set M during an alternating breadth-first search of G? An *alternating breadth-first search*, which has applications in some matching algorithms, is a breadth-first search in which only edges in the set U (M) can be followed in going from even (respectively, odd) to odd (respectively, even) levels.

Reference: Anderson [12], Greenlaw, Hoover, and Ruzzo, THIS WORK.

Hint: Anderson's proof was from a version of CVP composed of OR and NOT gates (Richard J. Anderson, Personal Communication, 1988). The new reduction we present is from NANDCVP, Problem A.1.5. Let $t_1, \ldots, t_k$ denote TRUE inputs, $f_1, \ldots, f_l$ denote FALSE inputs, and $g_1, \ldots, g_m$ denote NAND gates. A new vertex s is created from where the search will originate. For each t_i, $1 \le i \le k$, two new vertices t_i' and t_i'' are introduced; for each f_i, $1 \le i \le l$, a new vertex f_i' is introduced; and for each g_i, $1 \le i \le m$, a vertex v_i is introduced. f_i' is connected to s by an edge in U and to v_j, where j is such that f_i' was input to gate g_j, by an edge in M. t_i'' is connected to s by an edge in U, t_i'' is connected to t_i' by an edge in M, and t_i' is connected to v_j, where j is such that t_i' was input to gate g_j. If gate g_i has outputs to gates g_j and g_h, then (v_i, v_j) and (v_i, v_h) are edges in M. For each of these gates receiving inputs from g_i there are two additional vertices. For g_j they are called v_{ij} and v_{ij}'. (v_i, v_{ij}) is an edge in U, (v_{ij}, v_{ij}') is in M, and (v_{ij}', v_j) is in U. For gate g_h

similar vertices and edges are added. The circuit evaluates to TRUE (FALSE) if and only if the vertex corresponding to the output gate of the circuit is visited along an edge in M (respectively, U).

Remarks: The matching constructed by the search is not necessarily maximal. The problem of finding a *maximum matching* is in *RNC* (Mulmuley, Vazirani, and Vazirani [271]). The problem of finding a *perfect matching* is also in *RNC* (Karp, Upfal, and Wigderson [196], [271]). See Problems B.9.7 and B.9.8.

A.4   Combinatorial Optimization

A.4.1   Linear Inequalities (LI)

Given: An integer $n \times d$ matrix A and an integer $n \times 1$ vector b.

Problem: Is there a rational $d \times 1$ vector $x > 0$ such that $Ax \leq b$?
(It is not required to find such a x.) By $x > 0$ we mean all components of x are nonnegative and at least one is nonzero.

Reference: (Stephen A. Cook, Personal Communication, 1982), Khachian [207], Valiant [357].

Hint: LI is in P by [207]. Also see Karmarkar [192]. The following reduction of CVP to LI is from (Stephen A. Cook, Personal Communication, 1982).

1. If input x_i is TRUE (FALSE) it is represented by the equation $x_i = 1$ (respectively, $x_i = 0$).

2. A NOT gate with input u and output w, computing $w \leftarrow \neg u$ is represented by the inequalities $w = 1 - u$ and $0 \leq w \leq 1$.

3. An AND gate with inputs u and v computing $w \leftarrow u \wedge v$ is represented by the inequalities $0 \leq w \leq 1$, $w \leq u$, $w \leq v$, and $u + v - 1 \leq w$.

4. An OR gate is represented by the inequalities $0 \leq w \leq 1$, $u \leq w$, $v \leq w$, and $w \leq u + v$.

Note, for any gate if the inputs are 0 or 1, the output will be 0 or 1. To determine the output z of the circuit, add the inequalities required to force $z = 1$. If the system has a solution, the output is TRUE; otherwise, the output is FALSE.

Remarks: Remains P-complete if entries in A and b are restricted to $\{0, 1\}$. See also remarks for Problems A.4.2 and A.4.3.

A.4.2   Linear Equalities (LE)

Given: An integer $n \times d$ matrix A and an integer $n \times 1$ vector b.

Problem: Is there a rational $d \times 1$ vector $x > 0$ such that $Ax = b$? By $x > 0$ we mean all components of x are nonnegative and at least one is nonzero.

Reference: (Stephen A. Cook, Personal Communication, 1982), Khachian [207], Valiant [357].

Hint: LE is NC^1 reducible to LI since $Ax \leq b$ and $-Ax \leq -b$ if and only if $Ax = b$. Thus, LE is in P. For completeness an instance of LI can be reduced to LE as follows. For each inequality in LI there is a corresponding equality in LE with an additional "slack" variable that is used to make the inequality into an equality.

Remarks: If LE is restricted so the coefficients of A and b are either $-1, 0,$ or 1, LE is still P-complete. This follows from the reduction given by Itai [171]. The restricted version of LE is denoted $[-1,1]$ LE and is used in proving that Homologous Flow, Problem A.4.5, is P-complete. Cucker and Torrecillas proved that the problem of deciding whether a system of equations of *degree d*, for d greater than or equal to two, is solvable by substitution is P-complete [73].

A.4.3 Linear Programming (*) (LP)

Given: An integer $n \times d$ matrix A, an integer $n \times 1$ vector b, and an integer $1 \times d$ vector c.

Problem: Find a rational $d \times 1$ vector x such that $Ax \leq b$ and cx is maximized.

Reference: Dobkin, Lipton, and Reiss [93], Dobkin and Reiss [94], Khachian [207], Valiant [357].

Hint: Note that the problem is stated as a computation problem. LP is technically not in P, but is in FP by [207]. Also see Karmarkar [192]. Reduce LI to LP by picking any cost vector c, say $c = \vec{0}$, and checking whether the resulting linear program is feasible.

Remarks: The original reduction in [93] is from HORN, Problem A.6.2, to LP. In [94], LP and LI are shown to be logarithmic space equivalent by reducing LP to LI using *rational binary search* (Papadimitriou [277], Reiss [304]) to find the value of the maximum and a x that yields it. However, it is not clear how to perform this reduction in NC^1. Since LP and LI are complete via NC^1 reductions though, there must be an NC^1 reduction between the two problems. Although we know that LP and LI are NC^1 equivalent, the NC^1 reduction between them is not an obvious one. Serna shows it is P-complete to approximate a *solution approximation*, which requires finding a x' close to the optimal solution, and to approximate a *value approximation*, which requires finding a x' such that cx' is close to cx [327]. Megiddo gives a reduction of LP to Serna's approximate problem [257]. It is also P-hard to approximate cx to within any constant fraction, even given a feasible solution x' (Anne Condon, Personal Communication, 1991); reduction is from Discounted Markov Decision Process, Problem A.8.2. See Lin-Kriz and Pan [237] for some results on two variable linear programming. Dahlhaus observes that for d equal to 3 and values over the reals the problem is P-complete, whereas for d equal to 2, the problem is in NC [75]. The reader is referred to [75] for additional details.

A.4.4   Maximum Flow (MaxFlow)

Given: A directed graph $G = (V, E)$ with each edge e labeled by an integer capacity $c(e) \geq 0$, two distinguished vertices, source s and sink t, and a value f.

Problem: Is there a *feasible flow* of value f, that is, is the value of the maximum flow into the sink greater than or equal to f?

Reference: Goldschlager, Shaw, and Staples [128], Lengauer and Wagner [231].

Hint: The first P-completeness proof for a decision problem derived from Maximum Flow was for the problem of determining whether the flow is odd or even [128]. We give this reduction. (The proof given in [231] for the more natural threshold problem stated above is similar.) The reduction is from AM2CVP, Problem A.1.4, to MaxFlow. Gates v_i and connections e_{ij} of α are associated with vertices v_i' and edges e_{ij}' of G. G has additional vertices s and t, and an overflow edge for each v_i'. Each edge e_{ij} of α has a capacity and a flow associated with it. This capacity is 2^i, and the flow is 2^i if gate v_i is TRUE and 0 otherwise. A vertex v_i' with inputs v_j' and v_k' has a maximum possible inflow of $2^j + 2^k$, and outflow to other gates of $d2^i$ (d is the outdegree of v_i). The remaining flow is absorbed by the overflow edge from v_i' with capacity $2^j + 2^k - d2^i$. This overflow edge is directed toward t in case v_i is an AND gate and toward s in case v_i is an OR gate. Thus, the vertices must be topologically ordered with the output first and the inputs last, and the output gate must be an OR gate. Note that all edge capacities are even except the one from v_0 to t. Therefore, the maximum flow for G is odd if and only if α outputs TRUE.

Remarks: See Dinic [92] or Ford and Fulkerson [108] for basic definitions and polynomial time algorithms. This reduction produces exponential edge capacities in G. In a network with edge capacities expressed in unary, computing the magnitude of the maximum flow is in RNC^2 (Feather [103]) and a method for finding the flow in RNC is also known (Karp, Upfal, and Wigderson [196]). If the network is restricted to being acyclic, MaxFlow remains P-complete (Ramachandran [295]). Flows in planar networks can be computed in *NC* (Johnson [174], Johnson and Venkatesan [175]). *Two Commodity Flow* (2CF) is defined similar to MaxFlow except there are two sources and two sinks, and there are two separate flow functions for the commodities. Since MaxFlow is a special case of 2CF and 2CF is in *P* by results of Itai [171] and Khachian [207], it follows that 2CF is *P*-complete. Itai defined several other variants of 2CF that are also *P*-complete. They are defined below. (l, u)-2CF is a restricted form of 2CF in which there are lower and upper bounds on the capacity of each edge. Selective (l, u)-2CF is defined to be a 2CF with lower and upper bounds on the sum of the two flows on each edge. Stein and Wein show that, although there is an *RNC* algorithm to approximate maximum flow, approximating the minimum cost maximum flow is *P*-complete [339].

A.4.5 Homologous Flow (HF)

Given: A directed graph $G = (V, E)$ with each edge (v, w) labeled by a lower and upper bound on flow capacity $l(v, w), u(v, w) \geq 0$ and two distinguished vertices, source s and sink t.

Problem: Is there a feasible flow in the network? A *feasible flow* is one in which the flow assigned to each arc falls within the lower and upper bounds for the arc. A *homologous flow* is a flow in which pairs of edges are required to have the same flow.

Reference: Itai [171].

Hint: It follows that HF is in *P* by the results of [171] and Khachian [207]. We describe the reduction given in [171] and note that it is a logarithmic space reduction. The reduction is from [−1,1] LE, see remarks for Problem A.4.2. Let $\sum_{j=1}^{m} a_{ij} x_j = b_i$, for $i = 1, \ldots, n$ be an instance of [−1,1] LE. For $\sigma \in \{-1, 0, 1\}$, let $J_\sigma^i = \{j \mid a_{ij} = \sigma\}$. Another formulation of the original equations is $\sum_{j \in J_1^i} x_j - \sum_{j \in J_{-1}^i} x_j = b_i$, for $i = 1, \ldots, n$. There are n sections in the flow network constructed and each one has $m + 5$ vertices $\{v_1^i, \ldots, v_m^i, y^i, z^i, J_{-1}^i, J_0^i, J_1^i\}$. For $\sigma = -1, 0, 1$, if $j \in J_0^i$, then add (v_j^i, J_σ^i) as a *nonrestricted edge*, one with lower bound 0 and upper bound ∞, to the network. Add (J_1^i, z^i) with lower and upper capacities equal to b_i. (J_1^i, y^i) and (J_{-1}^i, y^i) are homologous nonrestricted edges. (J_1^i, z^i) and (J_1^i, y^i) are nonrestricted edges. An additional vertex z_0 is added as a source and z_n is the sink. For each j, $(z^0, v_j^1), (z^1, v_j^2), \ldots, (z^{n-1}, v_j^n)$ are pairwise nonrestricted homologous edges. Let f denote the flow. Given a solution x to the equations, a feasible flow is $x_j = f(z_0, v_j^1) = \cdots = f(z^{n-1}, v_j^{n-1})$ and given a feasible flow, it is easy to construct solution x.

A.4.6   Lexicographically First Blocking Flow (LFBF)

Given: A directed acyclic graph $G = (V, E)$ represented by fixed ordered adjacency lists with each edge e labeled by a capacity $c(e) \geq 0$, and two distinguished vertices, source s and sink t.

Problem: Is the value of the lexicographically first blocking flow odd? A *blocking flow* is a flow in which every path from s to t has a *saturated edge* — an edge whose flow is equal to its capacity. The *lexicographically first blocking flow* is the flow resulting from the standard sequential depth-first search blocking flow algorithm.

Reference: Anderson and Mayr [15].

Hint: The reduction given in Maximum Flow, Problem A.4.4, can be easily modified to show this problem is P-complete.

Remarks: The problem of finding the lexicographically first blocking flow in a three layered network is also P-complete. A *three layered network* is one in which all source to sink paths have length three. Cheriyan and Maheshwari also give an *RNC* algorithm for finding a blocking flow in a three layered network [54], also see Problem B.9.1. Goldberg and Tarjan give a parallel algorithm for finding a blocking flow in an acyclic network [120]. Their algorithm runs in parallel time $O(n \log n)$ and uses m processors on an EREW-PRAM, where the network has n vertices and m edges.

A.4.7   First Fit Decreasing Bin Packing (FFDBP)

Given: A list of n items $v_1, \ldots, v_n$, where each v_i is rational number between 0 and 1, and two distinguished indices i and b.

Problem: Is the ith item packed into the bth bin by the first fit decreasing bin packing heuristic?

Reference: Anderson, Mayr, and Warmuth [17].

Hint: Reduce AM2CVP, Problem A.1.4, to FFDBP. Without loss of generality, we can assume the gates $\beta_1, \ldots, \beta_n$ are numbered in topological order. The reduction transforms the sequence $\beta_1, \ldots, \beta_n$ into a list of items and bins. Let $\delta_i = 1 - i/(n+1)$ and $\epsilon = 1/(5(n+1))$, and T_i (F_i) denote any item of size δ_i (respectively, $\delta_i - 2\epsilon$). We describe how to construct the list of items and bins. For AND gate β_i with outputs to gates β_j and β_k construct bins of size δ_i, $2\delta_i - 4\epsilon$, $\delta_i + \delta_j - 3\epsilon$, and $\delta_i + \delta_k - 4\epsilon$; and items of size δ_i, δ_i, $\delta_i - 2\epsilon$, $\delta_i - 2\epsilon$, $\delta_i - 3\epsilon$, and $\delta_i - 4\epsilon$. For an OR gate β_i with outputs to gates β_j and β_k construct bins of size $2\delta_i - 4\epsilon$, δ_i, $\delta_i + \delta_j - 3\epsilon$, and $\delta_i + \delta_k - 4\epsilon$; and the same items as for the AND gate. The output gate β_n is treated specially and has bins of size δ_n and δ_n, and items of size δ_n, δ_n, $\delta_n - 2\epsilon$, and $\delta_n - 2\epsilon$. For gates receiving a constant circuit input, a T_i (F_i) is removed if the gate receives a FALSE (respectively, TRUE) input. The lists of bins are concatenated in the order of their corresponding gate numbers and similarly for the items. To get unit size bins let $u_1, \ldots, u_q$ be the non-increasing list of item sizes and let $b_1, \ldots, b_r$ be the list of variable bin sizes as constructed above. Let $B = \max\{b_i\}$ and $C = (2r + 1)B$. For $1 \le i \le 2r$, set $v_i = C - iB - b$, if $i \le r$ and $C - ib$, otherwise. Packing these $2r$ items into r bins of size C has the affect of leaving b_i space in the ith bin. By concatenating the "u" and "v" item lists and normalizing the bin sizes, a first fit decreasing bin packing of the items will place the item corresponding to the second T_n in β_n's list into the last bin if and only if the circuit evaluates to TRUE.

Remarks: The problem remains P-complete even if unary representations are used for the numbers involved. This is one of the first such problem where large numbers do not appear to be required for P-completeness (in contrast see MaxFlow, Problem A.4.4). The problem of determining if I is the packing produced by the *best fit decreasing algorithm* is also P-complete [17]. In [17] there is an *NC* algorithm that produces a packing within 11/9 of optimal. This is the same performance as for first fit decreasing. Mayr also describes *NC* approximation algorithms for bin packing [254].

A.4.8 General List Scheduling (GLS)

Given: An ordered list of n jobs $\{J_1, \ldots, J_n\}$, a positive integer execution time $T(J_i)$ for each job, and a non-preemptive schedule L. The jobs are to be scheduled on two identical processors.

Problem: Is the final offset produced by the list scheduling algorithm nonzero? The *final offset* is the difference in the total execution time of the two processors.

Reference: Helmbold and Mayr [154].

Hint: Reduce NORCVP, see Problem A.1.5, to GLS. Without loss of generality, assume the gates in the instance of NORCVP are numbered in reverse topological order. The input wires to gate i are numbered 4^{2i} and 4^{2i+1}. The output wire of gate one, the overall circuit output, is labeled four. Let V_i be the sum of the labels on the output wires of gate i. For gate i, seventeen jobs are introduced with the following execution times — one job at $2 * 4^{2i+1}$, fourteen jobs at $4^{2i}/2$, and two jobs at $(4^{2i} + V_i)/2$. The initial job has execution time equal to the sum of the labels of all TRUE input wires. The remaining jobs are listed in descending order of gate number. The final offset will be four (zero) if and only if the output gate i is TRUE (respectively, FALSE).

Remarks: The problem is in NC if the job times are small, that is $n^{O(1)}$. NC algorithms for scheduling problems with either intree or outtree precedence constraints are known (Helmbold and Mayr [153, 154]). Also see Problem A.4.9 for additional scheduling results. See Mayr [254] for NC approximation algorithms. Sunder and He show that List Scheduling is P-complete [349]. The differences between *List Scheduling* and GLS are that all jobs have unit time and the number of processors is an input to the problem. That is, it is not fixed at two as in GLS. Sunder and He prove their result via a reduction from Height-priority Schedule, Problem A.4.9. They also show that List Scheduling is in NC if the precedence constraints are an interval order. An *interval order* is a partial order $G = (V, E)$, where V is a set of intervals on the real line and $([l_1, r_1], [l_2, r_2]) \in E$ if and only if r_1 is less than l_2. Their algorithm runs in $O((\log n)^2)$ time using n^5 processors on a PRIORITY CRCW-PRAM. Another version of the algorithm runs in $O((\log n)^3)$ time using n^4 processors on the same model [349].

A.4.9   Height-priority Schedule (HPS)

Given: A directed, outforest $G = (V, E)$ specifying the precedence constraints among the $|V|$ unit time tasks that are represented by the vertices of G, a nondecreasing profile μ, a designated task j, and a time slot t. To define terms we follow the discussion given in [95]. A graph is an *outforest* if every task has at most one incoming edge. The *profile* μ is a function from N to $\mathsf{N} - \{0\}$, where $\mu(i)$ denotes the number of machines available at the ith *time slot*, that is, the interval $[i, i + 1)$. If a profile has only one value, m, then it is called *straight*. A schedule s for a graph G and a profile μ is a function from vertices of G onto an initial segment $\{0, \ldots, l - 1\}$ of N, such that

1. $|s^{-1}(r)| \leq \mu(r)$, for all r in $\{0, \ldots, l - 1\}$ and

2. if y is a successor of x in G, then $s(x)$ is less than $s(y)$.

l denotes the *length* of the schedule. A minimum length schedule is called *optimal*. A schedule is *greedy* if the maximum number of tasks is scheduled at every slot, that is, $|s^{-1}(k)| < \mu(k)$ implies that every y such that $s(y)$ is greater than k is a successor of some vertex s in $s^{-1}(k)$.

A *priority* q is a function from the set of tasks into $\mathbb{N}$. A schedule s is a *q-priority schedule* if vertices of higher priority are preferred over vertices of lower priority. Among the vertices of the same priority ties are broken arbitrarily. A q-priority schedule also has the property that $s(x)$ greater than $s(y)$ and $q(x)$ greater than $q(y)$ imply that x is a successor of some vertex z with $s(z)$ equal to $s(y)$. *Height* is typically used as a priority function. Vertices without successors have a height of zero.

A profile is called *nondecreasing* if $\mu(k) \le \mu(k+1)$ for every slot k.

Problem: Is task j scheduled in time slot t by the height-priority schedule?

Reference: Dolev, Upfal, and Warmuth [95].

Hint: The reduction is from a variant of Topologically Ordered Circuit Value, Problem A.1.2.

Remarks: Dolev, Upfal, and Warmuth show several other problems are P-complete. We mention a few of them here. Consult [95] for terms that are not defined here. *Height-priority schedule for an opposing forest and a straight line profile, height-priority schedule for a level order and straight line profile, weight-priority* (using only three different weights) *schedule for an outforest and a straight profile, greedy schedule*, and the *lexicographically first schedule for an outforest and a straight line profile* are all P-complete [95]. When the number of machines m is fixed and does not vary with time, and when the precedence constraints are given by a collection of *outtrees*; Dolev, Upfal, and Warmuth give EREW-PRAM algorithms for computing optimal schedules. In the former case the algorithm runs in $O(\log n)$ time using n^2 processors and in the latter case the algorithm runs in $O((\log n)^2)$ time using n processors. Also see Problem A.4.8 for additional scheduling results.

A.5 Local Optimality

A.5.1 MAXFLIP Verification (MAXFLIPV)

Given: An encoding $\overline{\alpha}$ of a Boolean circuit α constructed of AND, OR, and NOT gates, plus inputs $x = x_1, \ldots, x_n$. The circuit's m output values $y = y_1, \ldots, y_m$.

Problem: Is the circuit's output a local maximum among the neighbors of x when y is viewed as a binary number? The *neighbors of x* are Boolean vectors of length n whose Hamming distance differs from x by one. That is, they can be obtained from x by flipping one bit.

Reference: Johnson, Papadimitriou, and Yannakakis [178].

Hint: The problem is easily seen to be in P. The reduction is from Monotone Circuit Value, Problem A.1.3. Let α denote an instance of MCVP with input $x_1, \ldots, x_n$. Construct an instance of MAXFLIP as follows. The new circuit is the same as α except for a modification to the input. Add a "latch" input that is AND'ed with each of α's inputs before they are fed into later gates of α. Set the latch input to value 0. The output of the circuit constructed will be 0. The input $x_1, \ldots, x_n, 0$ will be locally optimal if and only if the output is 0 when the latch input is 1. This is true if and only if the output of α on its input is 0.

Remarks: The complementary problem, called the *FLIP Verification Problem*, in which the output is minimized, is also P-complete [178]. The general problems MAXFLIP and FLIP are *PLS*-complete [178]. *PLS* stands for *polynomially local search*. The class is defined in Section D.1. We note for most problems that are *PLS*-complete the problem of verifying local optimality turned out to be P-complete. However, Krentel shows that this is not always the case [222].

A.5.2 Local Optimality Kernighan-Lin Verification (LOKLV)

Given: An undirected graph $G = (V, E)$ with unit weights on the edges, and a partition of V into two equal size subsets A and B.

Problem: Is the cost of the partition, $c(A, B)$, a local optimum among the *neighbors of the partition*? The *cost of the partition* is defined to be the sum of the costs of all edges going between the sets A and B. We follow the presentation given by Johnson, Papadimitriou, and Yannakakis to define the neighbors [178]. A *swap* of partition (A, B) is a partition (C, D) such that (C, D) is obtained from (A, B) by swapping one element of A with an element of B. The swap (C, D) is a *greedy* swap if $c(C, D) - c(A, B)$ is minimized over all swaps of (A, B). If (C, D) is the lexicographically smallest over all greedy swaps, then (C, D) is said to be the *lexicographically greedy swap of* (A, B). A sequence of partitions (A_i, B_i), each obtained by a swap from the preceding partition, is *monotonic* if the differences $A_i - A_0$ and $B_i - B_0$ are monotonically increasing. A partition (C, D) is a neighbor of (A, B) if it occurs in the unique maximal monotonic sequence of lexicographic greedy swaps starting with (A, B).

Reference: Johnson, Papadimitriou, and Yannakakis [178], Savage and Wloka [319, 320].

Hint: Since the weights are one, the range of solution values is polynomial and the problem is in P. The reduction presented in [320] is from a variant of Monotone Circuit Value, Problem A.1.3.

Remarks: The reduction in [178] showed that the problem was P-complete if the edge weights were encoded in unary. A problem called *Weak Local Optimum for Kernighan-Lin Verification* in which the *neighborhoods* are larger is also P-complete [178]. The general versions of these problems, *Local Optimality Kernighan-Lin* and *Weak Local Optimality Kernighan-Lin*, in which the weights are encoded in binary are both *PLS*-complete [178]. Schäffer and Yannakakis deduce that a complete local search using Kernighan-Lin on graphs with unit weights is P-complete [324]. Since the result in Problem A.5.2 is for a single neighborhood, the result in [320] implies the one in [324].

A.5.3 Unweighted, Not-all-equal Clauses, 3SAT FLIP (*) (UNAE3SAT)

Given: A Boolean formula F in CNF with three positive literals per clause.

Problem: Find a locally optimal assignment for F. An assignment is *locally optimal* if it has maximum cost among its neighbors. The *cost* of the assignment is the number of not-all-equals clauses that are satisfied by the assignment; each clause has a weight of one. A

truth assignment satisfies a clause C under the *not-all-equals* crite-
rion if it is such that C has at least one TRUE and one FALSE literal.
The *neighbors* of an assignment s are assignments that can be obtained from s by flipping the value of one variable.
Reference: Papadimitriou, Schäffer, and Yannakakis [278], Schäffer
and Yannakakis [324].
Hint: The problem is stated as a search problem and so is technically *FP*-complete. The reduction is from NORCVP, see Problem
A.1.5.
Remarks: The weighted version of the problem in which each clause
is given an integer weight coded in binary is *PLS*-complete [278,
324]. If the weights are encoded in unary, the problem is *FP*-
complete.

A.5.4   Unweighted Maximum Cut SWAP (*) (UMCS)

Given: An undirected graph $G = (V, E)$.
Problem: Find a locally optimal subset of vertices. A subset is
locally optimal if it has maximum cost among its neighbors. The
cost is the sum of the number of edges leaving vertices in the subset;
each edge has a weight of one. A *neighbor* of a subset S is a set of
size $|S|$ whose symmetric difference with S contains one vertex.
Reference: Papadimitriou, Schäffer, and Yannakakis [278], Schäffer
and Yannakakis [324].
Hint: The problem is stated as a search problem and so is technically *FP*-complete. The reduction is from UNAE3SAT, Problem
A.5.3.
Remarks: The weighted version of the problem in which each edge
is given an integer weight encoded in binary is *PLS*-complete [278,
324]. If the edge weights are encoded in unary, the problem is *FP*-
complete. The *Different than Majority Labeling Problem* is equivalent to this problem [324]. A *different than majority labeling* of an
undirected graph $G = (V, E)$ is a labeling of the vertices with either
0 or 1 such that each vertex is labeled differently than at least half
of its neighbors. Luby describes an *NC* algorithm for a related problem [247]. Sarnath and He show that a lexicographic version of the
problem is *P*-complete [316], see Problem A.5.8.

A.5.5 Unweighted Two Satisfiability FLIP (*) (U2SATFLIP)

Given: A Boolean formula F in CNF with two literals per clause.
Problem: Find a locally optimal assignment for F. An assignment
is *locally optimal* if it has maximum cost among its neighbors. The
cost of the assignment is the number of clauses that are satisfied
by the assignment; each clause has a weight of one. The *neighbors*
of an assignment s are assignments that can be obtained from s by
flipping the value of one variable.
Reference: Papadimitriou, Schäffer, and Yannakakis [278], Schäffer
and Yannakakis [324].
Hint: The problem is stated as a search problem and so is technically *FP*-complete. The reduction is from UMCS, Problem A.5.4.
Remarks: The weighted version of the problem in which each edge
is given an integer weight encoded in binary is *PLS*-complete [278,
324]. If the edge weights are encoded in unary, the problem is *FP*-
complete.

A.5.6 Unweighted Graph Partitioning SWAP (*) (UGPS)

Given: An undirected graph $G = (V, E)$ with $2n$ vertices.
Problem: Find a locally optimal partition of V into two equal size
sets. The partition V_1 and V_2 is *locally optimal* if the number of
edges going between V_1 and V_2 a minimum among all neighbors of
the partition. A *neighbor* is a partition that can be obtained from
V_1 and V_2 by swapping one element of V_1 with one element of V_2.
Reference: Papadimitriou, Schäffer, and Yannakakis [278], Savage
and Wloka [319, 320], Schäffer and Yannakakis [324].
Hint: The problem is stated as a search problem and so is technically *FP*-complete. This problem is equivalent to UMCS, Problem
A.5.4 [324]. The reduction in [320] is from a variant of Monotone
Circuit Value, Problem A.1.3.
Remarks: The weighted version of the problem in which the weights
are encoded in binary is *PLS*-complete [278, 324]. If the weights
are encoded in unary, the problem is *FP*-complete (Johnson, Papadimitriou, and Yannakakis [178]). Another problem the *Fiduccia-
Mattheyses Heuristic Graph Partitioning SWAP* (FM-Graph Partitioning in [324]) is defined similarly to UGPS except for the neigh-

bors of a solution. The neighborhood of a solution may be ob-
tained by a sequence of up to $|V|$ swaps following the Fiduccia-
Mattheyses heuristic (see [324]). FM-Graph Partitioning is also *FP-
complete* [320, 324]. In fact, a simpler local search problem in which
each partition has just one neighbor, the one obtained after the first
step of the Fiduccia-Mattheyses heuristic, is also *FP*-complete [320,
324]. This problem is called FM in [320] and FM-SWAP in [324].
In [320] they also show that a simulated annealing based on a SWAP
neighborhood and a "cooling schedule" is *P*-complete. Several additional results are presented proving other graph partitioning strategies are *P*-hard. See [319, 320] for further details.

A.5.7   Stable Configuration in Connectionist Model (*) (SCCM)

Given: An undirected graph $G = (V, E)$ whose vertices and edges
have integer weights coded in unary, and a configuration C (see
definition below). The vertex (edge) weights are denoted w_i (respectively, w_{ij}). G is called a *Connectionist Model* and has associated
with it the following properties. Each vertex $v_i \in V$ has a *state* of
either 0 or 1 associated with it. (Some authors consider states of -1
and 1; it is known that this model is equivalent.) The state of vertex
v_i is denoted s_i. A *configuration* refers to the vector of vertex states,
$\vec{s} = (s_1, \ldots, s_{|V|})$. The *influence function* for vertex v_i is defined as
follows:

$$I_i(\vec{s}) = \sum_{v_j \in V} w_{ji} s_j \ + w_i.$$

The state of a vertex v_i is *stable* in a given configuration $\vec{s}$ if and
only if

1. $I_i(\vec{s}) = 0$, or
2. $I_i(\vec{s}) > 0$ and $s_i = 1$, or
3. $I_i(\vec{s}) < 0$ and $s_i = 0$.

A configuration is *stable* if the states of all vertices in the configuration are stable. Stable configurations coincide with *local maximum*
with respect to the following "energy" function:

$$H(\vec{s}) = \frac{1}{2} \sum_{(v_i, v_j) \in E} w_{ij} s_i s_j + \sum_{v_i \in V} w_i s_i.$$

Problem: Find a stable configuration of the Connectionist Model G.

Reference: Godbeer [119], Lipscomb [242], Papadimitriou, Schäffer, and Yannakakis [278], Schäffer and Yannakakis [324].

Hint: Note that the problem as stated is a search problem. It is in FP if the weights are encoded in unary. The reduction is from LFMIS, Problem A.2.1 [119]. Additional reductions are given in [119] and [324] for other versions of the problem.

Remarks: Many variants of this problem have been considered [119, 242, 324]. The complexity of the problem changes depending on the types of values (positive, negative, or both positive and negative) the weights are allowed to take on and depending on the encodings of the weights. In [119] directed and undirected versions of the problem are considered. Versions of the problem that are NP-complete, P-hard, and P-complete are given. For example, if the problem is restricted to just positive weights, the Monotone Circuit Value Problem can be reduced to it. Since this version is known to be in P, it is P-complete. In [242] several variants of the general problem are presented that are P-hard. In [324] they consider a slight variant of the problem and show that when it is restricted to edge weights of only -1, it is P-complete. The version of this problem in which the weights are encoded in binary is PLS-complete [278, 324]. DasGupta describes parallel complexity results for neural networks in [78]. He shows a *deterministic recurrent neural network* that has at least one stable state can learn any P-complete language; he gives conditions restricting the thresholds and weights that result in neural networks capable only of learning languages in NC [78].

A.5.8 Lexicographically First Different Than Majority Labeling (LFDTML)

Given: An undirected graph $G = (V, E)$ with a numbering on the vertices and a designated vertex v. A *different than majority labeling* is a labeling of the vertices with either 0 or 1 such that each vertex is labeled differently than at least half of its neighbors. A greedy sequential algorithm for solving this problem begins by initially assigning the value 0 to each vertex. The algorithm iterates through the vertices in order flipping a vertex's label if it is not correctly labeled. The flipping process is repeated until the overall labeling is a different than majority labeling. The labeling produced by this algorithm is called the *lexicographically first different than majority labeling.*

Problem: Is vertex v labeled 1 in the lexicographically first different than majority labeling?

Reference: Sarnath and He [316].

Hint: The reduction is from MCVP, Problem A.1.3.

Remarks: The parallel complexity of *Different Than Majority Labeling* (DTML) was posed as an open question by Luby [246]. DTML was also discussed by Godbeer [119] and the problem was reduced to a version of a connectionist model problem, see Problem A.5.7. Schäffer and Yannakakis proved the problem to be equivalent to Problem A.5.4 [324]. Therefore, the problem is P-complete. Sarnath and He show that LFDTML remains P-complete when restricted to planar graphs [316]. They also give another sequential algorithm for the problem and state that a decision problem based on this algorithm is also P-complete [316].

A.5.9   Traveling Salesman 2-Opt (*) (TS2Opt)

Given: A finite set $C = \{C_1, \ldots, C_n\}$ of cities, and a distance matrix D with entries (d_{ij}) that are positive integers $(1 \leq i, j \leq n)$, and an initial tour T_0.

Problem: Find a sequence of tours $T_0, \ldots, T_m$ such that T_i is the result of a 2-opt of T_{i-1}, the cost of T_i is less than the cost of T_{i-1}, and either T_m is a locally optimal tour or $m \geq n$. A *2-opt* refers to a neighborhood transformation done on the tours, see Lin and Kernighan [235].

Reference: Anderson [12].

Hint: The reduction is from a variant of Circuit Value, Problem A.1.1.

Remarks: Also see Problem A.2.15.

A.5.10   Maximum Satisfiability Approximation (MSA)

Given: A Boolean formula F with clauses $c_1, \ldots, c_m$ and variables $x_1, \ldots, x_n$, plus an integer l.

Problem: Does variable x_l get assigned a value TRUE by the *maximum satisfiability approximation algorithm*? The algorithm is sketched below. Its input is the same as for MSA.

```
      begin
          for i ← 1 to n do
              for j ← 1 to m do
                  fT(i, j) ←  the fraction of truth assignments for the
                              remaining variables of clause j that
                              satisfy clause j with xi set to TRUE;
              fF(i, j) ← 1 − fT(i, j);
              if (∑ⱼ₌₁ᵐ fT(i, j)) ≥ (∑ⱼ₌₁ᵐ fF(i, j)) then xi ← TRUE
                  else xi ← FALSE;
          update the clauses;
      end.
```

$$f_T(i,j) \leftarrow \text{ the fraction of truth assignments for the remaining variables of clause } j \text{ that satisfy clause } j \text{ with } x_i \text{ set to TRUE};$$

$$f_F(i,j) \leftarrow 1 - f_T(i,j);$$

$$\text{if } \left(\sum_{j=1}^{m} f_T(i,j) \right) \geq \left(\sum_{j=1}^{m} f_F(i,j) \right) \text{ then } x_i \leftarrow \text{TRUE else } x_i \leftarrow \text{FALSE};$$

Reference: Bongiovanni, Crescenzi, and De Agostino [38].
Hint: The reduction is from a variant of Circuit Value, Problem A.1.1, that consists of OR and NOT gates.
Remarks: The algorithm specified above 1/2 *approximates* MSA. The result shows that this sequential algorithm for approximating *Maximum Satisfiability* is unlikely to be made feasibly highly parallel.

A.5.11 Minimum Set Cover Approximation (MSCA)

Given: A finite set S, a collection C of subsets of S, a special subset t of S, and an integer i.
Problem: Is t a subset of s', where s' is the ith set chosen by the *minimum set cover approximation algorithm*? A *set cover* is a collection of sets C' such that each element of S is contained in at least one set from C'. A *minimum set cover* is a set cover of smallest cardinality. The minimum set cover approximation algorithm is outlined below. Its input is the same as for MSCA.

```
      begin
          solution ← ∅; uncovered ← S;
          while uncovered ≠ ∅ do
              choose s' a "remaining set" from C such that
                  |s'| is maximized;
              solution ← solution ∪ index(s');
              uncovered ← uncovered − s';
              remove the elements of s' from all remaining sets;
      end.
```

Reference: Bongiovanni, Crescenzi, and De Agostino [38].
Hint: The reduction is from a variant of Circuit Value, Problem A.1.1, that consists of OR and NOT gates.

Remarks: The *Minimum Set Cover Problem* is *NP*-complete (Garey and Johnson [113]). The algorithm specified above log *approximates* MSCA. The result shows that this sequential algorithm for approximating Minimum Set Cover is unlikely to be made feasibly highly parallel.

A.5.12 Two Layer Channel Router Column-swap Heuristic (*) (COLUMNS)

Given: An initial solution R_0 to a *two layer channel routing problem* and a time bound t. The reader is referred to [321] for background and definitions concerning routing problems.

Problem: Find the solution R_t obtained from R_0 by applying a local search algorithm for channel routing using the columns cost function and the subtrack swap neighborhood. We provide definitions as given in [321]. The *columns cost function* of a two layer channel routing is the number of overlapping vertical segments. The *subtrack swap neighborhood* of a channel routing solution is the set of channel routings obtained by swapping a pair of horizontal wires.

Reference: Savage and Wloka [321].

Hint: The reduction is from a variant of Monotone Circuit Value, Problem A.1.3.

Remarks: Savage and Wloka pose as open problems whether certain other routing heuristics are hard to parallelize [321]. They present an $O(\log n)$ time, n processor EREW-PRAM algorithm for two layer channel routing of VLSI designs in [318].

A.6 Logic

A.6.1 Unit Resolution (UNIT)

Given: A Boolean formula F in conjunctive normal form.
Problem: Can the empty clause $\square$ be deduced from F by *unit resolution*? An unit is a clause with only one term. For example, the unit resolvent of $A \vee B_1 \vee \cdots \vee B_m$ and the unit $\neg A$ is $B_1 \vee \cdots \vee B_m$.
Reference: Jones and Laaser [181].
Hint: Jones and Laaser provide a polynomial time algorithm for unit resolution [181]. To show B follows from the assumption $A_1 \wedge \cdots \wedge A_m$, negate B, add it to the set of clauses, and derive the empty clause. Reduce CVP to UNIT as described below. A gate in the circuit $v_k \leftarrow v_i \wedge v_j$ is represented by the clauses of $v_k \Leftrightarrow v_i \wedge v_j$. That is, $(\neg v_k \vee v_i) \wedge (\neg v_k \vee v_j) \wedge (v_k \vee \neg v_i \vee \neg v_j)$. Similarly, $v_k \leftarrow v_i \vee v_j$ is represented by the clauses of $v_k \Leftrightarrow v_i \vee v_j$, and $v_k \leftarrow \neg v_i$ is represented by the clauses of $v_k \Leftrightarrow \neg v_i$.
Remarks: See Chang and Lee [52] for an introduction to mechanical theorem proving. Under the appropriate definitions, it is known that approximating this problem is also P-complete (Serna and Spirakis [328]).

A.6.2 Horn Unit Resolution (HORN)

Given: A *Horn formula* F, that is, a conjunctive normal form (CNF) formula with each clause a disjunction of literals having at most one positive literal per clause.
Problem: Can the empty clause $\square$ be deduced from F by *unit resolution*?
Reference: Dobkin, Lipton, and Reiss [93], Jones and Laaser [181].
Hint: Reduce an arbitrary Turing machine to a CNF formula as in Cook [62]. All of the clauses are Horn clauses. Most clauses are of the form $\neg P_{i-1,t}^a \vee \neg P_{i,t}^b \vee \neg P_{i+1,t}^c \vee P_{i,t+1}^{f(a,b,c)}$, where P_i, t^a is TRUE if at time t tape cell i contains symbol a (or symbol (a, s) if the tape head is over the cell and the Turing machine is in state s). The function $f(a, b, c)$ depends on the Turing machine. For cells $i - 1, i$, and $i + 1$ containing symbols a, b, and c the value of cell i at the next time step is $f(a, b, c)$. Alternatively, one can reduce CVP to HORN as for UNIT, Problem A.6.1. The clauses for $v_k \leftarrow v_i \wedge v_j$ and for

$v_k \leftarrow \neg v_i$ are already in Horn form. For $v_k \leftarrow v_i \vee v_j$ the clauses of $v_k \Leftrightarrow v_i \vee v_j$ are not in Horn form, but replacing the OR by an AND gate and associated NOT gates using DeMorgan's laws results in a set of Horn clauses.

A.6.3 Propositional Horn Clause Satisfiability (PHCS)

Given: A set S of Horn clauses in the propositional calculus.
Problem: Is S satisfiable?
Reference: Kasif [202], Plaisted [290].
Hint: The reduction is straightforward from Alternating Graph Accessibility, Problem A.2.3.
Remarks: The problem remains P-complete when there are at most three literals per clause [290]. Plaisted has shown that two problems involving proofs of restricted depth are also P-complete. They are the *Two Literal Horn Clause Unique Matching Problem* and the *Three Literal Horn Clause Problem* [290]. Kasif observes that PHCS remains P-complete when the set of clauses is restricted so that implications have at most two atoms on their right-hand side Kasif [203].

A.6.4 Monadic Krom Satisfiability (MKS)

Given: A monadic Krom formula F. A *Krom formula* is a 2-CNF formula. That is, a formula in CNF with at most two disjuncts per clause. Let ϕ and ψ be predicate letters that may be preceded by a negation. A conjunct of F is *monadic* if it is of the form $(\phi y_1 y_1 \vee \psi y_1 y_1)$.
Problem: Is F satisfiable?
Reference: Denenberg and Lewis [89].
Hint: An algorithm showing the problem is in P is given in [89]. The reduction is from a Nonacceptance Problem for Pushdown Automata (Denenberg [88], [89]); see Problem A.7.8.

A.6.5 Multivalued Dependency (MVD)

Given: A set Σ of multivalued dependencies and a multivalued dependency σ. We follow the discussion presented by Denenberg in [88] to define these concepts. Let U denote the set of all attributes in the database and let X, Y, and Z denote sets of attributes. An *embedded multivalued dependency* (EMVD) is an expression of the form $X \rightarrow\rightarrow Y \mid Z$, where X, Y, and Z are disjoint sets of attributes in which Y and Z nonempty. A *multivalued dependency* (MVD) is an EMVD in which Z is equal to $U - XY$. A set Σ of MVDs *implies* a MVD σ if σ holds in every database in which every member of Σ holds.

Problem: Does Σ imply σ?

Reference: Denenberg [88].

Hint: The reduction is from a variant of Horn Unit Resolution, Problem A.6.2.

A.6.6 Relaxed Consistent Labeling (RCL)

Given: A relaxed consistent labeling problem G consisting of a set of variables $V = \{v_1, \ldots, v_n\}$ and a set of labels $L = \{L_1, \ldots, L_n\}$, where L_i consists of the possible labels for v_i. A binary predicate P, where $P_{ij}(x, y) = 1$ if and only if the assignment of label x to v_i is compatible with the assignment of label y to v_j. A designated variable X and a designated label f.

Problem: Is there a valid assignment of the label f to X in G?

Reference: Kasif [202], Greenlaw, Hoover, and Ruzzo, THIS WORK.

Hint: The original reduction is from Propositional Horn Clause Satisfiability, Problem A.6.3 [202]. The reduction we sketch is from NANDCVP, Problem A.1.5. A variable is introduced for each circuit input. The variable must have label 1 (0) if the circuit input is TRUE (respectively, FALSE). We view each NAND gate as being represented by three variables. Consider NAND gate k with inputs i and j, and outputs s and t. The variables for k will be denoted k, L_k, and R_k. The possible labels for a NAND gate (variable k) are 0, 1, T, T', and F. T and T' are used to denote TRUE values, and F is used to denote a FALSE value. The possible labels for variables L_k and R_k are 0 and 1. The constraints for variable k with its inputs are as follows: $P_{ik}(0, 1) = 1$, $P_{ik}(1, T) = 1$, $P_{ik}(0, T') = 1$, $P_{ik}(1, F) = 1$,

$P_{jk}(0,1) = 1$, $P_{jk}(0,T) = 1$, $P_{jk}(1,T') = 1$, and $P_{jk}(1,F) = 1$. The constraints on L_k and R_k are the same. When k has any label l from $\{1,T,T'\}$, then $P_{kL_k}(l,1) = 1$. When k has a label l from $\{0,F\}$, then $P_{kL_k}(l,0) = 1$. All other possible labelings are not allowed. The constraints involving NAND gate s (t) use L_k (respectively, R_k). Notice that since inputs have only one possible label, they must be assigned this label. The remainder of the labeling is done so that the circuit gets evaluated in a topological manner. Let o denote the number of the output gate of the NANDCVP instance. There is a valid assignment of label 1 to vertex L_o if and only if the output of gate o is TRUE.

Remarks: The *General Consistent Labeling Problem* is known to be *NP*-complete. Kasif shows that several decision problems based on *arc consistency* algorithms for solving constraint satisfaction problems are also *P*-complete [203, 204].

A.6.7 Generability (GEN)

Given: A finite set W, a binary operation $\bullet$ on W (presented as a table), a subset $V \subseteq W$, and $w \in W$.

Problem: Is w contained in the smallest subset of W that contains V and is closed under the operation $\bullet$?

Reference: Jones and Laaser [181].

Hint: The reduction is from Unit Resolution, Problem A.6.1. Define $a \bullet b$ to be the unit resolution of clauses a and b. Let W be all the subclauses of a formula F in an instance of UNIT, and V be all of its clauses. Let w be the empty clause.

Remarks: The problem remains *P*-complete if V is a singleton set and $\bullet$ is commutative (Barrington and McKenzie [25], [181]). If $\bullet$ is associative, GEN is complete for *NLOG*. The problem remains in *P* even with more than one operation. In [25] an alternative reduction is given from CVP showing that GEN is NC^1-complete for *P*. The complexities of several other versions of GEN are addressed in [25]. Under the appropriate definitions, it is known that approximating this problem is also *P*-complete (Serna and Spirakis [328]). Simons developed an $O(n)$ time parallel algorithm for the problem in 1987, where $n = |W|$ (Roger A. Simons, Personal Communication, 1992).

A.6.8 Path Systems (PATH)

Given: A path system $P = (X, R, S, T)$, where $S \subseteq X$, $T \subseteq X$, and $R \subseteq X \times X \times X$.

Problem: Is there an admissible vertex in S? A vertex x is *admissible* if and only if $x \in T$, or there exists admissible $y, z \in X$ such that $(x, y, z) \in R$.

Reference: Cook [64].

Hint: Jones and Laaser reduce Generability, Problem A.6.7, to PATH by defining $(x, y, z) \in R$ if and only if $x = y \bullet z$ [181].

Remarks: Cook defined path systems in [60]. This is the first problem shown to be logarithmic space complete for P. The original proof by Cook does a direct simulation of a Turing machine [64]. Under the appropriate definitions, it is known that approximating this problem is also P-complete (Serna and Spirakis [328]). Vitter and Simons give a $\sqrt{n}$ time parallel algorithm for the non-sparse version of the problem [366].

A.6.9 Unification (UNIF)

Given: Two symbolic terms s and t. Each term is composed of variables and function symbols. A *substitution* for x in a term u is the replacement of all occurrences of a variable x in u by another term v.

Problem: Is there a series of substitutions σ that unify s and t? That is, gives $\sigma(s) = \sigma(t)$. The two terms are called *unifiable* if such a σ exists.

Reference: Dwork, Kanellakis, and Mitchell [96], Dwork, Kanellakis, and Stockmeyer [97], Yasuura [375].

Hint: The reduction given in [96] is from Monotone Circuit Value, Problem A.1.3. The reductions given in [97] are from NANDCVP, Problem A.1.5. The reduction given in [375] begins with a variant of the Circuit Value Problem and proceeds through another problem on hypergraphs.

Remarks: Robinson defined unification in [305]. The reader is also referred to Chang and Lee [52] for some basic discussion about mechanical theorem proving. The *Unrestricted Unification Problem* is also P-complete [96]. *Unrestricted unification* is where substitutions are allowed to map variables to infinite terms. It is convenient to represent terms as labeled directed acyclic graphs. A term is *linear* if no variable appears more than once in it. The following two restricted versions of unification are also both P-complete: (a) both terms are linear, are represented by trees, and have all function symbols with arity less than or equal to two; (b) both terms are represented by trees, no variable appears in both terms, each variable appears at most twice in some term, and all function symbols have arity less than or equal to two [97]. A restricted problem called *Term Matching* can be solved in NC [96]. A term s *matches* a term t if there exists a substitution σ with $\sigma(s) = t$. Dwork, Kanellakis, and Mitchell used randomization to reduce the processor bound given in [96]. On a CREW-PRAM their algorithm runs in randomized time $O((\log n)^2)$ using $M(n)$ processors, where $M(n)$ denotes the complexity of an $n \times n$ matrix multiplication [97]. Vitter and Simons give a $\sqrt{n}$ time parallel algorithm for Unification when the instances of the problem are "dense" [366].

Kuper *et al.* give an NC algorithm for the problem of constructing the most specific anti-unifier [224]. This is the dual problem of unification. The *most specific anti-unifier* of m terms $t_1, \ldots, t_m$ is a term t_g such that

1. Each t_i is an instance of t_g.

2. t_g is an instance of any term with property one above.

Their algorithm produces a most specific anti-unifier for m terms of size $O(n)$ on a CREW-PRAM in time $O((\log mn)^2)$ using mn processors [224].

A.6.10   Logical Query Program (LQP)

Given: An extended logic program P, and a ground clause C of the form $p(\overline{x}) :\!-\, q_1(\overline{y}_1), \ldots, q_k(\overline{y}_k)$. A *ground clause* is one in which all arguments (e.g. $\overline{x}$ and $\overline{y}_i$ above) are constants. An *extended logic program* is a basic logic program plus an extensional data base instance. A *basic logic program* is a finite set of rules. A *rule* is a disjunction of literals having exactly one positive literal, called the *head*. The negative literals in the clause are called *subgoals*. The set of predicate symbols that appear only in subgoals is called the *Extensional Database*, or *EDB*. An *EDB fact* is an EDB predicate with constants as arguments. An *EDB instance* is a finite set of EDB facts. C is a *theorem* of P if the head of C is derivable from its subgoals in P.

Problem: Is C a theorem of P?

Reference: Ullman and Van Gelder [355].

Hint: Reduce Path Systems, Problem A.6.8, to LQP. Let (X, R, S, T) be an instance of PATH. Without loss of generality, assume $S = \{s\}$. Let $t(Y)$ be an EDB relation specifying that vertex Y is in T. Let $r(U, V, W)$ be an EDB relation specifying that the triple of vertices (U, V, W) is in R. The basic logic program consists of the two rules $a(Y) :- t(Y)$ and $a(Y) :- r(Y, V, W), a(V), a(W)$. The relation a models "admissibility" in the path system, so $a(s)$ is a theorem of P if and only if s is admissible in the path system.

Remarks: Remains P-complete even for very restricted programs. In NC for programs with the "polynomial fringe property." See [355] for details. Afrati and Papadimitriou classify *simple chain programs* according to their parallel complexities [4]. They show a certain subclass of simple chain programs are in NC and that all other simple chain programs are P-complete. Afrati describes additional classes of logic programs that can be solved in NC, and also provides sufficient conditions for single rule programs to be P-complete [3]. The reader is referred to [3] for definitions and further details. Numerous open problems are described in [3] as well.

A.6.11   Left-linear Semi-unification (LLSU)

Given: A set of pairs of terms $S = \{(M_1, N_1), \ldots, (M_k, N_k)\}$ that is left linear. We follow the discussion given in [155] for definitions. A *ranked alphabet* $\mathcal{A} = (F, a)$ is a finite set F of *function symbols* together with an *arity* function a that maps every element in F to a natural number. A function symbol of arity 0 is called a *constant*. The set of *variables* V is a denumerable infinite set that is disjoint from F. The *terms* over A and V is the set $T(\mathcal{A}, V)$ consisting of all strings generated by the grammar

$$M \rightarrow x \mid c \mid f(M, \ldots, M),$$

where f is a function symbol from $\mathcal{A}$ with arity k greater than 0, c is a constant, x is any variable from V, and M appears k times as an argument to f. Two terms M and N are equal, written $M = N$, if and only if they are identical as strings. A *substitution* σ is a mapping from V to $T(\mathcal{A}, V)$ that is the identity on all but a finite set of V. The set of variables on which σ is *not* the identity is the *domain* of σ. Every substitution $\sigma : V \rightarrow T(\mathcal{A}, V)$ can be extended to $\sigma : T(\mathcal{A}, V) \rightarrow T(\mathcal{A}, V)$ by defining

$$\sigma(f(M_1, \ldots, M_k)) = f(\sigma(M_1), \ldots, \sigma(M_k)).$$

A term M *subsumes* N, written $M \leq N$, if there is a substitution ρ such that $\rho(M) = N$. Given S a substitution σ is a *semi-unifier* of S if

$$\sigma(M_1) \leq \sigma(N_1), \ldots, \sigma(M_k) \leq \sigma(N_k).$$

S is *semi-unifiable* if it has a semi-unifier.

Problem: Is S semi-unifiable?

Reference: Henglein [155].

Hint: The proof is adopted from the one given by Dwork, Kanellakis, and Mitchell [96] to show Unification, Problem A.6.9, is P-complete.

Remarks: Define *kLLSU* to be the problem of left-linear semi-unifiability with exactly k *term inequalities* (same k as above) and *Monadic Semi-unification* (MSU) to be the problem of semi-unifiability for the alphabet $\mathcal{A} = (F, a)$, where $a(f)$ is greater than or equal to 1 for all $f \in F$ and $a(f)$ equals 1 for at least one f. 2LLSU and MSU are P-complete [155]. See Problem A.6.9 for related problems. Also see Problem B.3.2 for an open problem.

A.6.12   Mostowski Epimorphism (MostEpi)

Given: A *well-founded relation* (V, E) and $x_1, x_2 \in V$. Let f be the *Mostowski epimorphism* of the relation. The reader is referred to [74] for definitions.

Problem: Is $f(x_1) = f(x_2)$?

Reference: Dahlhaus [74].

Hint: The reduction is from Monotone Circuit Value, Problem A.1.3.

Remarks: The result indicates that the programming language SETL may not be well suited to parallelism [74]. See Problem B.3.1 for a related open problem.

A.6.13   Corporate Takeover Query (CTQ)

Given: A group of n companies $C_1, \ldots, C_n$ and a *partial* relation owns(C_i, C_j, S), where $1 \leq i, j \leq n$, and two distinct integers k and l. owns(C_i, C_j, S) indicates company C_i owns $S\%$ of company C_j's stock.

Problem: Has company C_k bought company C_l? A company B has *bought* company D whenever B controls more than 50% of D's stock. A company B *controls* itself, and also controls stock controlled by any other company B has bought.

Reference: Consens and Mendelzon [59].

Hint: The reduction is from Path Systems, Problem A.6.8.

Remarks: Other query languages are considered in [59]. For numerous of them, Consens and Mendelzon show any question that can be posed in the language can be resolved in *NC*.

A.6.14 Incomplete Table Recovery (ITR)

Given: A collection F of functional dependencies on a finite attribute set $\{A_1, \ldots, A_m\}$, a matrix $T = (T_{ij})$ for $0 \leq i \leq n$ and $1 \leq j \leq m$ called an *incomplete table* where $T_{0j} = A_j$ for $1 \leq j \leq m$, and the value of each T_{ij} is either a nonnegative integer or the null value $*$ for $1 \leq i \leq n$ and $1 \leq j \leq m$. The reader is referred to [267] for definitions regarding this problem.

Problem: Is T uniquely recoverable under F when the domain of each attribute A_j is the set of nonnegative integers?

Reference: Miyano and Haraguchi [267], Miyano, Shiraishi, and Shoudai [268].

Hint: The reduction is from Alternating Graph Accessibility, Problem A.2.3.

A.7 Formal Languages

A.7.1 Context-free Grammar Membership (CFGmem)

Given: A context-free grammar $G = (N, T, P, S)$ and a string $x \in T^*$.

Problem: Is $x \in L(G)$?

Reference: Jones and Laaser [181].

Hint: Reduce Generability, Problem A.6.7, to CFGmem. Let $(W, \bullet, V, w)$ be an instance of GEN. Construct the grammar $G = (W, \{a\}, P, w)$, where $P = \{x \to yz \mid y \bullet z = x\} \cup \{x \to \epsilon \mid x \in V\}$. It follows that $\epsilon \in L(G)$ if and only if w is generated by V.

Remarks: Goldschlager remarks it is the presence of ϵ-productions in the input grammar that make the membership question difficult [125]. Lewis, Stearns, and Hartmanis' $(\log n)^2$ space algorithm [234] and Ruzzo's AC^1 (hence NC^2) algorithm [307] for general context free language recognition can both be modified to work with an ϵ-free grammar given as part of the input. For a fixed grammar, unbounded fanin size $O(n^6)$ suffices [307]. Rytter shows context-free languages can be recognized on a cube connected computer in $O((\log n)^2)$ time using n^6 processors [309]. He also provides an $O(\log n)$ time n^7 processor COMMON CRCW-PRAM algorithm for the recognition of unambiguous context-free languages [310]. Klein and Reif give an $O(\log n)$ time n^3 processor CREW-PRAM algorithm for the recognition of deterministic context-free languages [216]. Dymond and Ruzzo give a somewhat simpler algorithm for this problem on the more restricted CROW-PRAM [101]. Kaji *et al.* prove *Parallel Multiple Context-free Grammar Membership* and *Multiple Context-free Grammar Membership*, which are problems involving generalizations of context-free grammars that are designed to model natural languages, are *P*-complete [182].

A.7.2 Context-free Grammar Empty (CFGempty)

Given: A context-free grammar $G = (N, T, P, S)$.

Problem: Is $L(G)$ empty?

Reference: Jones and Laaser [181], Goldschlager [125].

Hint: The reduction given in Problem A.7.1 suffices. The following reduction of Monotone Circuit Value, Problem A.1.3, to CFGempty (Martin Tompa, Personal Communication, 1991) is also of interest. Given a circuit α construct the grammar $G = (N, T, P, S)$ with non-terminals $N = \{i \mid v_i$ is a vertex in $\alpha\}$, terminals $T = \{a\}$, and start symbol $S = n$, where v_n is the output of α. Let $\nu(g)$ denote the value of gate g. The productions in P are of the following form.

1. For input v_i, $i \rightarrow a$ if $\nu(v_i)$ is TRUE,

2. $i \rightarrow jk$ if $v_i \leftarrow v_j \wedge v_k$, and

3. $i \rightarrow j \mid k$ if $v_i \leftarrow v_j \vee v_k$.

Then $\nu(v_i)$ is TRUE if and only if $i \stackrel{*}{\Rightarrow} \gamma$, where $\gamma \in \{a\}^+$.

Remarks: Note, this reduction and the one for CFGinf, Problem A.7.3, have no ϵ-productions yet remain complete. The original proof of Jones and Laaser reduced Generability, Problem A.6.7, to CFGempty. Their proof used the reduction for CFGmem, Problem A.7.1, and instead checked if $L(G)$ is empty [181].

A.7.3 Context-free Grammar Infinite (CFGinf)

Given: A context-free grammar $G = (N, T, P, S)$.
Problem: Is $L(G)$ infinite?
Reference: Goldschlager [125], Jones and Laaser [181].
Hint: Use a grammar similar to G in the proof for CFGempty, Problem A.7.2, except production $i \rightarrow a$ is replaced by $i \rightarrow x$, and the productions $x \rightarrow a$ and $x \rightarrow ax$ are also added.

A.7.4 Context-free Grammar ϵ-Membership (CFGϵmem)

Given: A context-free grammar $G = (N, T, P, S)$.
Problem: Is $\epsilon \in L(G)$?
Reference: Goldschlager [125], Jones and Laaser [181].
Hint: Use a grammar similar to G in the proof for CFGempty, Problem A.7.2, except production $i \rightarrow a$ is replaced by $i \rightarrow \epsilon$.

A.7.5   Forward Deterministic Growing Context-sensitive Grammar Membership (CSGmem)

Given: A forward deterministic growing context-sensitive grammar $G = (N, T, P, S)$ and a string $x \in T^*$. A context-sensitive grammar is *growing* if for each production $\alpha \rightarrow \beta \in P$, where $\alpha, \beta \in (N \cup T)^*$, $|\alpha|$ is less than $|\beta|$. A context-sensitive grammar is *forward deterministic* if whenever there are derivations of a sentential form u, $u \Rightarrow v$ and $u \Rightarrow v'$, then v equals v'.
Problem: Is $x \in L(G)$?
Reference: Sang Cho and Huynh [312].
Hint: The techniques used for the P-completeness proofs sketched in Problems A.7.1, A.7.2, A.7.3, and A.7.4 do not seem to apply to this problem because they involve grammars that are not forward deterministic and are not growing. The reduction given in [312] is from a version of Generic Machine Simulation, Problem A.12.1.
Remarks: The proof yields as a straightforward corollary that *Nondeterministic Growing Context-sensitive Grammar Membership* is *NP*-complete [312].

A.7.6   Straight-line Program Membership (SLPmem)

Given: A straight-line program over alphabet Σ, $|\Sigma| \geq 1$, with operations taken from $\Phi = \Sigma \cup \{\{\epsilon\}, \emptyset, \cup, \cdot\}$, and a string x.
Problem: Is x a member of the set constructed by the program? The *set constructed by the program*, when the last instruction involves $\cup$ or $\cdot$, is the set computed by the final instruction.
Reference: Goodrich [129], Greenlaw, Hoover, and Ruzzo, THIS WORK.
Hint: By noting there is a logarithmic space alternating Turing machine that "parses" x relative to the program, the problem is easily seen to be in P. Reduce Monotone Circuit Value, Problem A.1.3, to SLPmem by the following: TRUE $\rightarrow \{\epsilon\}$, FALSE $\rightarrow \emptyset$, AND $\rightarrow \cdot$, OR $\rightarrow \cup$, and $x \rightarrow \epsilon$.
Remarks: The original reduction was from Generability, Problem A.6.7. Remains in P if $\cap$ is allowed. The analogous membership question for regular languages presented as regular expressions or nondeterministic finite automata is complete for *NLOG*.

A.7.7 Straight-line Program Nonempty (SLPnonempty)

Given: A straight-line program over alphabet Σ, $|\Sigma| \geq 1$, with operations taken from $\Phi = \Sigma \cup \{\{\epsilon\}, \emptyset, \cup, \cdot\}$, and a string x.

Problem: Is the set constructed by the program nonempty? See Problem A.7.6 for definition.

Reference: Goodrich [129].

Hint: Same as Problem A.7.6.

Remarks: With $\cap$ added, SLPnonempty becomes complete for nondeterministic exponential time [129].

A.7.8 Two-way DPDA Acceptance (2DPDA)

Given: A two-way deterministic pushdown automaton $M = (Q, \Sigma, \Gamma, \delta, q_0, Z_0, F)$ and a string x.

Problem: Is x accepted by M?

Reference: Cook [61], Galil [111, 112], Ladner [225].

Hint: See, for example, Hopcroft and Ullman [162] for a definition of 2DPDAs. Cook gives a direct simulation of a polynomial time Turing machine by a logarithmic space *auxiliary* pushdown automaton [61]. Galil shows the existence of a P-complete language accepted by a 2DPDA, in effect showing that the logarithmic space work tape is not crucial to Cook's simulation [111, 112]. (See also Sudborough [348] for a general reduction of auxiliary PDAs to ordinary PDAs.) Ladner gives a much more direct proof by observing that a suitably encoded version of CVP is solvable by a 2DPDA, basically by doing a depth-first search of the circuit, using the stack for backtracking [225].

Remarks: Remains in P when generalized to nondeterministic and/or logarithmic space auxiliary PDAs [61]. When restricted to one-way PDAs, or other polynomial time PDAs, even with a logarithmic space work tape, the problem is in NC; specifically, it is complete for $LOGDCFL$ in the deterministic case, and for $LOGCFL = SAC^1$ in the nondeterministic case.

A.7.9 Labeled GAP (LGAP)

Given: A fixed context free language L over alphabet Σ, a directed graph $G = (V, E)$ with edges labeled by strings in Σ^*, and two vertices s and t.

Problem: Is there a path from s to t such that the concatenation of its edge labels is in L?

Reference: Ruzzo [306], Greenlaw, Hoover, and Ruzzo, THIS
WORK.

Hint: Reduce Two-way DPDA Acceptance, Problem A.7.8, to
LGAP. Let $M = (Q, \Sigma', \Gamma, \delta, q_0, Z_0, F)$ be a two-way DPDA (see
Hopcroft and Ullman [162] for details) and let $x \in \Sigma'$ be an input
string. Without loss of generality, the PDA has a unique final state
q_f and accepts with empty stack with its head at the right end of
the input. Let $\Sigma = \Gamma \cup \{\overline{Z} \mid Z \in \Gamma\}$. Let V be the set containing
the special vertex s, together with all "surface configurations" of the
PDA, that is, $Q \times \{1, \ldots, |x|\}$. There is an edge from $\langle p, i \rangle$ to $\langle q, j \rangle$
labeled $\alpha \in \Sigma^*$ if and only if when reading x_i the PDA has a move
from p to q that moves its input head $j - i \in \{-1, 0, 1\}$ cells to the
right, pops $Z \in \Gamma$, and pushes $\beta \in \Gamma^*$, where $\alpha = \overline{Z}\beta$. Additionally, there is an edge from the special vertex s to the initial surface
configuration $\langle q_0, 1 \rangle$ labeled Z_0 (the initial stack symbol). The des-
ignated vertex t is $\langle q_f, |x| \rangle$. Finally, L is the semi-Dyck language
$D_{|\Gamma|}$ on $|\Gamma|$ letters (Harrison [147, Section 10.4]), that is, L is the
language generated by the context-free grammar with productions
$\{S \rightarrow aS\overline{a}S \mid a \in \Gamma\} \cup \{S \rightarrow \epsilon\}$.

Remarks: Remains P-complete when L is D_2. An equivalent statement is that it is P-complete to decide, given a deterministic finite
state automaton M, whether $D_2 \cap L(M) = \emptyset$. If G is acyclic, the
problem is complete for $SAC^1 = LOGCFL$ [306].

A.7.10   Strong Bisimilarity in Transition Systems (SBTS)

Given: An encoding of a finite labeled transition system N, and
two designated states p and q. A *finite labeled transition system* is
a triple $M = \langle Q, \Sigma, T \rangle$, where Q is a finite set of states, Σ is a finite
alphabet, and $T \subseteq Q \times \Sigma \times Q$ is the set of transitions. A relation
$S \subseteq Q \times Q$ is a *strong bisimulation* of M if $(s_1, s_2) \in S$ implies for
all $x \in \Sigma$ that

1. whenever $(s_1, x, t_1) \in T$, then for some state t_2, $(s_2, x, t_2) \in T$
   and $(t_1, t_2) \in S$; and

2. whenever $(s_2, x, t_2) \in T$, then for some state t_1, $(s_1, x, t_1) \in T$
   and $(t_1, t_2) \in S$.

The *strong bisimulation relation* is defined as the union of all strong
bisimulations of M.

Problem: Are p and q strongly bisimilar? That is, is (p, q) in the strong bisimulation relation of N?

Reference: Àlvarez *et al.* [11], Balcázar, Gabarró, and Sántha [23].

Hint: The reduction is from SAM2CVP, Problem A.1.6. The key idea in the reduction is to modify the instance of SAM2CVP so that each AND gate receives at least one TRUE input and each OR gate receives at least one FALSE input. Call this the *input property*. The construction that accomplishes this is called an *alternating pattern*. It consists of alternating levels of two OR gates and two AND gates with unbounded fan-out. On OR (AND) levels in the alternating pattern one gate receives inputs of TRUE and FALSE (respectively, same) while the other receives FALSE (respectively, TRUE). The outputs of these gates are sent to gates on the next level to achieve the input property. The depth of the alternating pattern is the same as the circuit depth. The transition network consists of the modified circuit with all edges directed from the circuit output to the inputs. The vertices in this graph correspond to states. Each transition, which is represented by an edge, is assigned the same character from Σ. In fact, the alphabet can consist of a single character. p can be chosen as the state corresponding to the output gate of the circuit and q can be chosen as the TRUE OR gate in the last layer of the alternating pattern. The circuit will evaluate to TRUE if and only if p and q are strongly bisimilar.

Remarks: Notice that in the construction given above the transition system is nondeterministic. It is an open question whether the problem remains P-complete in the deterministic case [23], see Problem B.4.1. *Observation Equivalence* and *Observation Congruence* are two related problems that are both shown P-complete in [23]. Zhang and Smolka implement parallel algorithms for equivalence checking [378].

A.7.11 Propagating Set Systems (PSS)

Given: Let S be a set, and S_o and S_f elements of S. A *set system* consists of a finite set of productions P_S of the form $X \to Y$, where X and Y are subsets of S. A set $B \subseteq S$ *derives in one step* a set

$C \subseteq S$, written $B \Rightarrow C$, if and only if

$$C = \bigcup_{X \rightarrow Y \in P_S, X \subseteq B} Y.$$

$\overset{*}{\Rightarrow}$ denotes the reflexive, transitive closure of $\Rightarrow$. A *propagating set system* is a set system such that for every element $s \in S$, $\{s\} \rightarrow \{s\} \in P_S$.

Problem: Does $S_o \overset{*}{\Rightarrow} S'$ such that $S' \cap S_f \neq \emptyset$?

Reference: Monti and Roncato [269].

Hint: The reduction given in [269] is from a variant of Generic Machine Simulation, Problem A.12.1.

Remarks: The general version of the problem is *PSPACE*-complete.

A.7.12   Cellular Tree Automaton Acceptance (*) (CTAA)

Given: A sublinear time bounded *cellular tree automaton* (CTA) M and an input string x. See Ibarra, Jiang, and Chang [165] for the definition.

Problem: Does M accept x?

Reference: Ibarra, Jiang, and Chang [165].

Hint: A *trellis automaton* can accept a P-complete language (Ibarra and Kim [166]). This in turn can be simulated by a *linear iterative array* that in turn can be simulated by a cellular tree automaton. See [165] and [166] for definitions and further details.

Remarks: A sublinear time one-way bounded CTA can also accept a P-complete language [165]. In a *one-way* CTA, communication between vertices is bottom-up. Every language accepted by an one-way CTA can be accepted by a deterministic Turing machine in $(\log n)^2 / \log \log n$ space, where n is the size of the input [165].

A.7.13   Iterative Tree Array Acceptance (*) (ITAA)

Given: A *real-time* $\log n$ *depth bounded iterative tree array* M and an input string x of length n. See Ibarra, Jiang, and Chang [165] for definitions.

Problem: Does M accept x?

Reference: Ibarra, Jiang, and Chang [165].

Hint: Iterative tree arrays can simulate cellular tree automata. Combining this with the result of Problem A.7.12, the proof follows [165].

Remarks: Note that under the appropriate resource bounds cellular tree automata can simulate iterative tree arrays [165]. Also see Problem A.7.12.

A.7.14 Relation Coarsest Set Partition (RCSP)

Given: A finite set S, an initial partition π_0 of S, a designated set $S' \subseteq S$, and a set of binary relations $R_1, \ldots, R_k$ on S.

Problem: Is S' a member of the coarsest refinement π of π_0 such that for each pair of blocks B_1 and B_2 of π, and for each integer $i = 1, \ldots, k$ either

$$B_1 \subseteq \mathrm{PI}_i(B_2) \quad \text{or} \quad B_1 \cap \mathrm{PI}_i(B_2) = \varnothing,$$

where $\mathrm{PI}_i(B_2)$ is the pre-image set $\mathrm{PI}_i(B_2) = \{x \mid \text{there is a } y \in B_2 \text{ with } x \; R_i \; y\}$.

Reference: Sang Cho and Huynh [313].

Hint: In [313], they observe that Kanellakis and Smolka [183] showed the NC^1 equivalence of Relation Coarsest Set Partition to a P-complete variant of Strong Bisimilarity in Transition Systems, Problem A.7.10.

Remarks: Even if there is only a single relation, k equals one, the problem is P-complete [313]. Sang Cho and Huynh give a $\log n$ time, $O(n^2)$ processor CREW-PRAM algorithm for the *single function* Coarsest Set Partition Problem as well as a $\log n$ time, $O(n^3)$ processor EREW-PRAM algorithm for the same problem [313]. See also the remarks for Problems A.7.10 and B.4.1.

A.7.15 Iterated Shuffle (SHUF)

Given: A language L over a finite alphabet Σ described in terms of the operators $\cdot$, $*$, $\cup$, $\cap$, Δ, and $\dagger$; which denote concatenation, Kleene star, union, intersection, shuffle, and iterated shuffle, respectively; plus a designated word $w \in \Sigma^*$. The *shuffle* of two languages L_1 and L_2, denoted $L_1 \Delta L_2$, is

$$\{x_1 y_1 x_2 y_2 \cdots x_m y_m \mid x_1 x_2 \cdots x_m \in L_1, y_1 y_2 \cdots y_m \in L_2 \text{ and } x_i, y_i \in \Sigma^* \text{ for } i = 1, \ldots, m\}.$$

The *iterated shuffle* denoted $L^\dagger$ is

$$\{\epsilon\} \cup L \cup (L\Delta L) \cup (L\Delta L\Delta L) \cup \cdots.$$

Problem: Is $w \in L$?

Reference: Shoudai [332].

Hint: Note, certain restrictions must be placed on L in order for this problem to be in P. The reduction is from a variant of NORCVP, see Problem A.1.5.

Remarks: It is known that there are two deterministic context-free languages whose shuffle is NP-complete (Ogden, Riddle, and Rounds [274]). Here the intersection operation is used to force the problem into P [332].

A.8 Algebra

A.8.1 Finite Horizon Markov Decision Process (FHMDP)

Given: A *nonstationary* Markov decision process $M = (S, c, p)$ and an integer T. Before defining the problem, we present some background on Markov decision processes. The term *finite horizon* refers to the time bound T. S is a finite set of states and contains a designated initial state s_0. Let s_t denote the current state of the system for each time $t = 1, 2, \ldots$ Associated with each state $s \in S$ is a finite set of decisions D_s. A cost of $c(s, i, t)$ is incurred at time t by making decision $i \in D_{s_t}$. The next state s' has probability distribution given by $p(s, s', i, t)$. If c and p are independent of t, then the process is said to be *stationary*. A *policy* δ is a mapping that assigns to each time step t and each state s a decision $\delta(s, t)$. A policy is *stationary* if δ is independent of time, and can then be supplied as an input.

Problem: Is the minimum expected cost of

$$\sum_{t=0}^{T} c(s_t, \delta(s_t, t), t)$$

over all policies δ equal to 0?

Reference: Papadimitriou and Tsitsiklis [279].

Hint: There is a polynomial time algorithm for the problem that uses dynamic programming (Howard [164]). The reduction is from Monotone Circuit Value, Problem A.1.3. Let $c = ((a_i, b_i, c_i), i = 1, \ldots, k)$ denote an encoding of MCVP, where a_i denotes gate type, and b_i and c_i denote the numbers of gate i's inputs. A stationary Markov process $M = (S, c, p)$ is constructed from the circuit instance as follows. S has one state q_i for each i, $1 \leq i \leq k$. There is an additional state in S called q. If (a_i, b_i, c_i) corresponds to a circuit input, the corresponding state q_i has a single decision 0 with $p(q_i, q, 0) = 1$, and cost $c(q_i, 0) = 1$ (0) if a_i is a FALSE (respectively, TRUE) input. All other costs of this process are 0. There is one decision 0 for state q and $p(q, q, 0) = 1$. If a_i is an OR gate, there are two decisions 0 and 1 from state q_i. The associated probabilities are $p(q_i, q_{b_i}, 0) = 1$ and $p(q_i, q_{c_i}, 1) = 1$. The associated costs are both 0. If a_i is an AND gate, there are two decisions 0 and 1 from state q_i. $p(q_i, q_{b_i}, 0) = 1/2$ and $p(q_i, q_{c_i}, 1) = 1/2$ with associated costs 0. The initial state is k

corresponding to the output gate of the circuit. The time horizon T is k. It is easy to verify that the expected cost of the process is 0 if and only if the circuit evaluates to TRUE.

Remarks: The reduction shows that the finite horizon stationary version of the problem is P-hard. This problem is not known to be in P. The *deterministic* version of the FHMDP, which requires that p only has values 0 or 1, is in NC [279]. Note, this last result holds for both the stationary and nonstationary versions of the problem.

A.8.2 Discounted Markov Decision Process (DMDP)

Given: A stationary Markov decision process $M = (S, c, p)$ and a real number $\beta \in (0, 1)$. See Problem A.8.1 for definitions. This problem is *infinite horizon*, that is, there is no time bound.

Problem: Is the minimum expected cost of

$$\sum_{t=0}^{\infty} c(s_t, \delta(s_t, t))\beta^t$$

over all policies δ equal to 0?

Reference: Papadimitriou and Tsitsiklis [279].

Hint: The problem can be phrased as a linear programming problem and solved in polynomial time. The same construction as used in Problem A.8.1 can be used to show this problem is P-complete.

Remarks: The *Infinite Horizon, Discounted, Deterministic Problem* is in NC [279]. The *deterministic* problem requires that p only has values 0 or 1.

A.8.3 Average Cost Markov Decision Process (ACMDP)

Given: A stationary Markov decision process $M = (S, c, p)$. See Problem A.8.1 for definitions. This problem is *infinite horizon*, that is, there is no time bound.

Problem: Is the minimum expected cost of

$$\lim_{T \to \infty} \left(\sum_{i=0}^{T} c(s_t, \delta(s_t, t))/T \right)$$

over all policies δ equal to 0?

Reference: Papadimitriou and Tsitsiklis [279].

Hint: The problem can be phrased as a linear programming problem and solved in polynomial time. The reduction is from a synchronous variant of Monotone Circuit Value, see Problem A.1.6. The construction is a modification to that given in Problem A.8.1. Instead of having states corresponding to circuit inputs going to a new state q, they have transitions to the initial state. The limit is 0 if and only if the circuit instance evaluates to TRUE.

Remarks: The *Infinite Horizon, Average Cost, Deterministic Problem* is in *NC* [279]. The *deterministic* problem requires that p only has values 0 or 1.

A.8.4 Gaussian Elimination with Partial Pivoting (GEPP)

Given: An $n \times n$ matrix A with entries over the rationals and an integer l.

Problem: Is the pivot value for the lth column positive when Gaussian elimination with partial pivoting is performed on A? *Partial pivoting* is a technique used to obtain numerical stability in which rows of the matrix are exchanged so that the largest value in a given column can be used to perform the elimination.

Reference: Vavasis [361].

Hint: The standard Gaussian elimination algorithm requires $O(n^3)$ operations. Since the size of the numbers involved can be bounded by a polynomial in n (see [361]), the problem is in P. To show completeness reduce NANDCVP, Problem A.1.5, to GEPP. Without loss of generality, assume the inputs and gates of the circuit are numbered in topological order from 1 to G, where G numbers the output gate. A $2G \times 2G$ matrix $A = (a_{i,j})$ is constructed from the instance of NANDCVP. The entries of A are described below. A TRUE circuit input i contributes entry -3.9 in position $a_{2i-1,i}$ and entry 0 in position $a_{2i,i}$. For FALSE input i or NAND gate i, A has entry -3.9 in position $a_{2i-1,i}$ and 4.0 in position $a_{2i,i}$. If gate i is an input to gate k, then A has entry 0 in position $a_{2k-1,i}$ and entry 1 in position $a_{2k,i}$. For $1 \leq i \leq G$, A has entry $a_{2i,G+i} = 1$. All unspecified matrix entries have value 0. The pivot value used in eliminating column G is positive (negative) if and only if the circuit evaluates to FALSE (respectively, TRUE).

Remarks: The reduction does not rely on large numbers; therefore, it shows that the problem is strongly P-complete. Another decision problem that is strongly complete for P based on Gaussian elimination with partial pivoting is as follows: given matrix A, and integers i and j, is the pivot used to eliminate the jth column taken from the initial i^{th} row? Vavasis also shows that Gaussian elimination with complete pivoting is P-complete. In *complete pivoting* both rows and columns are interchanged so that the largest remaining matrix entry can be used as a pivot. Complete pivoting is known to be numerically stable. The reduction for complete pivoting does not show the problem is strongly P-complete. This question is open. Some additional references regarding the parallel complexities of this and related problems are (Borodin, von zur Gathen, and Hopcroft [43], Csanky [72], Ibarra, Moran, and Rosier [167], Mulmuley [270], and Pan and Reif [276]). For further open questions see Problems B.5.2 and B.5.4.

A.8.5   Iterated Mod (IM)

Given: Integers $a, b_1, \ldots, b_n$.
Problem: Is $((\cdots((a \bmod b_1) \bmod b_2) \cdots) \bmod b_n) = 0$?
Reference: Karloff and Ruzzo [190].
Hint: Reduce NANDCVP, Problem A.1.5, to IM. Without loss of generality, assume the gates are numbered in reverse topological order from G down to 1, where the output gate is numbered 1. Let $y_1, \ldots, y_r$ denote the inputs and $Y_l \in \{0,1\}$ denote the value of input y_l. The input wires to gate g are numbered $2g$ and $2g - 1$. Let a be a bit vector of length $2G + 1$ whose j^{th} bit is Y_l if edge j is incident from input y_l, and 1 otherwise. Let O_g represent the set of out-edge labels from gate g. For $1 \le g \le G$, we construct moduli $b_1, \ldots, b_{2G}$ as follows:

$$b_{2g} = 2^{2g} + 2^{2g-1} + \sum_{j \in O_g} 2^j \text{ and } b_{2g-1} = 2^{2g-1}.$$

The output gate in the NANDCVP instance has value 0 if and only if

$$((\cdots((a \bmod b_1) \bmod b_2) \cdots) \bmod b_{2G}) = 0.$$

In Lin [236] a direct simulation of a Turing machine by IM is given.
Remarks: The *Polynomial Iterated Mod Problem* is the problem in which $a(x), b_1(x), \ldots, b_n(x)$ are univariate polynomials over a field F and the question is to determine if

$$((\cdots((a(x) \bmod b_1(x)) \bmod b_2(x)) \cdots) \bmod b_n(x)) = 0?$$

This problem is in NC [190]. The proof technique used to show IM is P-complete can be modified to show the Superincreasing Knapsack Problem is also P-complete [190]. The *Superincreasing Knapsack Problem* is defined analogously to the Knapsack Problem (Garey and Johnson [113]) with weights $w_1, \ldots, w_n$, except for $2 \leq i \leq n$, $w_i > \sum_{j=1}^{i-1} w_j$. See Lin [236, 237] for additional work on IM. Mayr describes a fully NC approximation scheme for the $0 - 1$ *Knapsack Problem* in [254].

A.8.6 Generalized Word Problem (GWP)

Given: Let S be a finite set and F be the free group generated by S. Let $\underline{S} = \{s, s^{-1} \mid s \in S\}$, where s^{-1} denotes the inverse of s. Let $\underline{S}^*$ denote the set of all finite words over $\underline{S}$. Let $U = \{u_1, \ldots, u_m\} \subseteq \underline{S}^*$, where $m \in \mathbb{N}$ and let $x \in \underline{S}^*$.

Problem: Is $x \in \langle U \rangle$? That is, is x in the subgroup of F generated by U?

Reference: Avenhaus and Madlener [19], Stewart [340].

Hint: Stewart reported an error in [19]. The reduction in [19] is a generic one from a normal form Turing machine. However, it reduces a Turing machine computation to a version of GWP where S is a countably infinite set [340]. Stewart shows using the Nielsen reduction algorithm that this problem is still in P. Stewart calls this P-complete problem the *Generalized Word Problem for Countably-generated Free Groups* (GWPC). He shows that GWPC is logarithmic space reducible to GWP; thus, proving GWP is P-complete as well [340].

Remarks: For a natural number k, GWPC(k) and GWPC($\leq k$) are the generalized word problems for finitely-generated subgroups of countably-generated free groups where all words involved are of length exactly k and at most k, respectively. Stewart shows GWPC(k) and GWPC($\leq k$) are P-complete for k greater than two [341]. When k equals two the problems are complete for symmetric logarithmic space ($SLOG$). The *Word Problem for a Free Group* is to decide whether x equals the empty word in F. This problem is solvable in deterministic log space (Lipton and Zalcstein [243]).

A.8.7   Subgroup Containment (SC)

Given: Let S be a finite set and F be the free group generated by S. Let $\underline{S} = \{s, s^{-1} \mid s \in S\}$, where s^{-1} denotes the inverse of s. Let $\underline{S}^*$ denote the set of all finite words over $\underline{S}$. Let $U = \{u_1, \ldots, u_m\}, V = \{v_1, \ldots, v_p\} \subseteq \underline{S}^*$, where $m, p \in \mathbb{N}$.

Problem: Is the group generated by U a subgroup of the group generated by V?

Reference: Avenhaus and Madlener [19].

Hint: A variant of the Nielsen reduction algorithm can be used to show the problem is in P. The reduction is from Generalized Word, Problem A.8.6. Observe that for any $x \in \underline{S}^*$ and $U \subseteq \underline{S}^*$, $x \in \langle U \rangle$ if and only if $\langle x \rangle$ is a subgroup of $\langle U \rangle$.

Remarks: Since $\langle U \rangle$ is a subgroup of $\langle V \rangle$ if and only if $\langle U \cup V \rangle$ is normal in $\langle V \rangle$, it follows that the *Normal Subgroup Problem*, which is also in P, is P-complete. The problem of determining whether $\langle U \rangle$ is normal in $\langle U, x \rangle$ is also P-complete [19].

A.8.8   Subgroup Equality (SE)

Given: Let S be a finite set and F be the free group generated by S. Let $\underline{S} = \{s, s^{-1} \mid s \in S\}$, where s^{-1} denotes the inverse of s. Let $\underline{S}^*$ denote the set of all finite words over $\underline{S}$. Let $U = \{u_1, \ldots, u_m\}, V = \{v_1, \ldots, v_p\} \subseteq \underline{S}^*$, where $m, p \in \mathbb{N}$.

Problem: Is $\langle U \rangle = \langle V \rangle$?

Reference: Avenhaus and Madlener [19].

Hint: A variant of the Nielsen reduction algorithm can be used to show the problem is in P. The reduction is from Subgroup Containment, Problem A.8.7. Observe $\langle U \rangle$ is a subgroup of $\langle V \rangle$ if and only if $\langle U \cup V \rangle = \langle V \rangle$.

A.8.9   Subgroup Finite Index (SFI)

Given: Let S be a finite set and F be the free group generated by S. Let $\underline{S} = \{s, s^{-1} \mid s \in S\}$, where s^{-1} denotes the inverse of s. Let $\underline{S}^*$ denote the set of all finite words over $\underline{S}$. Let $U = \{u_1, \ldots, u_m\}, V = \{v_1, \ldots, v_p\} \subseteq \underline{S}^*$, where $m, p \in \mathbb{N}$.

Problem: Is $\langle U \rangle$ a subgroup of $\langle V \rangle$ with finite index in $\langle V \rangle$? The *index* of U in V is the number of distinct right cosets of U in V.

Reference: Avenhaus and Madlener [19].

Hint: A variant of the Nielsen reduction algorithm can be used to show the problem is in P. The reduction is from Subgroup Containment, Problem A.8.7. Note, $\langle U \rangle$ is a subgroup of $\langle V \rangle$ if and only if $\langle U \cup V \rangle$ has finite index in $\langle V \rangle$. Let $x \in \underline{S}^*$. The problem of determining whether $\langle U \rangle$ has finite index in $\langle U, x \rangle$ is also P-complete [19].

A.8.10 Group Independence (GI)

Given: Let S be a finite set and F be the free group generated by S. Let $\underline{S} = \{s, s^{-1} \mid s \in S\}$, where s^{-1} denotes the inverse of s. Let $\underline{S}^*$ denote the set of all finite words over $\underline{S}$. Let $U = \{u_1, \ldots, u_m\} \subseteq \underline{S}^*$, where $m \in \mathbb{N}$.

Problem: Is U *independent*? That is, does each $x \in \langle U \rangle$ have a unique freely reducible representation? A word w is *freely reducible* if it contains no segment of the form ss^{-1} or $s^{-1}s$.

Reference: Avenhaus and Madlener [19].

Hint: A variant of the Nielsen reduction algorithm can be used to show the problem is in P. The reduction is from an arbitrary polynomial time Turing machine [19].

A.8.11 Group Rank (GR)

Given: Let S be a finite set and F be the free group generated by S. Let $\underline{S} = \{s, s^{-1} \mid s \in S\}$, where s^{-1} denotes the inverse of s. Let $\underline{S}^*$ denote the set of all finite words over $\underline{S}$. Let $k \in \mathbb{N}$. Let $U = \{u_1, \ldots, u_m\} \subseteq \underline{S}^*$, where $m \in \mathbb{N}$.

Problem: Does $\langle U \rangle$ have rank k? The *rank* is the number of elements in a minimal generating set.

Reference: Avenhaus and Madlener [19].

Hint: A variant of the Nielsen reduction algorithm can be used to show the problem is in P. The reduction is from Group Independence, Problem A.8.10. Observe U is independent if and only if $\langle U \rangle$ has rank the number of elements in U.

A.8.12   Group Isomorphism (SI)

Given: Let S be a finite set and F be the free group generated by S. Let $\underline{S} = \{s, s^{-1} \mid s \in S\}$, where s^{-1} denotes the inverse of s. Let $\underline{S}^*$ denote the set of all finite words over $\underline{S}$. Let $U = \{u_1, \ldots, u_m\}, V = \{v_1, \ldots, v_p\} \subseteq \underline{S}^*$, where $m, p \in \mathbb{N}$.
Problem: Is $\langle U \rangle$ isomorphic to $\langle V \rangle$?
Reference: Avenhaus and Madlener [19].
Hint: A variant of the Nielsen reduction algorithm can be used to show the problem is in P. The reduction is from Group Independence, Problem A.8.10. U is independent if and only if $\langle U \rangle$ and $\langle \{s_1, \ldots, s_{|U|}\} \rangle$ are isomorphic.

A.8.13   Group Induced Isomorphism (GII)

Given: Let S be a finite set and F be the free group generated by S. Let $\underline{S} = \{s, s^{-1} \mid s \in S\}$, where s^{-1} denotes the inverse of s. Let $\underline{S}^*$ denote the set of all finite words over $\underline{S}$. Let $U = \{u_1, \ldots, u_m\}, V = \{v_1, \ldots, v_p\} \subseteq \underline{S}^*$, where $m = p \in \mathbb{N}$.
Problem: Does the mapping ϕ defined by $\phi(u_i) = v_i$ for $i = 1, \ldots, m$, induce an isomorphism from $\langle U \rangle$ to $\langle V \rangle$?
Reference: Avenhaus and Madlener [19].
Hint: A variant of the Nielsen reduction algorithm can be used to show the problem is in P. The reduction is from Group Independence, Problem A.8.10. U is independent if and only if ϕ as defined above induces an isomorphism from $\langle U \rangle$ to $\langle \{s_1, \ldots, s_{|U|}\} \rangle$.

A.8.14   Intersection of Cosets (IC)

Given: Let S be a finite set and F be the free group generated by S. Let $\underline{S} = \{s, s^{-1} \mid s \in S\}$, where s^{-1} denotes the inverse of s. Let $\underline{S}^*$ denote the set of all finite words over $\underline{S}$. Let $x, y \in \underline{S}^*$. Let $U = \{u_1, \ldots, u_m\}, V = \{v_1, \ldots, v_p\} \subseteq \underline{S}^*$, where $m = p \in \mathbb{N}$.
Problem: Is $\langle U \rangle x \cap y \langle V \rangle$ nonempty?
Reference: Avenhaus and Madlener [20].
Hint: A polynomial time algorithm for the problem is given in [20]. The reduction is from an arbitrary polynomial time Turing machine [20].
Remarks: The *Intersection of Right Cosets Problem* and the *Intersection of Left Cosets Problem* are subproblems of the Intersection

of Cosets Problems and they are both P-complete as well. For example, the Right Coset Problem is P-complete since $\langle U \rangle x \cap \langle V \rangle y$ is nonempty if and only if $\langle U \rangle x y^{-1} \cap e \langle V \rangle$ is nonempty, where e denotes the empty word.

A.8.15 Intersection of Subgroups (IS)

Given: Let S be a finite set and F be the free group generated by S. Let $\underline{S} = \{s, s^{-1} \mid s \in S\}$, where s^{-1} denotes the inverse of s. Let $\underline{S}^*$ denote the set of all finite words over $\underline{S}$. Let e denote the empty word. Let $U = \{u_1, \ldots, u_m\}, V = \{v_1, \ldots, v_p\} \subseteq \underline{S}^*$, where $m = p \in \mathbb{N}$.

Problem: Is $\langle U \rangle \cap \langle V \rangle \neq \langle e \rangle$?

Reference: Avenhaus and Madlener [20].

Hint: A polynomial time algorithm for the problem is given in [20]. The reduction is straightforward from Intersection of Right Cosets, see Problem A.8.14.

A.8.16 Group Coset Equality (GCE)

Given: Let S be a finite set and F be the free group generated by S. Let $\underline{S} = \{s, s^{-1} \mid s \in S\}$, where s^{-1} denotes the inverse of s. Let $\underline{S}^*$ denote the set of all finite words over $\underline{S}$. Let $x, y \in \underline{S}^*$. Let $U = \{u_1, \ldots, u_m\}, V = \{v_1, \ldots, v_p\} \subseteq \underline{S}^*$, where $m = p \in \mathbb{N}$.

Problem: Is $\langle U \rangle x = y \langle V \rangle$?

Reference: Avenhaus and Madlener [20].

Hint: A polynomial time algorithm for the problem is given in [20]. The reduction is from Intersection of Subgroups, see Problem A.8.15.

Remarks: The following three decision problems are also P-complete: *Equality of Right Cosets* — Does $\langle U \rangle x = \langle V \rangle y$?, *Equivalence of Cosets* — Are there x, y such that $\langle U \rangle x = y \langle V \rangle$?, and *Equivalence of Right Cosets* — Are there x, y such that $\langle U \rangle x = \langle V \rangle y$? [20].

A.8.17   Conjugate Subgroups (CS)

Given: Let S be a finite set and F be the free group generated by S. Let $\underline{S} = \{s, s^{-1} \mid s \in S\}$, where s^{-1} denotes the inverse of s. Let $\underline{S}^*$ denote the set of all finite words over $\underline{S}$. Let $U = \{u_1, \ldots, u_m\}, V = \{v_1, \ldots, v_p\} \subseteq \underline{S}^*$, where $m = p \in \mathbb{N}$.
Problem: Is there a $x \in \underline{S}^*$ such that $x^{-1}\langle U \rangle x = \langle V \rangle$?
Reference: Avenhaus and Madlener [20].
Hint: A polynomial time algorithm for the problem is given in [20]. The reduction is from Equivalence of Right Cosets, see Problem A.8.16.
Remarks: The problem of determining whether $x^{-1}\langle U \rangle x$ is a subgroup of $\langle V \rangle$ is also P-complete [20].

A.8.18   Uniform Word Problem for Finitely Presented Algebras (UWPFPA)

Given: A finitely presented algebra $\mathcal{A} = (M, A, \Gamma)$ and a pair of terms x and y. M is a finite set of *symbols* and $A : M \to \mathbb{N}$ defines the *arity* of each symbol. M is partitioned into two sets: $G = \{a \in M \mid A(a) = 0\}$ consists of *generator symbols* and $O = \{a \in M \mid A(a) > 0\}$ consists of *operator symbols*. The set of *terms* over M is the smallest subset of M^* such that

1. all elements of G are terms, and
2. if θ is m-ary and $x_1, \ldots x_m$ are terms, then $\theta(x_1, \ldots, x_m)$ is a term.

Let τ denote the set of terms. Γ is a set of unordered pairs of terms called *axioms*. $\equiv$ is the smallest congruence relation on τ satisfying the axioms of Γ.
Problem: Is $x \equiv y$?
Reference: Kozen [221].
Hint: A polynomial time algorithm for the problem is given in [221]. The reduction is from Monotone Circuit Value, Problem A.1.3. Let $\mathcal{B}$ be an instance MCVP represented as a list of assignments to variables $C_1, \ldots, C_n$ of the form $C_i = 0, C_i = 1, C_i = C_j \vee C_k$, or $C_i = C_j \wedge C_k$, where $i > j, k$. $\mathcal{B}$ is in MCVP provided value(C_n) $= 1$, where n denotes the output gate of the circuit. The reduction is as follows: $G = \{C_1, \ldots, C_n, 0, 1\}, O = \{\vee, \wedge\}, \Gamma = \mathcal{B} \cup \{0 \vee 0 \equiv 0, 0 \vee 1 \equiv 1, 1 \vee 0 \equiv 1, 1 \vee 1 \equiv 1, 0 \wedge 0 \equiv 0, 0 \wedge 1 \equiv 0, 1 \wedge 0 \equiv 0, 1 \wedge 1 \equiv 1\}$.

$\mathcal{B}$ is in MCVP if and only if $C_n \equiv 1$.

A.8.19 Finitely Presented Algebras Triviality (FPAT)

Given: A finitely presented algebra $\mathcal{A} = (M, A, \Gamma)$. See Problem A.8.18 for definitions.
Problem: Is $\mathcal{A}$ *trivial*? That is, does $\mathcal{A}$ contain only one element?
Reference: Kozen [221].
Hint: A polynomial time algorithm for the problem is given in [221]. The reduction is from Monotone Circuit Value, Problem A.1.3. Construct Γ as done in the proof hint for Problem A.8.18. Let $\Gamma' = \Gamma \cup \{C_n \equiv 0\}$. Using notation from Problem A.8.18, it follows that $\mathcal{B}$ is an instance of MCVP if and only if $C_n \equiv 1$. That is, if and only if $1 \equiv_{\Gamma'} 0$ if and only if $\tau/\equiv_{\Gamma'}$ is trivial.

A.8.20 Finitely Generated Subalgebra (FGS)

Given: A finitely presented algebra $\mathcal{A} = (M, A, \Gamma)$ and terms $x_1, \ldots, x_n, y$. Let $[x] = \{y \in \tau \mid x \equiv y\}$. See the Uniform Word Problem for Finitely Presented Algebras, Problem A.8.18, for definitions.
Problem: Is $[y]$ contained in the subalgebra generated by $[x_1], \ldots, [x_n]$?
Reference: Kozen [221].
Hint: A polynomial time algorithm for the problem is given in [221]. This problem is a general formulation of Generability, Problem A.6.7, and so it follows that it is also P-complete.

A.8.21 Finitely Presented Algebras Finiteness (FPAF)

Given: A finitely presented algebra $\mathcal{A} = (M, A, \Gamma)$. See the Uniform Word Problem for Finitely Presented Algebras, Problem A.8.18, for definitions.
Problem: Is $\mathcal{A}$ finite?
Reference: Kozen [221].
Hint: A polynomial time algorithm for the problem is given in [221]. The reduction is from Monotone Circuit Value, Problem A.1.3, and is similar to that used in Problem A.8.19. The algebra constructed in that proof is modified as follows: add another generator b to G, and the axioms

$\{b \wedge b \equiv 0, \ b \wedge 0 \equiv 0, \ 0 \wedge b \equiv 0, \ b \vee b \equiv 0, \ b \vee 0 \equiv 0, \ 0 \vee b \equiv 0\}$ to Γ' to obtain Γ''. Γ'' is finite if Γ' is trivial; otherwise, it is infinite.

A.8.22   Uniform Word Problem for Lattices (UWPL)

Given: Let E be a set of equations and $e_1 = e_2$ an equation. We present some preliminary definitions before defining the problem. A *lattice* is a set L with two binary operations $\{+, \cdot\}$ that satisfy the lattice axioms. Let $x, y, z \in L$. The *lattice axioms* are as follows:

1. associativity: $(x \cdot y) \cdot z = x \cdot (y \cdot z)$ and $(x + y) + z = x + (y + z)$,

2. commutativity: $x \cdot y = y \cdot x$ and $x + y = y + x$,

3. idempotence: $x \cdot x = x$ and $x + x = x$, and

4. absorption: $x + (x \cdot y) = x$ and $x \cdot (x + y) = x$.

Let $\mathcal{U}$ be a countably infinite set of *symbols*. The set of *terms* over $\mathcal{U}$, $W(\mathcal{U})$, is defined inductively as follows:

1. If α is in $\mathcal{U}$, then α is in $W(\mathcal{U})$.

2. If p and q are in $W(\mathcal{U})$, then $(p + q)$ and $(p \cdot q)$ are in $W(\mathcal{U})$.

Let e_1 and e_2 be terms over $\mathcal{U}$. An *equation* is a formula of the form $e_1 = e_2$. A *valuation* for a given lattice L is a mapping $\mu : \mathcal{U} \to L$. The valuation is extended to $W(\mathcal{U})$ by defining $\mu(p+q) = \mu(p) + \mu(q)$ and $\mu(p \cdot q) = \mu(p) \cdot \mu(q)$. A lattice satisfies an equation $e_1 = e_2$ under a valuation μ, denoted $L \models_\mu e_1 = e_2$, if and only if $\mu(e_1) = \mu(e_2)$. A lattice L satisfies a set of equations E, denoted $L \models_\mu E$, if and only if L satisfies every member of E under μ. E *implies* $e_1 = e_2$, denoted $E \models e_1 = e_2$, if and only if for every lattice L and valuation μ such that $L \models_\mu E$, it follows that $L \models_\mu e_1 = e_2$.

Problem: Does $E \models e_1 = e_2$?

Reference: Cosmadakis [71].

Hint: A polynomial time algorithm for the problem is given in [71]. The reduction is from the *Implication Problem for Propositional Horn Clauses* (Jones and Laaser [181]). See Problems A.6.1 and A.6.2. Let Σ be a set of propositional formulas of the form $x_i \wedge x_j \Rightarrow x_k$, where $x_1, x_2, \ldots$ are propositional variables. Let σ be the formula $x_1 \wedge x_2 \Rightarrow x_3$. The problem is to test if Σ implies σ. Let ϕ represent the formula $x_j \wedge x_j \Rightarrow x_k$. In the instance of UWPL, we construct the equation ϵ_ϕ as follows: $\alpha_i \cdot \alpha_j \cdot \alpha_k = \alpha_i \cdot \alpha_k$. Let $E_\Sigma = \{\epsilon_\phi \mid \phi \in \Sigma\}$. It follows that Σ implies σ if and only if $E_\Sigma \models \epsilon_\sigma$.

Remarks: The problem remains P-complete if we use inequalities instead of equations. Furthermore, the problem remains P-complete when $E = \emptyset$ and the terms are represented by directed acyclic graphs instead of trees. However, if $E = \emptyset$ and the terms are represented as trees, the problem is in $DLOG$ [71]. This problem is called the *Identity Problem for Lattices*.

A.8.23 Lattice Generators (LG)

Given: Let L be a lattice. Let E be a set of equations and $e, g_1, \ldots, g_n$ be terms over $\mathcal{U}$. Let $\mu : \mathcal{U} \to L$ be a valuation (see Problem A.8.22). We present some preliminary definitions first. Let $X \subseteq L$. The *sublattice generated* by X is the smallest subset of L that contains X and is closed under the operations of L. e *is generated by* $g_1, \ldots, g_n$ in L under μ, denoted $L \models_\mu \text{gen}(e, g_1, \ldots, g_n)$, if and only if $\mu(e)$ is in the sublattice of L generated by the set $\{\mu(g_i) \mid i = 1, \ldots, n\}$. E *implies that* e *is generated by* $g_1, \ldots, g_n$, denoted $E \models \text{gen}(g_1, \ldots, g_n)$, if and only if for every lattice L and valuation μ such that $L \models_\mu E$, it follows that $L \models_\mu \text{gen}(e, g_1, \ldots, g_n)$.
Problem: Does $E \models \text{gen}(e, g_1, \ldots, g_n)$?
Reference: Cosmadakis [71].
Hint: A polynomial time algorithm for the problem is given in [71]. The reduction is a continuation of the reduction used in Problem A.8.22. Since $E_\Sigma \models \epsilon_\sigma$ if and only if $E_\Sigma \models \text{gen}(\alpha_1 \cdot \alpha_2 \cdot \alpha_3, \alpha_1, \alpha_2)$, it follows that GPL is also P-complete.
Remarks: The problem remains P-complete when $E = \emptyset$ and the terms are represented by directed acyclic graphs instead of trees. However, if $E = \emptyset$ and the terms are represented as trees the problem is in $DLOG$ [71]. This problem is called the *Generator Problem for Free Lattices*.

A.8.24 Boolean Recurrence Equation (BRE)

Given: A four-tuple (M, B, F, j), where M is a $1 \times n$ Boolean vector, B is an $n \times n$ Boolean matrix, F is an $n \times 1$ Boolean vector, and j is an integer in the range 0 to n.
Problem: Is the first entry of $M * Y_j$ a 1? Y_j is defined recursively as $Y_0 = F$, $Y_k = B \cdot \overline{Y_{k-1}}$ for $k \geq 1$. $\overline{Y}$ denotes the complement of Y.
Reference: Bertoni *et al.* [34].
Hint: The reduction is from an alternating Turing machine that

uses $O(\log n)$ space.

Remarks: If $0 \leq j \leq (\log n)^k$, then the problem is complete for AC^k [34]. That is, the class of problems accepted by alternating Turing machines in $O(\log n)$ space and $O((\log n)^k)$ alternations.

A.8.25   Fill Slots (FILL)

Given: A Boolean matrix M, and three integers i, j, and k.

Problem: Is a 1 in row k used to cover values in column i when j is the highest row of the matrix that procedure Fill Slots is applied to? The *Fill Slots* procedure basically processes rows of the matrix from j downward. It looks for the first row r that does not contain a 1. A 1 is inserted in that row while "covering" the column whose bits if treated as an integer below r is largest (ties may be broken arbitrarily). The bits that were covered are then zeroed. The process is repeated until the bottom of the matrix is reached.

Reference: de la Torre, Greenlaw, and Schäffer [84].

Hint: The reduction is from a version of topologically ordered Monotone Circuit Value, Problem A.1.3. We sketch it below. Let α denote an instance of MCVP. The idea is to generate columns to simulate each gate in α. Any unspecified matrix value is a 0. Each gate is associated with a disjoint set of rows and columns. Each row is associated with some gate; each column is associated with a gate, except for the columns at the far left of the matrix which correspond to circuit inputs. A TRUE (FALSE) input is denoted by a column with a single 1 (respectively, all 0's) in it. An AND gate is associated with four consecutive rows and three consecutive columns. The topological ordering of the gates is translated into a left-to-right ordering of the gadget columns and a top-to-bottom ordering of the gadget rows.

The important part of the AND gadget is depicted below. These are the values that occupy the 4×3 submatrix of the rows and columns associated with the AND gate.

0	0	0
0	1	1
0	0	0
1	1	1

In the third column there are two additional 1's below the four rows shown — one (the other) in a row where the left (respectively, right) output of the gate is input. The left (right) input to an AND gate is "delivered" in a separate column to the first (respectively, third) row of the gadget. The OR gadget is similar and consists of the lower 3×2 left corner of the AND gadget. Inputs to an OR gate are "delivered" in separate columns to the second row of the gadget. Outputs of the OR gate are handled similar to the AND. Assume the output gate G of α is an OR gate. In the instance of FILL i is the second column of the gadget g corresponding to G, j is the first row of the overall matrix constructed, and k is the middle row of g.

Remarks: The Fill Slots procedure is similar to one used in [84] to prove that the *Edge Ranking Problem* is in P. The result suggests that their algorithm may not parallelize well. FILL seems interesting because it involves only Boolean values. Additional details can be found in de la Torre, Greenlaw, and Schäffer [83]. Also, see Problem B.1.2.

A.8.26 Multi-list Ranking (MLR)

Given: A set $L = \{l_1, \ldots, l_q\}$ of lists, where each list l_j, $1 \leq j \leq q$, contains one or more integers; an integer e, which is an element of some list; and a designated integer i.

Problem: Does element e receive a rank less than or equal to i? The *rank* of each element is computed iteratively as follows: assign a rank of one to all of the first elements of all lists; delete all occurrences of first elements from all lists; repeat this procedure on the updated lists after incrementing the value of the rank. The procedure is iterated as long as one list is nonempty.

Reference: Dessmark, Lingas, and Maheshwari [91].

Hint: The reduction is from Generic Machine Simulation, Problem A.12.1.

Remarks: If there are only $O((\log n)^k)$ lists, the problem can be solved in SC^{k+1}. The authors show that in this case the problem is hard for the class SC^k. For a variant of the problem with k lists, each of size at most n, they provide an $O(\log n)$ time, n^{k+1} processor CREW-PRAM algorithm. Several other restrictions of the problem are considered and polylogarithmic time PRAM algorithms are given for them. See [91] for further details. The original motivation for looking at this problem was to investigate the complexity of Successive Convex Hulls, Problem A.9.5.

A.8.27   Aperiodic Monoid Membership Variety B_2 (AMonMEMB)

Given: A set of total functions $a_1, \ldots, a_r$ and a designated function f, all from the set $\{1, 2, \ldots, m\}$ to itself, with the property that $\langle a_1, \ldots, a_r \rangle \in B_2$. $\langle a_1, \ldots, a_r \rangle$ denotes the set of all functions obtained by composing the functions a_i with one another. B_2 is a restricted class of *aperiodic monoids*. The reader is referred to [29] for definitions.

Problem: Does f belong to $\langle a_1, \ldots, a_r \rangle$?

Reference: Beaudry, McKenzie, and Thérien [29].

Hint: The reduction is from a variant of Generability, Problem A.6.7.

Remarks: The lattice of *aperiodic monoid varieties* is partitioned in [29] into the following five sublattices: B_1, B_2, B_3, B_4, and B_5. The membership problem for varieties in B_2 as described above is *P*-complete. For varieties in B_1 the problem is in AC^0; for B_3 it is *NP*-complete; for B_4 it is *NP*-hard; for B_5 it is *PSPACE*-complete [29].

A.9 Geometry

A.9.1 Plane Sweep Triangulation (PST)

Given: An n-vertex polygon Q that may contain holes, and a designated vertex u.

Problem: Is there a vertical edge connecting to u in the plane sweep triangulation of Q? The *plane sweep triangulation* is the triangulation produced by sweeping a horizontal line L from top to bottom. When L encounters a vertex v of Q, each diagonal from v to another vertex in Q, which does not cross a previously drawn diagonal, is added to the triangulation.

Reference: Atallah, Callahan, and Goodrich [18].

Hint: It is easy to see that the plane sweep triangulation algorithm runs in polynomial time. The reduction is from a variant of Planar CVP, Problem A.1.7. The new version of PCVP consists of NOT gates of fanout one, OR gates of fanout one, routing gates, and fanout gates that take one value and produce two copies of it. This instance of PCVP is required to be laid out on a planar grid in a special manner with alternating layers of routing and logic. The reduction involves constructing "geometric" gadgets for routing (left and right shifts in the grid), "vertical" wires, fanout one OR gates, and NOT gates. The presence (absence) of a vertical edge in the triangulation denotes a TRUE (respectively, FALSE) value. The vertex u is a special "target" vertex in the output gate of the circuit. A vertical line is connected to u in the triangulation if and only if the circuit evaluates to TRUE.

Remarks: The problem of finding some arbitrary triangulation is in *NC* (Goodrich [130]). If the polygon Q is not allowed to have holes, the complexity of the problem is open. In [18] they conjecture that this restricted version is in *NC*.

A.9.2 3-Oriented Weighted Planar Partitioning (3OWPP)

Given: A set of nonintersecting line segments $s_1, \ldots, s_n$ in the *Euclidean plane* ($\mathbb{R} \times \mathbb{R}$), a set of associated integer weights $w_1, \ldots, w_n$, and two designated segments r and t. The segments are *3-oriented* meaning that there are only three different possible slopes for the segments.

Problem: Do segments r and t "touch" in the partitioning of the plane constructed by extending segments in the order of their weights? Segments are extended until they reach another segment or a previous segment extension.

Reference: Atallah, Callahan, and Goodrich [18].

Hint: It is easy to see that the process of extending the segments can be performed in polynomial time. The reduction is from the same version of PCVP as used in Problem A.9.1. The gates of the instance of PCVP are numbered in topological order. Gadgets are constructed for routing and for logic. There are gadgets for right and left shifts, fanout gates, OR gates, NOT gates, and TRUE inputs. TRUE values in the circuit are transmitted as vertical extensions of segments. The most interesting gadget is the one for the NOT gate and we describe this. The gadgets for the other constructs all involve only two different sloped segments, whereas to simulate NOT gates three different slopes are required.

The instance of PCVP is laid out on a grid. We consider a NOT gate numbered i that receives its input on channel j and has its output on channel k. A *blocking segment* is one that is used to prevent the extension of another line segment and whose weight is very large. These segments do not play an active role in simulating the gate. The NOT gadget consists of six blocking segments and three additional segments — called "one," "two," and "three" indicating their relative weights. That is, segment one is processed first within the gadget, followed by two, and then three. Segment two is a horizontal segment whose potential extension spans channels j and k, and is blocked on both ends. Two lies directly to the left of channel j. Segment three is a vertical segment on channel k blocked "above" segment two but with the possibility of being extended downward across two's extension. Channel j, the input to NOT gate i, is blocked above segment two. Segment one has a slope of -1 and its potential extension is blocked at both ends. Segment one lies completely to the left of channel j. Its rightward extension would cross channel j as well as segment two's extension. We now describe how this gadget simulates a NOT gate. If the input to gate i is TRUE (FALSE), then the vertical segment on channel j has (respectively, has not) been extended to where it is blocked. This prevents (allows) segment one from being extended across segment two. Thus, segment two can be (respectively, cannot be) extended toward the right across channel k.

This prevents (allows) segment three from being extended across segment two's extension indicating a FALSE (respectively, TRUE) value for the output of the gate. The assignments of weights and the construction of all gadgets can be accomplished in logarithmic space. Segment r is the vertical segment corresponding to the output wire of the circuit. Segment t is a special output "pad." r will touch t when extended if and only if the circuit evaluates to TRUE.

Remarks: The complexity of the 2-oriented version of the problem is open [18]. In [18] they remark that the problem has been reduced to an instance of Monotone Circuit Value, Problem A.1.3, that has a very restricted topology, although not planar. Thus, it is open whether or not this version of the problem is in NC.

A.9.3 Visibility Layers (VL)

Given: A set of n nonintersecting line segments in the Euclidean plane and a designated segment s.

Problem: Is the label assigned to segment s by the visibility layering process congruent to one mod three? The *visibility layering process* is repeatedly to compute and delete the upper envelope of the remaining set of segments and label those segments with the current depth. The *upper envelope* consists of those segments visible from the point $(0, +\infty)$. A segment is *visible* from a point p if a ray cast from p can hit the segment before hitting any other segment.

Reference: Atallah, Callahan, and Goodrich [18], Hershberger [156].

Hint: The visibility layering process can be performed in polynomial time [156]. The reduction presented in [156] is from Monotone Circuit Value, Problem A.1.3. We sketch this reduction. The gates in the instance of MCVP are assumed to be numbered in topological order. A grid is constructed that consists of $V + 1$ rows and E columns, where V (E) is the number of vertices (respectively, edges) in the directed acyclic graph corresponding to the circuit. Gadgets are constructed for AND and OR gates. Gadgets consist of horizontal line segments of varying lengths. The gadget for AND gate k with inputs i and j ($i < j$), and outputs l and m ($l < m$) consists of three horizontal segments situated in row k of the grid. One segment spans column i, one segment spans column j, and another segment spans from column i through column m. The gadget for OR gate k with inputs i and j ($i < j$), and outputs l and m ($l < m$) consists of three horizontal segments situated in row k of the grid. One segment spans column j, one segment spans columns i through j, and another segment spans columns j through m. If an input associated with a given column is TRUE (FALSE), a horizontal segment is put (respectively, is not put) in to span that column in row 0. "Deepeners," which are horizontal line segments spanning single columns of the grid, are used to make sure gate input values arrive at the "right time" and also to make sure that once a gate has been evaluated its outputs affect only the desired gates. Segment s is the third horizontal segment in the gadget of the output gate. The output of the circuit is TRUE if and only if segment s has a label whose value is congruent to one mod three.

Remarks: The reduction given in [18] is similar and is also from a variant of MCVP. The main difference is in the way fanout is treated. The version of MCVP used in [18] consists of *crossing fanout gates*, single output AND gates, and single output OR gates. An instance consists of alternate routing and logic layers. Gadgets are constructed for the three types of gates and a similar decision problem to the one in [156] is posed to determine the output of the circuit. If the length of all segments is required to be the same, the complexity of the problem is not known [18]. In [18] they conjecture that this version of the problem is in NC.

A.9.4 Point Location on A Convex Hull (PHULL)

Given: An integer d, a set S of n points in $\mathbb{Q}^d$, and a designated point $p \in \mathbb{Q}^d$.
Problem: Is p on the convex hull of S?
Reference: Long and Warmuth [245].
Hint: The reduction is from Monotone Circuit Value, Problem A.1.3 [245].
Remarks: The result shows that Successive Convex Hulls, Problem A.9.5, for arbitrary dimension d is P-complete. See Problem A.9.5. The convex hull of n points in the Euclidean plane can be computed optimally on an EREW-PRAM in $O(\log n)$ time using n processors (see Dessmark, Lingas, and Maheshwari [91]).

A.9.5 Successive Convex Hulls (SCH)

Given: A set S of n points in the Euclidean plane, an integer k, and a designated point $p \in \mathbf{R} \times \mathbf{R}$.

Problem: Is p in the kth remaining convex hull that is formed by repeatedly finding and removing convex hulls from S?

Reference: Dessmark, Lingas, and Maheshwari [91].

Hint: Chazelle shows the problem is in P [53]. The reduction is from Multi-list Ranking, Problem A.8.26.

Remarks: See Problem A.9.4 for a closely related question.

A.10   Real Analysis

A.10.1   Real Analogue to CVP (*) (RealCVP)

Given: A feasible real function V defined on $(-\infty, +\infty)$. A real function f is *feasible* if, given a sufficiently accurate fixed-point binary approximation to $x \in [-2^n, 2^n]$, a fixed-point binary approximation to $f(x)$ with absolute error less than 2^{-n}, can be computed in time $n^{O(1)}$. Sufficiently accurate means that the error in approximating the input x is less than $2^{-n^{O(1)}}$. This fixes the number of input bits. The continuity of f limits its range; thus, it fixes the number of output bits. Both are polynomial in n.

Problem: Compute $V(x)$ with absolute error less than 2^{-n}.

Reference: Hoover [159, 158].

Hint: The reduction is from Circuit Value, Problem A.1.1. The function V computes the continuous analog of the circuit value function by mapping circuit descriptions, along with their possible inputs, onto the real line. To evaluate the circuit α on input x do the following: treat the encoding $\overline{\alpha}$ as an integer, the bits $\overline{x}$ as an n-bit fixed-point binary fraction, and add the two. The value of $V(\overline{\alpha}.\overline{x})$ is then a rational number that encodes the values of the gates of α on the input x. To make V continuous between these evaluation points, V is simply linearly interpolated.

Remarks: The same function yields a family of FP-complete polynomials $\{p_n\}$ computable by feasible-size-magnitude circuits. A $+$, $-$, $\times$ arithmetic circuit family is *feasible-size-magnitude* if the nth member is polynomial size and its output over the interval $[-2^n, +2^n]$ can be computed without generating any intermediate values with magnitude exceeding $2^{n^{O(1)}}$.

A.10.2   Fixed Points of Contraction Mappings (*)   (FPCM)

Given: An NC *real function* C that behaves as a contractor on some interval I contained in $(-\infty, +\infty)$. The endpoints of I are specified as integers. A real function f is in NC if an approximation to $f(x)$ with absolute error less than 2^{-n}, for $x \in [-2^n, +2^n]$, can be computed in NC (with the same input/output conventions as for RealCVP, Problem A.10.1).

Problem: Compute the fixed point of C in I with absolute error less than 2^{-n}.

Reference: Hoover [159].

Hint: The reduction is from Circuit Value, Problem A.1.1. The same basic technique as for RealCVP is used but the function C evaluates the circuit level by level, thus converging to a fixed point that encodes the final state of the circuit. Finding the fixed point is in FP since each iteration of the contraction mapping reduces the width of the interval by some constant factor.

Remarks: This provides an argument that fast numerical methods based on fixed points probably have to use contraction maps with better than linear rates of convergence, such as Newton's method.

A.10.3 Inverting An Injective Real Function (*) (IIRF)

Given: An NC *real function* f defined on $[0,1]$. The function is increasing and has the property that $f(0) < 0 < f(1)$. Thus, there is a unique root x_0 such that $f(x_0) = 0$. A real function f is in NC if an approximation to $f(x)$ with error less than 2^{-n}, for $x \in [-2^n, +2^n]$, can be computed in NC.

Problem: Compute x_0 with error less than 2^{-n}.

Reference: Ko [218].

Hint: Map intermediate configurations of a logarithmic space deterministic Turing machine onto the real line.

Remarks: This problem was expressed originally in terms of logarithmic space computability and reductions — if f is logarithmic space computable then $f^{-1}(0)$ is not logarithmic space computable, unless $DLOG$ equals P. The problem remains hard even if f is required to be differentiable.

A.11   Games

A.11.1   Two Player Game (GAME)

Given: A two player game $G = (P_1, P_2, W_0, s, M)$ defined by $P_1 \cap P_2 = \emptyset$, $W_0 \subseteq P_1 \cup P_2$, $s \in P_1$, and $M \subseteq P_1 \times P_2 \cup P_2 \times P_1$. P_i is the set of positions in which it is player i's turn to move. W_0 is the set of immediate winning positions (defined below) for player one, and s is the starting position. M is the set of allowable moves; if $(p, q) \in M$ and $p \in P_1$ (or P_2) then player one (respectively, or two) may move from position p to position q in a single step. A position x is *winning* for player one if and only if $x \in W_0$, or $x \in P_1$ and $(x, y) \in M$ for some winning position y, or $x \in P_2$ and y is winning for every move (x, y) in M.

Problem: Is s a winning position for the first player?

Reference: Jones and Laaser [181], Greenlaw, Hoover, and Ruzzo, THIS WORK.

Hint: Reduce AM2CVP, Problem A.1.4, to GAME. OR gates in the circuit correspond to winning positions for player one; AND gates to winning positions for player two. W_0 is the set of all inputs having value TRUE and s is the output. s is winning if and only if the output of the circuit is TRUE.

Remarks: The original reduction by Jones and Laaser was from Generability, Problem A.6.7, to GAME [181]. Given W, $\bullet$, V, and w construct the game $G = (W, W \times W, V, w, M)$, where the allowable moves are given by

$$M = \{(p, (q, r)) \mid q \bullet r = p\} \cup \{((p, q), p) \mid p, q \in W\} \cup \{((p, q), q) \mid p, q \in W\}.$$

Player one attempts to prove that a vertex p is generated by V. One does this by exhibiting two elements q and r, also claimed to be generated by V, such that $p = q \bullet r$. Player two attempts to exhibit an element of the pair that is not generated by V. Since GAME is an instance of AND/OR Graph Solvability, it follows that determining whether an AND/OR graph has a solution is also P-complete (Kasif [202]).

A.11.2   Cat and Mouse (CM)

Given: A directed graph $G = (V, E)$ with three distinguished vertices c, m, and g.

Problem: Does the mouse have a *winning strategy* in the game? The game is played as follows. The cat starts on vertex c, the mouse on vertex m, and g represents the goal vertex. The cat and mouse alternate moves with the mouse moving first. Each move consists of following a directed edge in the graph. Either player has the option to pass by remaining on the same vertex. The cat is not allowed to occupy the goal vertex. The mouse wins if it reaches the goal vertex without being caught. The cat wins if the mouse and cat occupy the same vertex.

Reference: Chandra and Stockmeyer [50], (Larry J. Stockmeyer, Personal Communication, 1984).

Hint: The reduction is from a logarithmic space alternating Turing machine M. Assume that M starts in an existential configuration I, has a unique accepting configuration A that is existential, and each existential (universal) configuration has exactly two immediate successors, both of which are universal (respectively, existential). A directed graph is constructed with the number of vertices in the graph proportional to the number of configurations of M. We illustrate only how existential configurations can be simulated and do not account for the cat or mouse being able to pass on a move. There are two copies of each configuration C, denoted C and C', in the graph we construct. The graph has additional vertices as well. Consider an existential configuration X of M with its two succeeding universal configurations Y and Z. Assume that the cat is on X, the mouse is on X' and it is the mouse's turn to move. X is directly connected to Y and Z, whereas X' is connected to two intermediate vertices Y_1 and Z_1. Y (Z) is connected to Y_2 (respectively, Z_2). Y_1 (Z_1) is connected to both Y' and Y_2 (respectively, Z' and Z_2). Both Y_2 and Z_2 are connected to g. The mouse simulates an existential move of M by moving to either Y_1 or Z_1. If the mouse moves to Y_1 (Z_1), then the cat must move to Y (respectively, Z). Otherwise, the mouse's next move can be to Y_2 (respectively, Z_2) and from there onto g uncontested. From Y_1 (Z_1) the mouse must move to Y' (respectively, Z') and a universal move is ready to be simulated. The simulation of universal moves is fairly similar with the cat moving first. The game starts with the cat on I and the mouse on I'. There is an edge from A' to g. M will accept its input if and only if the mouse has a winning strategy.

A.11.3   Acyclic Geography Game (AGG)

Given: An acyclic directed graph $G = (V, E)$. We describe the game as it is presented in Chandra and Tompa [51]. The *Acyclic Geography Game* is played on G by two players. A *configuration* of the game is a vertex $u \in V$. Players take turns choosing an edge $(u, v) \in G$, thereby changing the game configuration from u to v. The initial configuration is $u = 1$. The first player with no move left loses.

Problem: Does player one have a winning strategy on G?

Reference: Chandra and Tompa [51].

Hint: The reduction is from Monotone Circuit Value, Problem A.1.3.

Remarks: Chandra and Tompa show that a depth constrained version of the Geography Game, called *SHORTGEOG*, is complete for AC^1 [51].

A.11.4   Longcake (LONGCAKE)

Given: Two players H and V, a token, and a $m \times n$ Boolean matrix M. We first describe how the game is played. Initially, the token is placed on position m_{11} of M, it is H's turn to move, and the current submatrix is M. The term *current submatrix* denotes the portion of M that the game is currently being played on. H's turn consists of moving the token horizontally within the current submatrix to some entry $m_{ij} = 1$. At this point, either all columns to the left of j or all columns to the right of j are removed from the current submatrix, depending on which causes fewer columns to be removed. Note that the token occupies a corner of the current submatrix again. V's turn is similar except V moves vertically and rows are removed. The first player with no moves left loses.

Problem: Does H have a winning strategy on M?

Reference: Chandra and Tompa [51].

Hint: The reduction is from the Acyclic Geography Game, Problem A.11.3.

Remarks: The game *Shortcake* is the same as Longcake except the larger portion of the current submatrix is thrown away. Shortcake is complete for AC^1 [51]. Another variant of these games called *Semicake* is complete for $LOGCFL = SAC^1$ [51].

A.11.5 Game of Life (LIFE)

Given: An initial configuration of the Game of Life, a time bound T expressed in unary, and a designated cell c of the grid. The *Game of Life* is played on an infinite grid. *Cells*, squares on the grid, are either *live* or *dead*. Each cell has eight *neighbors*. An *initial configuration* specifies that certain cells are live at the beginning of the game. The rules of the game are as follows:

1. A cell that is dead at time t becomes live at time $t+1$ if it had exactly three live neighbors at time t.

2. A cell dies at time $t+1$ unless it had two or three live neighbors at time t.

Problem: Is cell c live at time T?

Reference: Berlekamp, Conway, and Guy [33, pages 817–850], Greenlaw, Hoover, and Ruzzo, THIS WORK.

Hint: Berlekamp, Conway, and Guy sketch a reduction that the Game of Life is capable of universal computation. We translated this result into the statement of a P-complete problem. Since the time bound is expressed in unary, the decision problem can be answered in polynomial time. The reduction given in [33] is from CVP, Problem A.1.1. The key to the reduction is to use Life forms such as *glider guns*, *gliders*, and *eaters* to simulate NOT, OR, and AND gates. Inputs are represented by *glider streams* that can be thinned, redirected, and copied. Suppose A represents a stream of gliders. The stream can be complemented by using a glider gun to cause a *vanishing reaction*. That is, gliders shot from the glider gun collide with those in the stream and disappear. If there is not a glider present in A at a particular point to collide with, then the glider shot from the gun proceeds to the output stream. Thus, performing the function of a NOT gate. An OR (AND) gate of fanout one can be built from two (respectively, one) glider gun(s) and an eater. Glider streams can be copied using glider guns and eaters. The cell c will be live at time T if and only if the output gate of the circuit evaluates to TRUE. Additional details of the reduction are given in [33].

Remarks: The Game of Life is an example of a two dimensional cellular automata, see Problem A.12.3. It is not known whether a one dimensional version of the Game of Life can simulate a Turing machine. See Problem A.12.3 for more details about one dimensional cellular automata.

A.11.6   Zero-sum Bimatrix Game (ZSBG)

Given: Two $m \times n$ matrices A and B that have integer entries, and a designated natural number k, $1 \le k \le m$. The game involves two players. Simultaneously, player one chooses a row i and player two chooses a column j. The result of these choices is that player one (two) receives a_{ij} (respectively, b_{ij}) points. A strategy i of player one *dominates* a strategy i' of player one if $a_{ij} \ge a_{i'j}$ for $j = 1, \ldots, n$. A strategy j of player two *dominates* a strategy j' of player two if $b_{ij} \ge b_{ij'}$ for $i = 1, \ldots, m$. It is easy to see that all dominated strategies can be removed from both one and two's matrix without affecting the outcome of the game. A *reduced* game is one in which all dominated strategies have been eliminated. The game is *zero-sum* if $A + B = \mathcal{O}$, where $\mathcal{O}$ denotes the $m \times n$ matrix with all 0 entries.

Problem: Is row k of matrix A deleted in the reduced game? In a bimatrix game the reduced game is unique up to row and column permutations (Knuth, Papadimitriou, and Tsitsiklis [217]); thus, the elimination order will not affect the answer to this question.

Reference: Knuth, Papadimitriou, and Tsitsiklis [217].

Hint: In [217] they give a polynomial time algorithm for the general problem, that is, the game is not required to be a zero-sum game. The reduction proving completeness is from a variant of Monotone Circuit Value, Problem A.1.3. The variant requires that AND gates have only OR gates as inputs, OR gates are allowed everything expect inputs from other OR gates, the output of the circuit come from an AND gate, no two OR gates have the same inputs, and the fanout of circuit inputs is one. This variant is similar to Problem A.1.4 and is obviously P-complete. Let α be an instance of this restricted version of MCVP. The reduction involves constructing a matrix A. Matrix B equals $-A$. Therefore, the game is zero-sum. Let n denote the number of OR gates in α and m the number of inputs plus AND gates. A will be a $(m + 1) \times (m + n)$ matrix. The first m rows of A correspond to circuit inputs and AND gates. The first n columns correspond to OR gates. k will be chosen as the row corresponding to the output AND gate. The description of A's entries is broken into three parts. A left submatrix, A's last row, and the remaining right submatrix of size $m \times m$.

We first describe the submatrix entries a_{ij}, $1 \le i \le m$ and $1 \le j \le m$.

1. $a_{ij} = 3$ if row i corresponds to an AND gate that receives an input from the OR gate represented by column j.

2. $a_{ij} = -3$ if row i corresponds to an input of the OR gate represented by column j.

3. $a_{ij} = 2$ if row i corresponds to a FALSE input that is not input to the OR gate represented by column j.

4. All a_{ij} not falling into one of these categories are given a 0 entry.

The last row of matrix A is all 1's.
The entries $a_{i,n+j}$, for $i, j = 1, \ldots, m$ are as follows:

1. -3 if $i = j$,

2. 2 if $i \neq j$ and i is a FALSE circuit input, and

3. -1 otherwise.

The entries of A are constructed so that a row or column of A is eliminated if and only if it corresponded to a gate or input in the circuit that was TRUE.

A.11.7 Two-person Pebble Game Fixed Rank (PEBBLE)

Given: A fixed rank pebble game. We present the definitions given by Kasai, Adachi, and Iwata in [201]. A *pebble game* is a four tuple $G = (X, R, S, t)$ with the following properties.

1. X is a finite set of vertices.

2. $R \subseteq \{(x, y, z) \mid x, y, z \in X, x \neq y, y \neq z, z \neq x\}$ is called the set of *rules*. For $A, B \subseteq X$, we write $A \vdash B$ if $(x, y, z) \in R$, $x, y \in A$, $z \notin A$, and $B = (A - \{x\}) \cup \{z\}$. The *move* $A \vdash B$ is made by the rule (x, y, z). The symbol $\overset{*}{\vdash}$ denotes the reflexive and transitive closure of $\vdash$.

3. S is a subset of X.

4. $t \in X$ is the *terminal* vertex.

A pebble game has *fixed rank* if the number of vertices in S is fixed. In a *two-person* pebble game two players P_1 and P_2 alternate moving pebbles with P_1 moving first. The *winner* is the first player who can pebble t or who can force the other player into a no move situation.

Problem: Does player P_1 have a winning strategy?

Reference: Kasai, Adachi, and Iwata [201].

Hint: The reduction is from a logarithmic space bounded alternating Turing machine.

Remarks: A pebble game is *solvable* if there exists $A \subseteq X$ such that $S \overset{*}{\vdash} A$ and $t \in A$. The *one-person pebble game*, which is to determine if the game is solvable, of fixed ranked is $NLOG$-complete [201]. For questions with a similar flavor see Problems A.11.1 and A.11.2. For additional remarks about pebbling see Section 5.4.

A.12 Miscellaneous

A.12.1 Generic Machine Simulation Problem (GMSP)

Given: A string x, a description $\overline{M}$ of a Turing machine M, and an integer t coded in unary. (To be precise, the input is the string $x\#\overline{M}\#^t$, where $\#$ is a delimiter character not otherwise present in the string.)

Problem: Does M accept x within t steps?

Reference: Folklore.

Hint: A proof is given in Chapter 4.

Remarks: Buss and Goldsmith show a variant of this problem is complete with respect to *quasilinear time reductions* for $N^m P_l$, a subclass of P. See [48] for the appropriate definitions. They also show variants of Problems A.1.2 and A.7.2 are complete in this setting.

A.12.2 General Deadlock Detection (GDD)

Given: A multigraph $D = (V, E)$ with $V = \pi \cup \rho$, where $\pi = \{p_1, \ldots, p_n\}$ is the set of *process vertices* and $\rho = \{r_1, \ldots, r_m\}$ is the set of *resource vertices*; and a set $T = \{t_1, \ldots, t_m\}$, where t_i denotes the number of units of r_i. The bipartite multigraph D represents the state of the system. The edges in V are of the form (p_i, r_j) denoting a *request* of process p_i for resource r_j or of the form (r_j, p_i) denoting an allocation of resource r_j to process p_i.

Problem: Is D a *deadlock state*? A deadlock state is one in which there is a nontrivial subset of the processes that cannot change state and will never change state in the future.

Reference: Spirakis [337].

Hint: The reduction is from Monotone Circuit Value, Problem A.1.3. Let $\alpha = (\alpha_1, \ldots, \alpha_n)$ denote an instance of MCVP. There will be one process p_i associated with each α_i and one additional special process p_0. The representation of gates is as follows:

1. If α_i is an input with a FALSE (TRUE) value, the edge (p_i, rf_i) (respectively, (rt_i, p_i)) is in D. The rf_i's (rt_i's) denote single unit resource vertices representing FALSE (respectively, TRUE).

2. Suppose $\alpha_{i_1} = \alpha_{i_2} = \alpha_j$ AND α_k, where $j, k < i_1, i_2$ (the AND gate has fanout two). Then edges $(p_{i_1}, r_{i_1 j})$, $(p_{i_1}, r_{i_1 k})$, $(r_{i_1 j}, p_j)$, and $(r_{i_1 k}, p_k)$ are added to D for α_{i_1}, and edges $(p_{i_2}, r_{i_2 j})$, $(p_{i_2}, r_{i_2 k})$, $(r_{i_2 j}, p_j)$, and $(r_{i_2 k}, p_k)$ are added to D for α_{i_2}. The resource vertices are all single unit resources.

3. Suppose $\alpha_{i_1} = \alpha_{i_2} = \alpha_j$ OR α_k, where $j, k < i_1, i_2$ (the OR gate has fanout two). Then edges $(p_{i_1}, r_{i_1 jk})$, $(r_{i_1 jk}, p_j)$, and $(r_{i_1 jk}, p_k)$ are added to D for α_{i_1}, and edges $(p_{i_2}, r_{i_2 jk})$, $(r_{i_2 jk}, p_j)$, and $(r_{i_2 jk}, p_k)$ are added to D for α_{i_2}. The resource vertices are two unit resources.

The subscripts on the resource vertices are used only to uniquely identify the vertices and do not have any other meaning associated with them. Edges are also added for the special process p_0 as follows: for $1 \leq i \leq n$ add (rf_i, p_0) and (p_0, rt_i), and for $1 \leq j, k \leq n - 1$ add (p_0, r_{nj}) and (p_0, r_{njk}). The graph D is not in a deadlock state if and only if α_n is TRUE.

Remarks: Note that in the reduction the maximum number of units of any resource is two. The problem is in NC if t_i equals 1 for all i [337]. That is, if there is only one unit of each resource. If the system states are *expedient*, the resource allocator satisfies them as soon as possible, and at most one request can be connected to any process at a given time, then the problem is in NC [337].

A.12.3　One Dimensional Cellular Automata (CA)

Given: An initial configuration of a *one dimensional cellular automata*, a time bound T expressed in unary, a state q, and a designated cell c of the bi-infinite lattice. Each square of the one dimensional bi-infinite lattice is called a *site*. Each site may take on a finite set of values from an alphabet Σ, where $|\Sigma| = k$. The *range r* of each site denotes the number of neighbors to each side of the site that can directly influence it. The variables at each site, denoted σ_i, take on values based on a local transition rule $\phi : \Sigma^{2r+1} \rightarrow \Sigma$, where $\sigma_i(t+1) = \phi(\sigma_{i-r}(t), \sigma_{i-r+1}(t), \ldots, \sigma_{i+r}(t))$. Thus, for a value of r equal to one, the value of σ_i at time $t + 1$ is determined by $\phi(\sigma_{i-1}(t), \sigma_i(t), \sigma_{i+1}(t))$, that is, the values of its two neighbors and itself at time t.

Problem: Is cell c in state q at time T?

Reference: Lindgren and Nordahl [239], Smith [333], Albert and

Culik [8], Greenlaw, Hoover, and Ruzzo, THIS WORK.

Hint: It is well known that one dimensional cellular automata are capable of universal computation. We translated this result into a P-complete decision problem. Since the time bound is expressed in unary, the problem is in P. The reduction is based on the direct simulation of an arbitrary Turing machine. The idea is to have most of the sites in the cellular automata "asleep." Some site holds the Turing machine's state; its position in the lattice reflects the Turing machine's tape head position. The site simulates one move, awakens its left or right neighbor as appropriate, passes the new state as appropriate, and puts itself to sleep. Cell c of the automata will be in state q at time T if and only if the Turing machine accepts its input.

Remarks: Lindgren and Nordahl [239] construct a universal one dimensional cellular automata from the four tape symbol and seven state universal Turing machine of Minsky [262]. For $r = 1$ ($r = 2$) implying a three (respectively, five) neighbor rule, their construction requires seven (respectively, four) states. Both of these results require *periodic* background. Using a *uniform* background, their constructions require nine (five) states for the three (respectively, five) neighbor rule.

A.12.4 Fluid Invasion (FLUID)

Given: A graph $G = (V, E)$, a source s and a sink s', a distinguished vertex u, a time t, nonnegative real conductances k_{ij} for each edge $\{i, j\}$, and nonnegative real capacities ϕ_l for each vertex $l \in V$.

Problem: Is vertex u filled by the invading fluid at time t according to the fluid invasion algorithm? Informally, the *fluid invasion algorithm* proceeds by adding vertices to the cluster one at a time depending on when they fill up with the fluid being inserted at the source s. The *cluster* consists of those vertices that have been filled by the invading fluid. The evolution of the fluid configuration is governed by Darcy's law. The reader is referred to Machta [249] for additional details of the fluid model.

Reference: Machta [249].

Hint: The reduction is from NORCVP, see Problem A.1.5. A gadget is constructed to simulate the circuit in which a vertex in the gadget fills with fluid if and only if the corresponding gate in the circuit evaluates to TRUE. One of the key ideas in the reduction is that fluid can be blocked from preceding along a particular path P_1 even after it has "started down" P_1. In terms of the circuit instance this means values can be kept from propagating forward in the circuit.

Remarks: Fluid Invasion remains P-complete when G is restricted to being a $l \times l$ two dimensional lattice in which s (s') is connected to all sites on one face (respectively, the opposite face) of the lattice and with all of the conductances equal to one [249]. The proof that this restricted version is P-complete is complicated and does not seem to follow easily from the result for FLUID. Additional schemes designed to model pattern formation processes are studied from a computational complexity point of view in Greenlaw and Machta [142, 141]. There they provide NC algorithms to compute *percolation clusters* for three different models — *invasion percolation*, *invasion percolation with trapping*, and *ordinary percolation*.

A.12.5   Eden Growth (EG)

Given: An undirected graph $G = (V, E)$ in which each vertex in V has an $O(|V|)$ fixed length, label sequence of m distinct numbers from $\{1, \ldots, m\}$, a designated source vertex s, and a designated vertex t.

Problem: Is vertex t added to the *Eden cluster* formed on G? The initial cluster consists of vertex s. At each step i, $1 \leq i \leq m$, the vertex adjacent to the current cluster, whose i^{th} label is smallest, is added to the cluster.

Reference: (Jonathan Machta and Raymond Greenlaw, Personal Communication, 1993).

Hint: Topological ordered NORCVP, see Problem A.1.5, is reduced to a directed space-time version of Eden growth. This version is then converted to an instance of Eden growth as stated in the problem definition.

Remarks: Eden growth is a process that is used for studying tumor growth. See Machta and Greenlaw [250] for additional information about the parallel complexity of Eden growth and related growth models.

A.12.6   Lempel-Ziv Data Compression (LZDC)

Given: Two binary strings: s and t.

Problem: Is string t added to the dictionary when string s is encoded using the LZ2 coding algorithm? The *LZ2* algorithm reads string s from left to right. The dictionary is initially empty. When a prefix of the unparsed portion of s is not in the dictionary, the prefix

is added to the dictionary. All but the last character of the prefix are compressed by replacing them with a pointer to the dictionary.
Reference: De Agostino [79].
Hint: The reduction is from a variant of Circuit Value, Problem A.1.1, that consists of OR and NOT gates.
Remarks: De Agostino also shows that two standard variations of the algorithm yield *P*-complete problems. They are the *next character heuristic* and the *first character heuristic*. Both are proved *P*-complete by reductions from the same version of CVP [79]. De Agostino and Storer show that if given in advance a dictionary containing n strings under the appropriate assumptions, they can compute the optimal compression in $O(\log n)$ time using n^2 processors on a CREW-PRAM or alternatively in $O((\log n)^2)$ time using n processors [80]. They show the techniques can be generalized to the *sliding window* method. For such an approach De Agostino and Storer obtain an $O(\log n)$ time algorithm using n^3 processors again on the CREW-PRAM.

A.12.7   Greedy Alphabet Reducing (GAR)

Given: A finite alphabet $\Sigma = \{a_1, \dots, a_n\}$ with n greater than two, two sets $P, N \subseteq \Sigma^*$ with $P \cap N = \emptyset$, and a positive integer k less than or equal to n.
Problem: Is the size of the alphabet Γ obtained by the greedy alphabet reducing algorithm less than k? The *greedy alphabet reducing algorithm* is given below.

> begin
> $\quad \Gamma \leftarrow \Sigma$;
> $\quad \psi(a) \leftarrow a$ for each $a \in \Sigma$;
> $\quad$ repeat
> $\qquad$ for each $(a, b) \in \Gamma \times \Gamma$ with $a \neq b$
> $\qquad\quad$ let $\varphi_{a \rightarrow b}$ be a mapping obtained by letting $\psi(\sigma) = b$,
> $\qquad\qquad$ for all $\sigma \in \Sigma$ with $\psi(\sigma) = a$;
> $\qquad$ choose $\varphi_{a \rightarrow b}$ satisfying $\tilde{\varphi}_{a \rightarrow b}(P) \cap \tilde{\varphi}_{a \rightarrow b}(N) = \emptyset$ and
> $\qquad\quad$ minimizing $|\tilde{\varphi}_{a \rightarrow b}(P) \cup \tilde{\varphi}_{a \rightarrow b}(N)|$;
> $\quad$ (Note, $\tilde{\varphi}_{a \rightarrow b}$ denotes the natural homomorphism associated with $\varphi_{a \rightarrow b}$.)
> $\qquad$ remove a from Γ;
> $\quad$ until no more replacements are found;
> end.

Reference: Shimozono and Miyano [330].

Hint: The reduction is from NANDCVP, Problem A.1.5.

Remarks: Shimozono and Miyano also show that the general *Alphabet Indexing Problem* is *NP*-complete, and the *Alphabet Indexing Local Search Problem* in the weighted case is *PLS*-complete and in the unweighted case is *P*-complete [330].

A.12.8   Network Simulation (NetSim)

Given: A fully connected undirected network with N vertices, a capacity $C(i,j)$ for each link $\{i,j\}$ (counted in "trunks"), a list of tuples specifying call arrival and holding times, and a designated call c.

Problem: During the simulation of the network (see Greenberg, Lubachevsky, and Wang [132] for details) is call c blocked?

Reference: Greenberg, Lubachevsky, and Wang [132].

Hint: The reduction is from Monotone Circuit Value, Problem A.1.3.

Remarks: They also prove that *multirate* simulation, in which a call may require more than one trunk on each link on its route, is *P*-complete even for N equal to two. See Problem B.8.7 for a related question.

Appendix B

Open Problems

This appendix contains a list of open problems. Many of these open questions are stated as search problems to be as general as possible. The goal is to classify each problem with respect to its computational complexity by, for example, finding an NC algorithm or a P-completeness proof for the problem.

For each question, we specify references indicating (to the best of our knowledge) who first examined the parallel complexity of the problem. The references also provide a good starting point for beginning research on a given problem. The remarks provided explain what is known about other versions of the problem. They often give additional references.

The problems listed are divided into the following categories.

B.1	graph theory
B.2	combinatorial optimization and flow
B.3	logic
B.4	formal languages
B.5	algebraic
B.6	geometry
B.7	real analysis

The open problem list is followed by a list of problems in the complexity class CC and by a list of problems in RNC. These classes are related to P and NC in the following ways:

$$CC \subseteq P \text{ and } NC \subseteq RNC$$

but, thus far, CC is incomparable with either NC or RNC, and RNC is incomparable with P. That is, the classes cannot be related using the $\subseteq$ relation.

We conclude our remarks about open problems in this section by noting that to our knowledge none of the four remaining open problems in (Garey and Johnson [113]) are known to be P-hard. The problems are as follows: Graph Isomorphism [OPEN1] (see remarks for Problems B.1.1 and B.9.9), Precedence Constrained 3-Processor Scheduling [OPEN8] (see remarks for Problems A.4.8 and A.4.9), Composite Number [OPEN11], and Minimum Length Triangulation [OPEN12] [113].

B.1 Graph Theory

B.1.1 Bounded Degree Graph Isomorphism (BDGI)

Given: Two undirected graphs $G = (V, E)$ and $H = (V', E')$. The vertices in G and H have maximum degree at most k, a constant independent of the sizes of G and H.

Problem: Are G and H isomorphic? $G = (V, E)$ and $H = (V', E')$ are *isomorphic* if and only if there are two bijections $f : V \to V'$ and $g : E \to E'$ such that for every edge $e = \{u, v\} \in E, \{f(u), f(v)\} = g(e) \in E'$.

Reference: Furst, Hopcroft, and Luks [110].

Remarks: Luks showed the problem is in P [110]. Without the degree bound, the problem is in NP but not known to be in P, nor is it known to be either P-hard or NP-complete. Lindell shows that the *Tree Isomorphism Problem* is in NC; see remarks for Problem B.9.9. *Subtree Isomorphism* is in RNC (Gibbons *et al.* [118], Lingas and Karpinski [241]). See Problem B.9.9 for additional details.

B.1.2 Edge Ranking (ER)

Given: A tree $T = (V, E)$.

Problem: Find an optimal edge ranking of T. An *edge ranking* of a tree is a labeling of the edges using positive integers such that the path between two edges with the same label contains an intermediate edge with a higher label. An edge ranking is *optimal* if the highest label used is as small as possible.

Reference: de la Torre, Greenlaw, and Schäffer [84].

Remarks: This problem was proved to be in P in [84]. They give a NC approximation algorithm for the problem that finds an edge ranking within a factor of two of optimal. An NC algorithm for constant degree trees is also given in [84]. A similar problem called the *Node Ranking Problem* for trees in which the vertices are labeled, instead of the edges, was proved to be in NC (de la Torre and Greenlaw [81], de la Torre, Greenlaw, and Przytycka [82]). See Problem A.8.25 for a related P-complete problem. Karloff and Shmoys give NC algorithms for several versions of edge ranking multigraphs [191], a problem having a similar flavor. See Problems A.2.6 and B.9.3 for a description of their results.

B.1.3   Edge-weighted Matching (EWM)

Given: An undirected graph $G = (V, E)$ with positive integer weights on the edges.

Problem: Find a matching of maximum weight. A *matching* is a subset of edges $E' \subseteq E$ such that no two edges in E' share a common endpoint.

Reference: Karp, Upfal, and Wigderson [196].

Remarks: EWM is in *RNC* if all weights are polynomially bounded [196]. Even in this restricted case, the problem is not known to be in *NC*. Define rank(e) to be the position of edge e's weight in the sorted list of edge weights, where the sorting is done in increasing order. Lexicographically First Maximal Matching, Problem B.8.2 (and hence all of *CC*), is *NC* reducible to EWM, by assigning weight $2^{\mathrm{rank}(e)}$ to edge e.

B.1.4   Graph Closure (GC)

Given: An undirected graph $G = (V, E)$ and a designated edge $e = \{u, v\}$.

Problem: Is e in the *closure* of G? That is, the graph obtained from G by repeatedly joining nonadjacent pairs of vertices u and v whose degree sum is at least $|V|$.[1]

Reference: Khuller [208].

Remarks: With the following modification, the problem becomes *P*-complete (see Problem A.2.19): add a set of designated edges E' such that only vertices whose degree sum is at least $|V|$ and whose corresponding edge is in E' may be added to the closure [208].

B.1.5   Low Degree Subgraph (LDS)

Given: An undirected graph $G = (V, E)$ and an integer k.

Problem: Find a maximal induced subgraph with maximum degree at most k.

Reference: Godbeer [119], Greenlaw [134].

Remarks: The *Maximal Independent Set Problem* is a LDS with k equal to zero, see Problem A.2.1. Godbeer shows that LDS can be

---

[1] Angelo Monti very recently solved this problem by proving it is *P*-complete (Sergio De Agostino, Personal Communication, 1994).

viewed as a *Connectionist Model* problem in which edge weights have value -1 [119], see Problem A.5.7. Two decision problems based on low degree subgraph computations are proved *NP*-complete in [134].

B.1.6 Maximal Independent Set Hypergraph (MISH)

Given: A hypergraph $H = (V, E)$, where the elements in E are subsets (called *hyperedges*) of V.
Problem: Find a maximal independent set I. A set $I \subseteq V$ is *independent* if for all $e \in E$ there is at least one $v \in e$ such that $v \notin I$. An independent set I is *maximal* if for every $v \in V - I$, $I \cup \{v\}$ is not independent.
Reference: Beame and Luby [27].
Remarks: If the edges are two element sets ("dimension two"), the problem becomes the *Maximal Independent Set Problem*, which is known to be in *NC*, see Problem A.2.1. Beame and Luby give an *RNC* algorithm for dimension $O(1)$. Kelsen cites a personal communication to Beame indicating that Beame and Luby's analysis in fact only holds for dimension three [206]. Beame and Luby also give an algorithm for the general problem that is conjectured to be *RNC*. Kelsen shows this algorithm is in *RNC* for constant dimension [206]. Dahlhaus, Karpinski, and Kelsen give an *NC* algorithm for dimension three [77]. Let n denote the number of vertices in the hypergraph and m the number of edges. Their algorithm runs in $O((\log n)^4)$ time and uses $n + m$ processors on an EREW-PRAM.

B.1.7 Restricted Lexicographically First Maximal Independent Set (RLFMIS)

Given: An undirected, planar, bipartite graph $G = (V, E)$ with a numbering on the vertices in V.
Problem: Find the lexicographically first maximal independent set.
Reference: Miyano [265].
Remarks: See Problem A.2.1. Finding the lexicographically first maximal subgraph of maximum degree one in planar, bipartite graphs of degree at most three is *P*-complete [265].

B.1.8   Lexicographically First Maximal Three-cycle Free Edge Induced Subgraph (LF3Edge)

Given: An undirected graph $G = (V, E)$ with an ordering on the edges in E and having a maximum degree of five or less.

Problem: Compute the lexicographically first maximal three-cycle free edge induced subgraph of G. That is, the lexicographically first maximal edge induced subgraph that does not contain any cycles of size three or more.

Reference: Miyano [264, 265].

Remarks: Numerous variants of this problem are P-complete. See Problem A.2.21 for a description of several of them. LF3Edge is in NC^2 when the degree restriction on G is four. For planar graphs, the complexity of the problem is also open. That is, there is no known degree restriction for LF3Edge that makes the problem P-complete nor is it clear when the problem is in NC [264]

B.2   Combinatorial Optimization

B.2.1   Optimal Two Variable Integer Linear Programming (Opt2ILP)

Given: A linear system of inequalities $Ax \leq b$ over $\mathbf{Z}$, where A is an $n \times 2$ matrix and b is an $n \times 1$ vector, and an ordered pair $u \in \mathbf{Z}^2$.

Problem: Find a 2×1 vector x, with $x^T \in \mathbf{Z}^2$ (T denotes transpose), such that $Ax \leq b$ and ux is a maximum.

Reference: Deng [90], Shallcross, Pan, and Lin-Kriz [329].

Remarks: This problem is NC-equivalent to the problem of computing the remainders produced by the Euclidean algorithm, see Problem B.5.1, [90, 329]. Shallcross, Pan, and Lin-Kriz illustrate reductions among problems NC-equivalent to this and related problems [329]. See [90] and the remarks for Problems B.2.2 and B.5.1 as well.

B.2.2   Two Variable Linear Programming (TVLP)

Given: A linear system of inequalities $Ax \leq b$ over $\mathbf{Q}$, where each row of A has at most two nonzero elements. A is an $n \times d$ matrix and b is an $n \times 1$ vector.

Problem: Find a feasible solution if one exists.

Reference: Lueker, Megiddo, and Ramachandran [248].

Remarks: There is a polylogarithmic algorithm that uses $n^{(\log n)^{O(1)}}$ processors on a CREW-PRAM [248]. See also Problems A.4.1, A.4.2, A.4.3, and B.2.1.

B.3 Logic

B.3.1 Canonical Labeling Well-founded Extensional Relation (CLWER)

Given: A *well-founded relation* (V, E). The reader is referred to [74] for definitions.

Problem: Compute a *canonical labeling* of the relation.

Reference: Dahlhaus [74].

Remarks: See Problem A.6.12 for a related P-complete problem.

B.3.2 One Left-linear Semi-unification (1LLSU)

Given: A set of pairs of terms $S = \{(M_1, N_1), \ldots, (M_k, N_k)\}$ that is left linear. See Problem A.6.11 for definitions.

Problem: Is S semi-unifiable?

Reference: Henglein [155].

Remarks: 2LLSU is P-complete [155]; see Problem A.6.11. Henglein conjectures that 1LLSU is P-complete [155].

B.4 Formal Languages

B.4.1 Strong Bisimilarity in Deterministic Transition Systems (SBDTS)

Given: An encoding of a finite labeled deterministic transition system N, and two designated states p and q. A *finite labeled transition system* is a triple $M = \langle Q, \Sigma, T \rangle$, where Q is a finite set of states, Σ is a finite alphabet, and $T \subseteq Q \times \Sigma \times Q$ is the set of transitions. The system is *deterministic* if for each $a \in \Sigma$ and $q' \in Q$ there is a unique triple in T, (q', a, p'), where $p' \in Q$. A relation $S \subseteq Q \times Q$ is a *strong bisimulation* of M if $(s_1, s_2) \in S$ implies for all $x \in \Sigma$ that

1. whenever $(s_1, x, t_1) \in T$, then for some state t_2, $(s_2, x, t_2) \in T$ and $(t_1, t_2) \in S$; and

2. whenever $(s_2, x, t_2) \in T$, then for some state t_1, $(s_1, x, t_1) \in T$ and $(t_1, t_2) \in S$.

The *strong bisimulation relation* is defined as the union of all strong bisimulations of M.

Problem: Are p and q strongly bisimilar? That is, is (p, q) in the strong bisimulation relation of N?

Reference: Àlvarez *et al.* [11], Balcázar, Gabarró, and Sántha [23].

Remarks: The problem is P-complete if the system is allowed to be nondeterministic [23], see Problem A.7.10. The complexity of the problem is also open if states are restricted to have indegree one [23].

B.4.2   Witness for Unambiguous Finite Automata (LFWITNESS)

Given: Let $M = (Q, \Sigma, \delta, s, F)$ be an unambiguous finite automaton and n an integer encoded in unary. A finite automaton is *unambiguous* if all strings accepted by the machine have a unique accepting computation.

Problem: Find the lexicographically first witness string for M. The *lexicographically first witness string* is the lexicographically first string that "witnesses" the inequality $L(M) \cap \Sigma^{\leq n} \neq \Sigma^{\leq n}$, where $L(M)$ denotes the language accepted by M and $\Sigma^{\leq n}$ denotes all strings over Σ of length less than or equal to n.

Reference: Sang Cho and Huynh [314].

Remarks: In [314] the problem is proved to be in P. For deterministic finite automata the problem is NC^1-complete for $NLOG$ [314]. See [314] for other results regarding related problems.

B.5 Algebra

B.5.1 Extended Euclidean Algorithm (ExtendedGCD)

Given: Two n-bit positive integers a and b.
Problem: Compute integers s and t such that $as + bt = \gcd(a, b)$.
Reference: Borodin, von zur Gathen, and Hopcroft [43].
Remarks: The analogous problem for n^{th} degree polynomials is in NC [43]. Deng shows several other problems are NC-equivalent to a closely related problem [90]. Two of these are expanding the continued fraction of the ratio of two integers and computing the sequence of convergents of two integers. See also Shallcross, Pan, and Lin-Kriz [329] and remarks following Problem B.2.1.

B.5.2 Gaussian Elimination with Partial Pivoting over Finite Fields (GEPPFF)

Given: An $n \times n$ matrix A with entries over a finite field and an integer l.
Problem: What is the smallest row index in the lth column that is nonzero when Gaussian elimination with partial pivoting is performed on A?
Reference: (Allan Borodin, Personal Communication, 1991).
Remarks: Vavasis shows the analogous problem for unrestricted fields is P-complete [361], see Problem A.8.4.

B.5.3 Integer Greatest Common Divisor (IntegerGCD)

Given: Two n-bit positive integers a and b.
Problem: Compute the greatest common divisor (gcd) of a and b, denoted $\gcd(a, b)$.
Reference: von zur Gathen [368].
Remarks: For n^{th} degree polynomials $p, q \in \mathbb{Q}[x]$, computing $\gcd(p, q)$ is in NC^2 via an NC^1 reduction to *Determinant* (Cook and Sethi [69], Borodin, Cook, and Pippenger [42]). IntegerGCD is NC^1 reducible to Short Vectors Dimension 2, Problem B.7.2 [368]. Kannan, Miller, and Rudolph give a sublinear

CRCW-PRAM algorithm for computing the gcd of two n-bit integers [184]. Their algorithm requires $O(n \log \log n / \log n)$ time and $n^2 (\log n)^2$ processors. Chor and Goldreich give a CRCW-PRAM algorithm for the same problem with time bound $O(n / \log n)$ and processor bound $n^{1+\epsilon}$, for any positive constant ϵ [56]. Sorenson presents an algorithm called the k-ary gcd algorithm [335, 336] whose sequential version is practical and whose parallel version has bounds that match those given in [56]. Also see (Deng [90], Lin-Kriz and Pan [237], Shallcross, Pan, and Lin-Kriz [329]) for additional research on IntegerGCD and related problems.

B.5.4   LU Decomposition (LUD)

Given: An $n \times n$ matrix A with entries over the rationals.
Problem: Find a numerically stable LU decomposition of A.
Reference: (Allan Borodin, Personal Communication, 1991).
Remarks: Vavasis shows that the LU decomposition arising from Gaussian elimination with partial pivoting is P-complete [361], see Problem A.8.4. The problem here is to find another method for constructing a LU decomposition in NC. This question is important because one often solves the same system of equations multiple times. Having the LU decomposition means the solution for different vectors can easily be obtained via back substitution.

B.5.5   Modular Inversion (ModInverse)

Given: An n-bit prime p and an n-bit positive integer a, such that p does not divide a.
Problem: Compute b such that $ab \bmod p = 1$.
Reference: Tompa [354].
Remarks: ModInverse is reducible to ExtendedGCD, Problem B.5.1. The reduction is to compute s and t such that $as + pt = gcd(a, p) = 1$. ModInverse is also reducible to ModPower, Problem B.5.6, even restricted to prime moduli. The idea is to compute $a^{p-2} \bmod p$ and apply Fermat's Little Theorem. Zeugmann considers a slight variant of the problem where p is replaced by a smooth modulus [377]. A number is *smooth* if all its prime factors are small. In this case Zeugmann gives a logarithmic space uniform Boolean family of circuits that solve the problem in $O(\log n \log \log n)$ depth

and $n^{O(1)}$ size. Zeugmann gives analogous results for polynomials over finite fields [376].

B.5.6 Modular Powering (ModPower)

Given: Positive n-bit integers a, b, and c.
Problem: Compute a^b mod c.
Reference: Cook [67].
Remarks: The complexity of the problem is open even for finding a single bit of the desired output. The problem is in NC for *smooth c*, that is, for c having only small prime factors (von zur Gathen [369]). Zeugmann improves on the circuit depth required to solve this problem in [377]. He presents logarithmic space uniform Boolean circuits of depth $O(\log n \log \log n)$ and polynomial size. Similar results for polynomials are given in [376]. Zeugmann also considers the problem of taking *discrete roots* and shows that for smooth modulus this problem can be solved using logarithmic space uniform Boolean circuits of depth $O(\log n \log \log n)$ and polynomial size [377]. In the special case when c is a prime (the antithesis of smooth), the problem is open. ModInverse, Problem B.5.5, is reducible to this restricted case. The analogous problems when a and c are n^{th} degree polynomials over a finite field of small characteristic, *Modular Polynomial Exponentiation* and *Polynomial Exponentiation*, are in NC^2 (Fich and Tompa [106]). They are open for finite fields having large (superpolynomial) characteristic. Note that ModPower can be reduced to the polynomial version with exponential characteristic simply by considering degree 0 polynomials.

B.5.7 Relative Primeness (RelPrime)

Given: Two n-bit positive integers a and b.
Problem: Are a and b relatively prime?
Reference: Tompa [354].
Remarks: This problem is a special case of IntegerGCD, Problem B.5.3.

B.5.8   Sylow Subgroups (SylowSub)

Given: A group G.
Problem: Find the Sylow subgroups of G.
Reference: Babai, Seres, and Luks [21].
Remarks: The problem is known to be in P (Kantor [185]), however, the NC question is open even for solvable groups [21]. For a permutation group G, testing membership in G, finding the order of G, finding the center of G, and finding a composition series of G are all known to be in NC [21]. Babai, Seres, and Luks present several other open questions involving group theory [21].

B.6   Geometry

B.6.1   Limited Reflection Ray Tracing (LRRT)

Given: A set of n flat mirrors of lengths $l_1, \ldots, l_n$, their placements at rational points in the plane, a source point S, the trajectory of a single beam emitted from S, and a designated mirror M.
Problem: Is M hit by the beam emitted from S within n reflections? At the mirrors, the angle of incident of the beam equals the angle of reflection.
Reference: Greenlaw, Hoover, and Ruzzo, THIS WORK.
Remarks: The *General Ray Tracing Problem* is to determine if a mirror is ever hit by the beam. When the mirrors are points, that is have no length, the general problem is in NC (Pilar de la Torre and Raymond Greenlaw, Personal Communication, 1990). In two or more dimensions, the general problem is in $PSPACE$ (Reif, Tygar, and Yoshida [303]). In three dimensions, with mirrors placed at rational points, the general problem is $PSPACE$-hard [303]. The general problem is open for all mirrors of a fixed size as well. See [303] for a detailed discussion.

B.6.2   Restricted Plane Sweep Triangulation (SWEEP)

Given: An n-vertex polygon P without holes.
Problem: Find the triangulation computed by the *plane sweep triangulation algorithm*. See Problem A.9.1 for a description of the

algorithm.

Reference: Atallah, Callahan, and Goodrich [18].

Remarks: The problem of finding some arbitrary triangulation is in *NC* (Goodrich [130]). If the polygon is allowed to have holes, the problem is *P*-complete [18]. See Problem A.9.1.

B.6.3   2-Oriented Weighted Planar Partitioning (2OWPP)

Given: A set of nonintersecting segments $s_1, \ldots, s_n$ in the Euclidean plane, a set of associated integer weights $w_1, \ldots, w_n$, and two designated segments r and t. The segments are *2-oriented* meaning that there are only two different possible slopes for the segments.

Problem: Do segments r and t "touch" in the partitioning of the plane constructed by extending segments in the order of their weights? Segments are extended until they reach another segment or a previous segment extension.

Reference: Atallah, Callahan, and Goodrich [18].

Remarks: The 3-oriented version, Problem A.9.2, in which three different slopes are allowed, is *P*-complete [18].

B.6.4   Unit Length Visibility Layers (ULVL)

Given: A set of n unit length, horizontal, nonintersecting line segments in the Euclidean plane, a designated segment s, and an integer d.

Problem: Is the label assigned to segment s by the visibility layering process d? The *visibility layering process* is repeatedly to compute and delete the upper envelope of the remaining set of segments and label those segments with the current depth. The *upper envelope* consists of those segments visible from the point $(0, +\infty)$.

Reference: Atallah, Callahan, and Goodrich [18].

Remarks: The problem is *P*-complete if the restriction on unit lengths is removed [18]. See Problem A.9.3.

B.7   Real Analysis

B.7.1   Short Vectors (SV)

Given: Input vectors $a_1, \ldots, a_n \in \mathbf{Z}^n$ that are linearly independent over $\mathbf{Q}$.

Problem: Find a nonzero vector x in the $\mathbf{Z}$-module (or "lattice") $M = \sum a_i \mathbf{Z} \subseteq \mathbf{Z}^n$ such that $\|x\| \leq 2^{(n-1)/2}\|y\|$ for all $y \in M - \{\vec{0}\}$, where $\|y\| = (\sum y_i^2)^{1/2}$ is the L_2 norm.

Reference: von zur Gathen [368].

Remarks: Lenstra, Lenstra, and Lovász show that the problem is in P [232]. IntegerGCD, Problem B.5.3, is NC^1 reducible to SV [368]. For additional remarks about related problems, see Bachem and Kannan [22].

B.7.2   Short Vectors Dimension 2 (SV2)

Given: Input vectors $a_1, a_2 \in \mathbf{Z}^2$ that are linearly independent over $\mathbf{Q}$, and a rational number $c \geq 1$.

Problem: Find a nonzero vector x such that $\|x\| \leq c\|y\|$ for all $y \in M - \{\vec{0}\}$.

Reference: von zur Gathen [368].

Remarks: IntegerGCD, Problem B.5.3, is NC^1 reducible to SV2 [368]. For additional remarks about related problems, see Bachem and Kannan [22].

B.7.3   Polynomial Root Approximation (PRA)

Given: An nth degree polynomial $p \in \mathbf{Z}[x]$, and an integer μ.

Problem: For each (real or complex) root z_i, $1 \leq 1 \leq n$, of p, an approximation $\tilde{z}_i$ such that $|z_i - \tilde{z}_i| < 2^{-\mu}$.

Reference: Ben-Or *et al.* [30].

Remarks: If all the roots are real, the problem is in NC [30].

B.7.4 Univariate Polynomial Factorization over $\mathbb{Q}$ (UPFQ)

Given: An nth degree polynomial $p \in \mathbb{Q}[x]$.
Problem: Compute the factorization of p over $\mathbb{Q}$.
Reference: von zur Gathen [368].
Remarks: UPFQ is NC^1 reducible to Short Vectors, Problem B.7.1 [368].

B.8 *CC*

Several researchers (including Anderson, Cook, Gupta, Mayr, and Subramanian) suggested looking at the complexity of the Comparator Circuit Value Problem, or CCVP, Problem B.8.1. This problem is defined below, Problem B.8.1. *CC* is defined as the class of problems *NC* many-one reducible to CCVP (Mayr and Subramanian [255]). Problems in this section are all equivalent to, that is, *NC* many-one interreducible with CCVP.

While the evidence is less compelling than that for *RNC* problems (see Section B.9), it is generally considered unlikely that these problems are *P*-complete, because of the lack of fanout in comparator circuits. On the other hand, no fast parallel algorithms are known for them, with the partial exception of $\sqrt{n}(\log n)^{O(1)}$ algorithms for CCVP and some related problems. Such algorithms were independently discovered by Danny Soroker (unpublished) and by Mayr and Subramanian [255]. Richard J. Anderson (also unpublished) has improved the algorithms so as to use only $\sqrt{n}$ processors. Mayr and Subramanian note that these algorithms are *P*-complete, in the sense of Chapter 8.

It is known that $NLOG \subseteq CC \subseteq P$ [255]. At present *NC* and *CC* are incomparable as are *RNC* and *CC*. That is, the classes cannot be related using the $\subseteq$ relation.

The majority of the results described in this appendix come from Mayr and Subramanian [255]. See also (Feder [104], Ramachandran and Wang [298], Subramanian [346, 347]) for more research on *CC*.

B.8.1   Comparator Circuit Value Problem (CCVP)

Given: An encoding $\overline{\alpha}$ of a circuit α composed of comparator gates, plus inputs $x_1, \ldots, x_n$, and a designated output y. A *comparator* gate outputs the minimum of its two inputs on its first output wire and outputs the maximum of its two inputs on its second output wire. The gate is further restricted so that each output has fanout at most one.

Problem: Is output y of α TRUE on input $x_1, \ldots, x_n$?

Reference: (Stephen A. Cook, Personal Communication, 1982), Mayr and Subramanian [255].

Remarks: Cook shows that CCVP is *NC* equivalent to computing the lexicographically first maximal matching in a bipartite graph. Mayr and Subramanian show that this matching problem is *NC* equivalent to Stable Marriage, Problem B.8.3 [255]. Sairam, Vitter, and Tamassia address the "incremental" complexity of CCVP in [311].

B.8.2   Lexicographically First Maximal Matching (LFMM)

Given: An undirected graph $G = (V, E)$ with an ordering on its edges and a distinguished edge $e \in E$.

Problem: Is e in the lexicographically first maximal matching of G? A matching is *maximal* if it cannot be extended.

Reference: (Stephen A. Cook, Personal Communication, 1982), Mayr and Subramanian [255].

Remarks: LFMM is *NC* equivalent to Comparator Circuit Value, Problem B.8.1 [255]. This problem resembles Lexicographically First Maximal Independent Set, Problem A.2.1, that is *P*-complete. A *P*-completeness proof for LFMM would imply that Edge-weighted Matching, Problem B.1.3, is also *P*-complete.

B.8.3   Stable Marriage (SM)

Given: A set of n men and a set of n women. For each person a ranking of the opposite sex according to their preference for a marriage partner. Note that a preference list does not need to include a ranking for every member of the opposite sex. This problem is sometimes called the *Stable Roommates Problem*.

Problem: Does the given instance of the problem have a set of marriages that is stable? The set is *stable* (or a set of *stable marriages*) if there is no unmatched pair $\{m, w\}$ such that both m and w prefer each other to their current partners.

Reference: Mayr and Subramanian [255], Pólya, Tarjan, and Woods [291].

Remarks: See, for example, Gibbons [116] or [291] for background on SM. If the preference lists are complete, the problem always has a solution [291]. SM is *NC* equivalent to Comparator Circuit Value, Problem B.8.1 [255]. Several variations of SM are also known to be equivalent to CCVP. For example, the *Male-optimal Stable Marriage Problem* in which there is a designated couple $\{m, w\}$ and the question asked is whether man m is married to woman w in the male-optimal stable marriage? [255]. The *male-optimal* stable marriage is the one formed by the algorithm given in [291]. It finds a matching in which no man could do any better in a stable marriage. Several other versions of SM are discussed in Problems B.8.4, B.8.5, and B.8.6.

B.8.4 Stable Marriage Fixed Pair (SMFP)

Given: A set of n men and a set of n women, for each person a ranking of the opposite sex according to their preference for a marriage partner, and a designated couple Alice and Bob.

Problem: Are Alice and Bob a *fixed pair* for the given instance of the problem? That is, is it the case that Alice and Bob are married to each other in *every* stable marriage?

Reference: Mayr and Subramanian [255], Subramanian [346].

Remarks: The reduction is from Comparator Circuit Value, Problem B.8.1 [346].

B.8.5 Stable Marriage Stable Pair (SMSP)

Given: A set of n men and a set of n women, for each person a ranking of the opposite sex according to their preference for a marriage partner, and a designated couple Alice and Bob.

Problem: Are Alice and Bob a *stable pair* for the given instance of the problem? That is, is it the case that Alice and Bob are married to each other in *some* stable marriage?

Reference: Mayr and Subramanian [255], Subramanian [346].

Remarks: The reduction is from Comparator Circuit Value, Problem B.8.1 [346].

B.8.6   Stable Marriage Minimum Regret (SMMR)

Given: A set of n men and a set of n women, for each person a ranking of the opposite sex according to their preference for a marriage partner, and an integer k, $1 \leq k \leq n$.

Problem: Is there a stable marriage in which every person has regret at most k? The *regret* of a person in a stable marriage is the position of her mate on her preference list.

Reference: Mayr and Subramanian [255], Subramanian [346].

Remarks: The goal in this problem is to minimize the maximum regret of any person. The reduction is from Comparator Circuit Value, Problem B.8.1 [346].

B.8.7   Telephone Connection (TC)

Given: A telephone line with a fixed channel capacity k, an integer l, and a sequence of calls $(s_1, f_1), \ldots, (s_n, f_n)$, where s_i (f_i) denotes the starting (respectively, finishing) time of the ith call. The ith call can be *serviced* at time s_i if the number of calls being served at that time is less than k. If the call cannot be served, it is discarded. When a call is completed, a channel is freed up.

Problem: Is the lth call serviced?

Reference: Ramachandran and Wang [298].

Remarks: TC is *NC* equivalent to Comparator Circuit Value, Problem B.8.1 [298].   Ramachandran and Wang give an $O(\min(\sqrt{n}, k) \log n)$ time EREW-PRAM algorithm that uses n processors for solving TC [298]. Also see Problem A.12.8.

B.9 *RNC*

The problems in this appendix are all known to be in *RNC* or *FRNC*, but not known to be in *NC* or *FNC*. A proof that any of them is *P*-complete would be almost as unexpected as a proof that *NC* equals *P*. Of course, $NC \subseteq RNC$ but *RNC* and *P* are at present incomparable. That is, the classes cannot be related using the $\subseteq$ relation. See Section 3.2.3 for more discussion of these issues. Here we use *RNC* (*NC*) to represent both *RNC* and *FRNC* (respectively, *NC* and *FNC*) depending on context.

B.9.1 Blocking Flow in a Three Layered Network (BF3)

Given: A three layered network $G = (V, E)$ with each edge labeled with a capacity $c_i \geq 0$, and two distinguished vertices, source s and sink t. A *three layered network* is one in which all source to sink paths have length three.

Problem: Find a blocking flow. A *blocking flow* is a flow in which every path from s to t has a *saturated edge* — an edge whose flow is equal to its capacity.

Reference: Cheriyan and Maheshwari [54].

Remarks: The problem is in *RNC* [54]. The problem of finding the lexicographically first blocking flow in a three layered network is *P*-complete (Anderson and Mayr [15]). See Problem A.4.6. The problem of finding a blocking flow in an acyclic network is also open [120]. In this case Goldberg and Tarjan give an EREW-PRAM algorithm that uses $O(n \log n)$ time and m processors for an n-vertex, m-edge network [120].

B.9.2 Directed or Undirected Depth-first Search (DFS)

Given: A graph $G = (V, E)$ and a vertex s.

Problem: Construct the depth-first search numbering of G starting from vertex s.

Reference: Aggarwal and Anderson [5], Aggarwal, Anderson, and Kao [6].

Remarks: *RNC* algorithms are now known for both the undi-

rected [5] and directed [6] cases, subsuming earlier RNC results for
planar graphs (Smith [334]). For directed acyclic graphs, DFS is in
NC (de la Torre and Kruskal [85, 86], Greenlaw [135]).

B.9.3 Edge Coloring (EC)

Given: An undirected graph $G = (V, E)$ with Δ equal to the maximum degree of any vertex in V.

Problem: Find an edge coloring of G that uses less than or equal to $\Delta + 1$ colors. An *edge coloring* is an assignment of colors to the edges such that no incident edges receive the same color.

Reference: Karloff and Shmoys [191].

Remarks: An NC algorithm is known for polylogarithmic Δ [191]. Karloff and Shmoys give an RNC algorithm on the COMMON CRCW-PRAM that uses $\Delta + 20 * \Delta^{1/2+\epsilon}$ colors with running time $(\log |V|)^{O(1)}$ and processors $|V|^{O(1)}$, where the running time is for a fixed $\epsilon > 0$ and the processor bound is independent of ϵ. Also see Problems A.2.6 and B.1.2.

B.9.4 Maximal Path (MP)

Given: An undirected graph $G = (V, E)$ with a numbering on the vertices in V and a designated vertex r.

Problem: Find a *maximal path* originating from r. That is, a path that cannot be extended without encountering a vertex already on the path.

Reference: Anderson and Mayr [16], Anderson [13].

Remarks: Anderson shows that the problem of computing a maximal path is in RNC [13]. Lexicographically First Maximal Path, Problem A.3.1, is P-complete even when restricted to planar graphs with maximum degree three. If the maximum degree of any vertex in G is at most Δ, there is an algorithm that can find a maximal path in $O(\Delta(\log n)^3)$ time using n^2 processors [16]. There is also an NC algorithm for finding a maximal path in planar graphs [16].

B.9.5 Maximum Disjoint Paths (MDP)

Given: An undirected graph $G = (V, E)$ and a set of vertices $U \subseteq V$.

Problem: Find a maximum cardinality set of nontrivial vertex disjoint paths that have their endpoints in U.

Reference: Anderson [12].

Remarks: MDP is first reduced to a bidirectional flow problem that is in turn reduced to a matching problem [12]. See Problem A.3.2.

B.9.6 0-1 Maximum Flow (0-1 MaxFlow)

Given: A directed graph $G = (V, E)$ with each edge labeled in unary with a capacity $c_i \geq 0$, and two distinguished vertices, source s and sink t.

Problem: Find a maximum flow.

Reference: Feather [103], Karp, Upfal, and Wigderson [196].

Remarks: Feather shows the problem of finding the *value* of the maximum flow to be in *RNC* [103]. Karp, Upfal, and Wigderson show how to construct a maximum flow, also in *RNC* [196]. Both problems remain in *RNC* when capacities are polynomially bounded. Both are *P*-complete when capacities are arbitrary, see Problem A.4.4. Karpinski and Wagner show that when G is given by its *vertex multiplicity graph* representation the *Unary Network Flow Problem* becomes *P*-complete [200].

B.9.7 Maximum Matching (MM)

Given: An undirected graph $G = (V, E)$.

Problem: Find a maximum matching of G. The concept of matching is defined in Problem B.1.3. A matching is *maximum* if no matching of larger cardinality exists.

Reference: Feather [103], Karp, Upfal, and Wigderson [196], Mulmuley, Vazirani, and Vazirani [271].

Remarks: Feather shows that the problem of finding the *size* of a maximum matching is in *RNC* [103]. Karp, Upfal, and Wigderson gave the first *RNC* algorithm for *finding* the maximum matching [196]. A more efficient algorithm was given by Mulmuley, Vazirani, and Vazirani [271]. Karloff shows how any *RNC* algorithm for matching can be made errorless [188]. *Maximum Edge-*

weighted Matching for unary edge weights and *Maximum Vertex-weighted Matching* for binary vertex weights are also known to be in *RNC* [196, 271].

B.9.8   Perfect Matching Existence (PME)

Given: An undirected graph $G = (V, E)$.
Problem: Does G have a perfect matching? A *perfect matching* is a matching where each vertex is incident to one edge in the matching.
Reference: Karp, Upfal, and Wigderson [196], Mulmuley, Vazirani, and Vazirani [271].
Remarks: See remarks for Problem B.9.7.   PME seems to be the simplest of the matching problems not known to be in *NC*. Dahlhaus, Hajnal, and Karpinski show that a perfect matching can be found in a "dense" graph in NC^2 [76]. Karpinski and Wagner show that when G is given by its *vertex multiplicity graph* representation the problem becomes P-complete [200]. Using such succinct graph representations they are also able to show that the *Perfect Bipartite Matching Problem* is P-complete [200]. Grigoriev and Karpinski show that if the *permanent* of G is polynomially bounded, one can decide whether G has a perfect matching in NC^2. They show how to construct such a matching in NC^3 [143]. See Grigoriev, Karpinski, and Singer [144] and Karpinski [199] for additional related work. Osiakwan and Akl designed an EREW-PRAM algorithm for solving the *Maximum Weight Perfect Matching Problem* for complete weighted graphs. Their algorithm runs in $O(n^3/p + n^2 \log n)$ time for $p \le n$, where n is the number of vertices in the graph and p is the number of processors [275].

B.9.9   Subtree Isomorphism (STI)

Given: Two unrooted trees $T = (V, E)$ and $T' = (V', E')$.
Problem: Is T isomorphic to a subtree of T'? See Problem B.1.1 for the definition of isomorphism.
Reference: Gibbons *et al.* [118], Lingas and Karpinski [241].
Remarks: RNC^3 algorithms for the problem were developed independently in [118, 241]. Each uses randomization solely to solve a number of *Bipartite Matching Problems*, see Problem B.9.8. Lindell shows that the problem of determining whether two unrooted

trees are isomorphic, namely the *Tree Isomorphism Problem*, can be solved in $DLOG$; therefore, on an EREW-PRAM in $\log n$ time using $n^{O(1)}$ processors [238].

Appendix C

Notation

In this appendix we describe the notation used throughout the book. For standard concepts we do not present a definition here but simply explain our notation. Items not defined in the book but that are perhaps less familiar are defined here. For concepts that are defined in the book, we reference the page on which the concept is defined.

RAM   Random access machine.

PRAM   Parallel random access machine.

$\mathbb{R}$ The set of real numbers.

$\mathbb{Q}$ The set of rational numbers.

$\mathbb{Z}$ The set of integers.

$\mathbb{Z}_2$ The integers mod 2.

$\mathbb{N}$ The set of natural numbers.

$\lceil x \rceil$ The least integer not less than x.

$\lfloor x \rfloor$ The greatest integer not exceeding x.

$\log n$ The maximum of 1 and $\lceil \log_2 n \rceil$. (Note, sometimes we include $\lceil \ \rceil$ for emphasis.)

$|x|$ The length of string x or the absolute value of number x.

$\|x\|$ The L_2 norm of vector x. That is, $\left(\sum x_i^2\right)^{1/2}$.

$|S|$ The cardinality of set S.

(x, y) The ordered pair consisting of x and y. If x and y are vertices in a graph, this pair is often the directed edge from x to y.

$\vee$ The OR function.

$\wedge$	The AND function.
$\oplus$	Exclusive OR, also denoted XOR.
ϵ	The empty string.
Σ	A finite alphabet.
Σ^*	All finite strings over the alphabet Σ.
$\Sigma^{\leq n}$	All strings over the alphabet Σ of length less than or equal to n.
$\equiv$	Is equivalent to.
$\cdot$	Concatenation of strings or concatenation of languages (depending on context).

$O(f(n))$ The set of functions of growth rate order $f(n)$. Let f and g be two functions whose domains are the natural numbers and whose ranges are the positive real numbers. $g(n) = O(f(n))$ (or more precisely, $g(n) \in O(f(n))$) if and only if there exist constants $c > 0$ and $n_0 \in \mathbb{N}$ such that $g(n) \leq cf(n)$ for all natural numbers $n \geq n_0$. For example $g(n) = O(1)$ means that $g(n)$ is bounded above by some constant. The following three items are special cases of this. (See Graham, Knuth, and Patashnik for a general discussion of asymptotic notation [131].)

$n^{O(1)}$ The set of polynomially bounded functions. $f(n) = n^{O(1)}$ means that f is bounded above by some polynomial.

$f(n)^{O(1)}$ The set of functions that are polynomial in $f(n)$; equivalently

$$f(n)^{O(1)} = \bigcup_{k \geq 0} f(n)^k.$$

$(\log n)^{O(1)}$ A polylogarithmic bounded function; the set of functions that are polynomial in $\log n$; equivalently

$$f(n)^{O(1)} = \bigcup_{k \geq 0} (\log n)^k.$$

$\Omega(f(n))$ The set of functions whose growth rate is at least order $f(n)$. Let f and g be two functions whose domains are the natural numbers and whose ranges are the positive real numbers. $g(n) = \Omega(f(n))$ if and only if there exist constants $c > 0$ and $n_0 \in \mathbb{N}$ such that $g(n) \geq cf(n)$ for all natural numbers $n \geq n_0$.

$o(f(n))$ Functions growing asymptotically slower than $f(n)$. Let f and g be two functions whose domains are the natural numbers and whose ranges are the positive real numbers. $g(n) = o(f(n))$ if and only if

$$\lim_{n \to \infty} \frac{g(n)}{f(n)} = 0.$$

$\omega(f(n))$ Functions growing asymptotically faster than $f(n)$. Let f and g be two functions whose domains are the natural numbers and whose ranges are the positive real numbers. $g(n) = \omega(f(n))$ if and only if

$$\lim_{n \to \infty} \frac{g(n)}{f(n)} = \infty.$$

$\tilde{O}(f(n))$ The set of functions of growth rate order $(\log n)^k f(n)$. Let f and g be two functions whose domains are the natural numbers and whose ranges are the positive real numbers. $g(n) = \tilde{O}(f(n))$ (or more precisely, $g(n) \in \tilde{O}(f(n))$) if and only if there exist constants $c > 0$, $k > 0$, and $n_0 \in \mathbb{N}$ such that $g(n) \leq c(\log n)^k f(n)$ for all natural numbers $n \geq n_0$.

$\leq_m$ Many-one reducibility, see page 47.

$\leq_m^{NC}$ NC many-one reducibility, see page 47.

$\leq_m^{NC^k}$ NC^k many-one reducibility (for $k \geq 1$), see page 47.

$\leq_m^{log}$ Many-one logarithmic space reducibility, see page 54.

$\leq_T$ Turing reducibility, see page 50.

$\leq_T^{NC}$ NC Turing reducibility for PRAM, see page 50.

$\leq_T^{NC}$ NC Turing reducibility for circuits, see page 53.

$\leq_T^{NC^k}$ NC^k Turing reducibility for circuits (for $k \geq 1$), see page 53.

Appendix D

Complexity Classes

In this appendix we provide a list of the complexity classes mentioned in the book. When appropriate, we present the "name" of the class. For those classes that are formally defined in the book, we give a page reference to the definition. Other classes that are mentioned but not defined in the text are defined here. Often a class can be defined in terms of several different models; we present just one definition. After listing the classes, we provide a brief section exhibiting some of the relationships among the classes. An excellent reference for complexity class definitions, alternative definitions, and for a broader view of how all the classes interrelate is Johnson [177].

D.1 Definitions

In what follows n denotes the size of the input.

- AC^k

    - The class AC^k, for each $k \geq 0$, is the set of all languages L, such that L is recognized by a uniform, unbounded fanin, circuit family $\{\alpha_n\}$ with $\text{size}(\alpha_n) = n^{O(1)}$ and $\text{depth}(\alpha_n) = O((\log n)^k)$.

    - The type of uniformity usually applied in the definition is logarithmic space uniformity, except for AC^0 which is usually defined with $DLOGTIME$ uniformity. That is, the circuit description can be computed by a random access deterministic Turing machine in $O(\log n)$ time.

- *AC*

  - The class $AC = \bigcup_{k \geq 0} AC^k$.

- *ALOG*

  - Alternating logarithmic space, sometimes denoted $ASPACE(\log n)$.
  - The class *ALOG* is the set of all languages L that are decidable by alternating Turing machines whose space is bounded by $O(\log n)$.

- *CC*

  - Comparator Circuit Value.
  - The class *CC* is the set of all languages L that are logarithmic space reducible to Comparator Circuit Value, Problem B.8.1.

- *DET*

  - Determinant
  - The class *DET* is the set of all languages that are NC^1 Turing reducible to the Integer Determinant Problem. The *Integer Determinant Problem* is the problem of computing the determinant of an $n \times n$ matrix having n-bit integer entries.

- *DLOG*

  - Deterministic logarithmic space, sometimes denoted $DSPACE(\log n)$ or *DL*.
  - The class *DLOG* is the set of all languages L that are decidable by deterministic Turing machines whose space is bounded by $O(\log n)$.

- *DLOGTIME*

  - Deterministic logarithmic time.
  - The class *DLOGTIME* is the set of all languages L that are decidable by random access deterministic Turing machines in time $O(\log n)$.

- FNC^k

  - The class FNC^k, for each $k \geq 1$, is the set of all functions F, such that F is computable by a uniform, bounded fanin, circuit family $\{\alpha_n\}$ with $\text{size}(\alpha_n) = n^{O(1)}$ and $\text{depth}(\alpha_n) = O((\log n)^k)$.

  - The type of uniformity usually applied in the definition is logarithmic space uniformity, except for FNC^1 where $DLOGTIME$ uniformity is appropriate.

- FNC

  - Function NC.

  - The class $FNC = \bigcup_{k \geq 1} FNC^k$.

- FP

  - Function P.

  - The class FP is the set of all functions F that are computable in sequential time $n^{O(1)}$.

- $FRNC^k$

  - The class $FRNC^k$, for each $k \geq 1$, is the set of all functions F, such that F is computable by a uniform probabilistic circuit family $\{\alpha_n\}$ with $\text{size}(\alpha_n) = n^{O(1)}$ and $\text{depth}(\alpha_n) = O((\log n)^k)$ and having error probability at most $1/4$.

  - The type of uniformity usually applied in the definition is logarithmic space uniformity, except for $FRNC^1$ where $DLOGTIME$ uniformity is appropriate.

- $FRNC$

  - Function RNC.

  - The class $FRNC = \bigcup_{k \geq 1} FRNC^k$.

- $LOGCFL$

  - The class $LOGCFL$ is the set of all languages L that are logarithmic space reducible to a context-free language.

- *LOGDCFL*

  - The class *LOGDCFL* is the set of all languages L that are
    logarithmic space reducible to a deterministic context-free
    language.

- NC^k

  - NC k (for $k \geq 1$), see definition on page 45.

- NC^1

  - NC one, see definition on page 45.

- NC^0

  - NC zero

  - The class NC^0 is the set of all languages L such that L
    is recognized by a *DLOGTIME* uniform Boolean circuit
    family $\{\alpha_n\}$ with $\text{size}(\alpha_n) = n^{O(1)}$ and $\text{depth}(\alpha_n) = O(1)$.

- *NC*

  - Nick's Class, see definitions on pages 44 and 45.

- *NLOG*

  - Nondeterministic logarithmic space, sometimes denoted
    NSPACE$(\log n)$ or *NL*.

  - The class *NLOG* is the set of all languages L that are de-
    cidable by nondeterministic Turing machines whose space
    is bounded by $O(\log n)$.

- *NP*

  - Nondeterministic polynomial time.

  - The class *NP* is the set of all languages L that are decid-
    able by a nondeterministic Turing machine in time $n^{O(1)}$.

- $\#P$

  - Number P, or sharp P.

- We present the definition given in Johnson [177]. A *counting Turing machine* (CTM) is a nondeterministic Turing machine whose output on a given input string is the number of accepting computations for that input.
- The class $\#P$ is the set of all functions F that are computable by CTMs that run in polynomial time.

• *P*

  - Polynomial time, see definition page 44.

• *PH*

  - Polynomial time hierarchy.
    Let $\Sigma_0^P = P$.
  - The class Σ_{k+1}^P, for $k \geq 0$, is the set of all languages L that are decidable in nondeterministic polynomial time with an oracle to a problem in Σ_k^P.
  - The class $PH = \bigcup_{k \geq 0} \Sigma_k^P$.

• *PLS*

  - Polynomial local search.
  - The following definitions are taken from Schäffer and Yannakakis [324]. A local search problem P_s is a computation problem (search problem) such that each feasible solution S to an instance x (the set of feasible solutions is denoted $\mathcal{F}(x)$, so $S \in \mathcal{F}(x)$) has an integer measure $\mu(S, x)$. $\mu(S, x)$ will be either maximized or minimized. Every solution $S \in \mathcal{F}(x)$ also has a set of neighboring solutions denoted $\mathcal{N}(S, x)$. A solution S is *locally optimal* if it does not have a strictly better neighbor. That is, one with larger (smaller) measure in the case of a maximization (respectively, minimization) problem. The specification of P_s includes a set of instances $\mathcal{I}$. A *local search problem* is given an input instance $x \in \mathcal{I}$ to find a locally optimal solution.
  - A local search problem P_s is in the class *PLS* of *polynomial local time search problems* if the following three polynomial time algorithms exist.
    1. Algorithm A, on input $x \in \mathcal{I}$, computes an initial feasible solution belonging to $\mathcal{F}(x)$.

   2. Algorithm M, on input $x \in \mathcal{I}$ and $S \in \mathcal{F}(x)$, computes $\mu(S, x)$.

   3. Algorithm C, on input $x \in \mathcal{I}$ and $S \in \mathcal{F}(x)$, either determines that S is locally optimal or finds a better solution in $\mathcal{N}(S, x)$.

- *PSPACE*

  - Polynomial space.

  - The class *PSPACE* is the set of all languages L that are decidable by Turing machines whose space is bounded by $n^{O(1)}$.

- *RNC*

  - Random *NC*, see definition on page 46.

- *SAC^k*

  - The class *SAC^k*, for each $k \geq 1$, is the set of all languages L, such that L is decidable by a uniform circuit family $\{\alpha_n\}$ with size(α_n) = $n^{O(1)}$ and depth(α_n) = $O((\log n)^k)$, where OR gates are allowed to have unbounded fanin and AND gates are required to have bounded fanin.

  - The type of uniformity usually applied in the definition is logarithmic space uniformity.

- *SAC*

  - Semi-unbounded circuits.

  - The class $SAC = \bigcup_{k \geq 1} SAC^k$.

- *SC^k*

  - The class *SC^k*, for $k \geq 1$, is the set of all languages L that are decidable by deterministic Turing machines whose space is bounded by $O((\log n)^k)$ and whose time is simultaneously bounded by $n^{O(1)}$.

- *SC*

  - Steve's Class.

  - The class $SC = \bigcup_{k \geq 1} SC^k$.

- *SLOG*

  - Symmetric logarithmic space, sometimes denoted SL.
  - The class $SLOG$ is the set of all languages L that are decidable by symmetric Turing machines whose space usage on an input of length n is bounded by $O(\log n)$.

- *SP*

  - Semi-efficient parallel time.
  - The class SP consists of those problems whose sequential running time $t(n)$ can be improved to $T(n) = t(n)^\epsilon$, $\epsilon < 1$, using $P(n) = t(n)^{O(1)}$ processors.

D.2 Relationships   Among   Complexity Classes

In this section we mention some of the relationships among the complexity classes discussed in this book. (Note that we have abused notation slightly to include relations between language classes like AC and function classes like DET.)

$$SAC^0 \subseteq AC^0 \subseteq NC^1 \subseteq SAC^1 \subseteq AC^1 \subseteq \cdots \subseteq NC^k \subseteq SAC^k \subseteq AC^k$$

$$NC = SAC = AC \subseteq P$$

$$NC^1 \subseteq DLOG = SC^1 \subseteq SLOG \subseteq NLOG \subseteq LOGCFL = SAC^1$$

$$DLOG \subseteq LOGDCFL \subseteq LOGCFL$$

$$NLOG \subseteq DET \subseteq AC^1$$

$$LOGDCFL \subseteq SC^2 \subseteq SC^3 \subseteq \cdots \subseteq SC \subseteq P$$

$$DLOG \subseteq SLOG \subseteq NLOG \subseteq ALOG = P$$

$$CC \subseteq P \subseteq NP = \Sigma_1^P \subseteq \Sigma_2^P \subseteq \cdots \subseteq \Sigma_k^P \subseteq PH \subseteq PSPACE$$

$$NP \subseteq \#P \subseteq PSPACE$$

Bibliography

The numbers in parentheses at the end of each entry in the bibliography are the page numbers on which that item is referenced.

[1] K. R. Abrahamson, N. Dadoun, D. G. Kirkpatrick, and T. Przytycka. A simple parallel tree contraction algorithm. *Journal of Algorithms*, 10(2):287–302, 1989.   (66)

[2] K. R. Abrahamson, M. Fellows, and C. Wilson. Parallel self-reducibility. In W. W. Koczkodaj, P. E. Lauer, and A. A. Toptsis, editors, *Proceedings of the Fourth International Conference on Computing and Information*, pages 67–70, Toronto, Ont., Canada, May 1992. IEEE.   (40)

[3] F. Afrati. The parallel complexity of single rule logic programs. *Discrete Applied Mathematics*, 40(2):107–126, 10 December 1992. (173)

[4] F. Afrati and C. H. Papadimitriou. The parallel complexity of simple logic programs. *Journal of the ACM*, 40(4):891–916, September 1993.   (173)

[5] A. Aggarwal and R. J. Anderson. A Random *NC* algorithm for depth first search. *Combinatorica*, 8(1):1–12, 1988.   (145, 239, 240)

[6] A. Aggarwal, R. J. Anderson, and M.-Y. Kao. Parallel depth-first search in general directed graphs. *SIAM Journal on Computing*, 19(2):397–409, April 1990.   (145, 239, 240)

[7] A. V. Aho, J. E. Hopcroft, and J. D. Ullman. *The Design and Analysis of Computer Algorithms*. Addison-Wesley, revised edition, 1975.   (96)

[8] J. Albert and K. Culik, II. A simple universal cellular automata and its one-way totalistic versions. *Complex Systems*, 1(1):1–16, 1987.   (217)

[9] E. W. Allender. *P*-uniform circuit complexity. *Journal of the ACM*, 36(4):912–928, October 1989.   (15, 32)

[10]   N. Alon, L. Babai, and A. Itai. A fast and simple randomized par-
       allel algorithm for the maximal independent set problem. *Journal of
       Algorithms*, 7(4):567–583, December 1986.   (128)

[11]   C. Àlvarez, J. L. Balcázar, J. Gabarró, and M. Sántha. Parallel com-
       plexity in the design and analysis of concurrent systems. In E. Aarts,
       J. van Leeuwen, and M. Rem, editors, *PARLE '91 Parallel Architec-
       tures and Languages Europe: Volume I*, volume 505 of *Lecture Notes
       in Computer Science*, pages 288–303, Eindhoven, The Netherlands,
       June 1991. Springer-Verlag.   (181, 228)

[12]   R. J. Anderson. *The Complexity of Parallel Algorithms*. PhD thesis,
       Stanford University, 1985. Computer Science Department Technical
       Report STAN-CS-86-1092.   (89, 94–96, 102, 145, 146, 148, 164, 241)

[13]   R. J. Anderson. A parallel algorithm for the maximal path problem.
       Combinatorica, 7(4):315–326, 1987.   (144, 240)

[14]   R. J. Anderson and E. W. Mayr. A *P*-complete problem and ap-
       proximations to it. Technical Report STAN-CS-84-1014, Stanford
       University, 1984.   (133)

[15]   R. J. Anderson and E. W. Mayr. Parallelism and greedy algorithms.
       In *Advances in Computing Research*, volume 4, pages 17–38. JAI
       Press, 1987.   (154, 239)

[16]   R. J. Anderson and E. W. Mayr. Parallelism and the maximal path
       problem. *Information Processing Letters*, 24(2):121–126, 1987.
                                                            (99, 144, 240)

[17]   R. J. Anderson, E. W. Mayr, and M. K. Warmuth. Parallel approx-
       imation algorithms for bin packing. *Information and Computation*,
       82(3):262–277, September 1989.   (93, 95, 112, 154, 155)

[18]   M. J. Atallah, P. Callahan, and M. T. Goodrich. *P*-complete geo-
       metric problems. In *Proceedings of the 1990 ACM Symposium on
       Parallel Algorithms and Architectures*, pages 317–326, Crete, Greece,
       July 1990.   (201–204, 233)

[19]   J. Avenhaus and K. Madlener. The Nielsen reduction and *P*-complete
       problems in free groups. *Theoretical Computer Science*, 32(1,2):61–
       76, 1984.   (189–192)

[20]   J. Avenhaus and K. Madlener. On the complexity of intersection and
       conjugacy in free groups. *Theoretical Computer Science*, 32(3):279–
       295, 1984.   (192–194)

[21]   L. Babai, S. Seres, and E. M. Luks. Permutation groups in *NC*. In
       *Proceedings of the Nineteenth Annual ACM Symposium on Theory
       of Computing*, pages 409–420, New York, NY, May 1987.   (232)

[22] A. Bachem and R. Kannan. Lattices and the basis reduction algorithm. Technical Report CMU-CS-84-112, Carnegie-Mellon University, Dept. of Computer Science, 1984.   (234)

[23] J. L. Balcázar, J. Gabarró, and M. Sántha. Deciding bisimilarity is P-complete. *Formal Aspects of Computing*, 4(6A):638–648, 1992.
                                                                      (181, 228)

[24] D. A. M. Barrington, N. Immerman, and H. Straubing. On uniformity within NC^1. *Journal of Computer and System Sciences*, 41(3):274–306, December 1990.   (15, 32, 33)

[25] D. A. M. Barrington and P. McKenzie. Oracle branching programs and logspace versus P. *Information and Computation*, 95(1):96–115, November 1991.   (170)

[26] P. W. Beame, S. A. Cook, and H. J. Hoover. Log depth circuits for division and related problems. *SIAM Journal on Computing*, 15(4):994–1003, November 1986.   (32, 53)

[27] P. W. Beame and M. Luby. Parallel search for maximal independence given minimal dependence. In *Proceedings of the First Annual ACM-SIAM Symposium on Discrete Algorithms*, pages 212–218, San Francisco, CA, January 1990. ACM.   (225)

[28] M. Beaudry, P. McKenzie, and P. Péladeau. Circuits with monoidal gates. In Finkel et al. [107], pages 555–565.   (127)

[29] M. Beaudry, P. McKenzie, and D. Thérien. The membership problem in aperiodic transformation monoids. *Journal of the ACM*, 39(3):599–616, July 1992.   (200)

[30] M. Ben-Or, E. Feig, D. C. Kozen, and P. Tiwari. A fast parallel algorithm for determining all roots of a polynomial with real roots. *SIAM Journal on Computing*, 17(6):1081–1092, December 1988.
                                                                      (234)

[31] B. Berger. The fourth moment method. In *Proceedings of the Second Annual ACM-SIAM Symposium on Discrete Algorithms*, pages 373–383, San Francisco, CA, January 1991. ACM.   (141)

[32] B. Berger and P. W. Shor. Approximation algorithms for the maximum acyclic subgraph problem. In *Proceedings of the First Annual ACM-SIAM Symposium on Discrete Algorithms*, pages 236–243, San Francisco, CA, January 1990. ACM.   (141)

[33] E. R. Berlekamp, J. H. Conway, and R. K. Guy. *Winning Ways for Your Mathematical Plays*, volume 2: Games in Particular. Academic Press, 1982.   (211)

[34] A. Bertoni, M. C. Bollina, G. Mauri, and N. Sabadini. On characterizing classes of efficiently parallelizable problems. In P. Bertolazzi and F. Luccio, editors, *VLSI: Algorithms and Architectures, Proceedings of the International Workshop on Parallel Computing and VLSI*, pages 13–26, Amalfi, Italy, May 1984 (published 1985). North-Holland.   (197, 198)

[35] G. E. Blelloch. Scans as primitive parallel operations. In *International Conference on Parallel Processing*, pages 355–362, 1987. (64)

[36] G. E. Blelloch. Prefix sums and their applications. In Reif [302], chapter 1, pages 35–60.   (64)

[37] J. A. Bondy and U. S. R. Murty. *Graph Theory with Applications*. MacMillan, 1976. Revised paperback edition, 1977.   (132)

[38] G. Bongiovanni, P. Crescenzi, and S. De Agostino. Two *P*-complete approximation algorithms. Manuscript, submitted 1993.   (165)

[39] R. B. Boppana and J. C. Lagarias. One way functions and circuit complexity. In A. L. Selman, editor, *Structure in Complexity Theory*, volume 223 of *Lecture Notes in Computer Science*, pages 51–66, Berkeley, CA, June 1986. Springer-Verlag.   (126)

[40] A. Borodin. On relating time and space to size and depth. *SIAM Journal on Computing*, 6(4):733–744, December 1977.
                                         (15, 16, 19, 27, 31, 54, 64, 67, 68, 119)

[41] A. Borodin. Structured *vs.* general models in computational complexity. *L'Enseignement Mathématique*, XXVIII(3-4):171–190, July-December 1982. Also in [244, pages 47–65].   (61)

[42] A. Borodin, S. A. Cook, and N. J. Pippenger. Parallel computation for well-endowed rings and space-bounded probabilistic machines. *Information and Control*, 58(1-3):113–136, 1983.   (229)

[43] A. Borodin, J. von zur Gathen, and J. E. Hopcroft. Fast parallel matrix and GCD computations. *Information and Control*, 52(3):241–256, 1982.   (188, 229)

[44] D. P. Bovet, S. De Agostino, and R. Petreschi. Parallelism and the feedback vertex set problem. *Information Processing Letters*, 28(2):81–85, June 1988.   (139, 140)

[45] J. F. Boyar and H. J. Karloff. Coloring planar graphs in parallel. *Journal of Algorithms*, 8(4):470–479, 1987.   (132)

[46] A. Z. Broder. How hard is it to marry at random? (On the approximation of the permanent). In *Proceedings of the Eighteenth Annual ACM Symposium on Theory of Computing*, pages 50–58, Berkeley, CA, May 1986. Errata: *Proceedings of the Twentieth Annual ACM Symposium on Theory of Computing*, page 551, Chicago, IL, May 1988.   (142, 143)

[47]   R. L. Brooks. On coloring the nodes of a network. *Proceedings of the Cambridge Philosophical Society*, 37:194–197, 1941.   (132)

[48]   J. F. Buss and J. Goldsmith. Nondeterminism within *P*. In C. Choffrut and M. Jantzen, editors, *STACS 91: 8th Annual Symposium on Theoretical Aspects of Computer Science*, volume 480 of *Lecture Notes in Computer Science*, pages 348–359, Hamburg, Germany, February 1991. Springer-Verlag.   (215)

[49]   A. K. Chandra, D. C. Kozen, and L. J. Stockmeyer. Alternation. *Journal of the ACM*, 28(1):114–133, January 1981. (19, 32, 66, 129)

[50]   A. K. Chandra and L. J. Stockmeyer. Alternation. In *17th Annual Symposium on Foundations of Computer Science*, pages 98–108, Houston, TX, October 1976. IEEE. Preliminary Version.
                    (15, 68, 209)

[51]   A. K. Chandra and M. Tompa. The complexity of short two-person games. *Discrete Applied Mathematics*, 29(1):21–33, November 1990.
                    (210)

[52]   C. L. Chang and R. C. T. Lee. *Symbolic Logic and Mechanical Theorem Proving*. Academic Press, 1973.   (167, 171)

[53]   B. Chazelle. On the convex layers of a planar set. *IEEE Transactions on Information Theory*, IT-31(4):509–517, 1985.   (205)

[54]   J. Cheriyan and S. N. Maheshwari. The parallel complexity of finding a blocking flow in a 3-layer network. *Information Processing Letters*, 31(3):157–161, 1989.   (154, 239)

[55]   B. Chlebus, K. Diks, W. Rytter, and T. Szymacha. Parallel complexity of lexicographically first problems for tree-structured graphs. In A. Kreczmar and G. Mirkowska, editors, *Mathematical Foundations of Computer Science 1989: Proceedings, 14th Symposium*, volume 379 of *Lecture Notes in Computer Science*, pages 185–195, Porąbka-Kozubnik, Poland, August-September 1989. Springer-Verlag.   (132, 146)

[56]   B. Chor and O. Goldreich. An improved parallel algorithm for integer GCD. *Algorithmica*, 5:1–10, 1990.   (230)

[57]   R. Cole and U. Vishkin. The accelerated centroid decomposition technique for optimal tree evaluation in logarithmic time. *Algorithmica*, 3(3):329–346, 1988.   (66)

[58]   A. Condon. A theory of strict *P*-completeness. In A. Finkel and M. Jantzen, editors, *STACS 92: 9th Annual Symposium on Theoretical Aspects of Computer Science*, volume 577 of *Lecture Notes in Computer Science*, pages 33–44, Cachan, France, February 1992. Springer-Verlag.   (103–107)

[59] M. P. Consens and A. O. Mendelzon. Low complexity aggregation in GraphLog and Datalog. In S. Abiteboul and P. C. Kanellakis, editors, *ICDT '90. Third International Conference on Database Theory Proceedings*, volume 470 of *Lecture Notes in Computer Science*, pages 379–394, Paris, France, 12-14 December 1990. Springer-Verlag. (175)

[60] S. A. Cook. Path systems and language recognition. In *Conference Record of Second Annual ACM Symposium on Theory of Computing*, pages 70–72, Northampton, MA, May 1970. (171)

[61] S. A. Cook. Characterizations of pushdown machines in terms of time-bounded computers. *Journal of the ACM*, 18(1):4–18, January 1971. (66, 179)

[62] S. A. Cook. The complexity of theorem proving procedures. In *Conference Record of Third Annual ACM Symposium on Theory of Computing*, pages 151–158, Shaker Heights, OH, May 1971. (75, 167)

[63] S. A. Cook. An observation on time-storage trade off. In *Conference Record of Fifth Annual ACM Symposium on Theory of Computing*, pages 29–33, Austin, TX, April-May 1973. (13, 14)

[64] S. A. Cook. An observation on time-storage trade off. *Journal of Computer and System Sciences*, 9(3):308–316, December 1974.
(14, 54, 171)

[65] S. A. Cook. Deterministic CFL's are accepted simultaneously in polynomial time and log squared space. In *Conference Record of the Eleventh Annual ACM Symposium on Theory of Computing*, pages 338–345, Atlanta, GA, April-May 1979. See also [367]. (15, 32, 67)

[66] S. A. Cook. Towards a complexity theory of synchronous parallel computation. *L'Enseignement Mathématique*, XXVII(1–2):99–124, January-June 1981. Also in [244, pages 75–100]. (21)

[67] S. A. Cook. A taxonomy of problems with fast parallel algorithms. *Information and Control*, 64(1–3):2–22, January/February/March 1985. (53, 78, 88, 89, 92, 128, 231)

[68] S. A. Cook and P. W. Dymond. Parallel pointer machines. *Computational Complexity*, 3(1):19–30, 1993. (19)

[69] S. A. Cook and R. Sethi. Storage requirements for deterministic polynomial time recognizable languages. *Journal of Computer and System Sciences*, 13(1):25–37, 1976. (69, 229)

[70] T. H. Cormen, C. E. Leiserson, and R. L. Rivest. *Introduction to Algorithms*. MIT Press, 1990. (71)

[71] S. S. Cosmadakis. The word and generator problems for lattices. *Information and Computation*, 77(3):192–217, 1988. (196, 197)

[72] L. Csanky. Fast parallel matrix inversion algorithms. *SIAM Journal on Computing*, 5(4):618–623, 1976. (188)

[73] F. Cucker and A. Torrecillas. Two *P*-complete problems in the theory of the reals. *Journal of Complexity*, 8(4):454–466, December 1992. (124, 151)

[74] E. Dahlhaus. Is SETL a suitable language for parallel programming — a theoretical approach. In E. Börger, H. Kleine Büning, and M. M. Richter, editors, *CSL '87: 1st Workshop on Computer Science Logic*, volume 329 of *Lecture Notes in Computer Science*, pages 56–63, Karlsruhe, West Germany, October 1987 (published 1988). Springer-Verlag. (174, 227)

[75] E. Dahlhaus. The complexity of subtheories of the existential linear theory of reals. In E. Börger, H. Kleine Büning, and M. M. Richter, editors, *CSL '89: 3rd Workshop on Computer Science Logic*, volume 440 of *Lecture Notes in Computer Science*, pages 76–89, Kaiserslautern, FRG, October 1989 (published 1990). Springer-Verlag. (152)

[76] E. Dahlhaus, P. Hajnal, and M. Karpinski. Optimal parallel algorithm for the Hamiltonian cycle problem on dense graphs. In *29th Annual Symposium on Foundations of Computer Science*, pages 186–193, White Plains, NY, October 1988. IEEE. (242)

[77] E. Dahlhaus, M. Karpinski, and P. Kelsen. An efficient parallel algorithm for computing a maximal independent set in a hypergraph of dimension 3. *Information Processing Letters*, 42(6):309–313, 24 July 1992. (225)

[78] B. DasGupta. Learning capabilities of recurrent neural networks. In *Proceedings SOUTHEASTCON '92, volume 2*, pages 822–823, Birmingham, AL, 12-15 April 1992. IEEE. (163)

[79] S. De Agostino. *P*-complete problems in data compression. *Theoretical Computer Science*, 127:181–186, 1994. (219)

[80] S. De Agostino and J. A. Storer. Parallel algorithms for optimal compression using dictionaries with the prefix property. In J. A. Storer and M. Cohn, editors, *Data Compression Conference*, pages 52–61, Snowbird, UT, March 1992. IEEE. (219)

[81] P. de la Torre and R. Greenlaw. Super critical tree numbering and optimal tree ranking are in *NC*. In *Proceedings of the Third IEEE Symposium on Parallel and Distributed Processing*, pages 767–773, Dallas, TX, December 1991. IEEE. (223)

[82] P. de la Torre, R. Greenlaw, and T. Przytycka. Optimal tree ranking is in *NC*. *Parallel Processing Letters*, 2(1):31–41, March 1992. (223)

[83] P. de la Torre, R. Greenlaw, and A. A. Schäffer. Optimal edge ranking of trees in polynomial time. Technical Report 92-10, University of New Hampshire, 1992. To appear, *Algorithmica*.   (199)

[84] P. de la Torre, R. Greenlaw, and A. A. Schäffer. Optimal edge ranking of trees in polynomial time. In *Proceedings of the Fourth Annual ACM-SIAM Symposium on Discrete Algorithms*, pages 138–144, Austin, TX, January 1993. ACM.   (198, 199, 223)

[85] P. de la Torre and C. P. Kruskal. Fast parallel algorithms for all sources lexicographic search and path finding problems. Technical Report Technical Report CS-TR 2283, University of Maryland, 1989. To appear, *Journal of Algorithms*.   (146, 148, 240)

[86] P. de la Torre and C. P. Kruskal. Fast and efficient parallel algorithms for single source lexicographic depth-first search, breadth-first search and topological-first search. In *International Conference on Parallel Processing*, volume 20, pages III–286–III–287, 1991. (146, 148, 240)

[87] A. L. Delcher and S. R. Kosaraju. An *NC* algorithm for evaluating monotone planar circuits. Manuscript, 1991.   (124)

[88] L. Denenberg. *Computational Complexity of Logical Problems*. PhD thesis, Harvard University, 1984.   (168, 169)

[89] L. Denenberg and H. R. Lewis. The complexity of the satisfiability problem for Krom formulas. *Theoretical Computer Science*, 30(3):319–341, 1984.   (168)

[90] X. Deng. On the parallel complexity of integer programming. In *Proceedings of the 1989 ACM Symposium on Parallel Algorithms and Architectures*, pages 110–116, Santa Fe, NM, June 1989.
                                                          (226, 229, 230)

[91] A. Dessmark, A. Lingas, and A. Maheshwari. Multi-list ranking: complexity and applications. In Finkel et al. [107], pages 306–316.
                                                          (199, 204, 205)

[92] E. A. Dinic. Algorithm for solution of a problem of maximum flow in a network with power estimation. *Soviet Math. Doklady*, 11(5):1277–1280, 1970.   (152)

[93] D. P. Dobkin, R. J. Lipton, and S. P. Reiss. Linear programming is log-space hard for *P*. *Information Processing Letters*, 8(2):96–97, February 1979.   (151, 167)

[94] D. P. Dobkin and S. P. Reiss. The complexity of linear programming. *Theoretical Computer Science*, 11(1):1–18, 1980.   (151)

[95] D. Dolev, E. Upfal, and M. K. Warmuth. The parallel complexity of scheduling with precedence constraints. *Journal of Parallel and Distributed Computing*, 3(4):553–576, 1986.   (156, 157)

[96] C. Dwork, P. C. Kanellakis, and J. C. Mitchell. On the sequential nature of unification. *Journal of Logic Programming*, 1(1):35–50, 1984. (171, 172, 174)

[97] C. Dwork, P. C. Kanellakis, and L. J. Stockmeyer. Parallel algorithms for term matching. *SIAM Journal on Computing*, 17(4):711–731, August 1988. (171, 172)

[98] P. W. Dymond. *Simultaneous Resource Bounds and Parallel Computation*. PhD thesis, University of Toronto, August 1980. Department of Computer Science Technical Report 145/80. (19)

[99] P. W. Dymond and S. A. Cook. Hardware complexity and parallel computation. In *21st Annual Symposium on Foundations of Computer Science*, pages 360–372, Syracuse, NY, October 1980. IEEE. (19, 68, 124)

[100] P. W. Dymond and S. A. Cook. Complexity theory of parallel time and hardware. *Information and Computation*, 80(3):205–226, March 1989. (19, 68, 124)

[101] P. W. Dymond and W. L. Ruzzo. Parallel random access machines with owned global memory and deterministic context-free language recognition. In L. Kott, editor, *Automata, Languages, and Programming: 13th International Colloquium*, volume 226 of *Lecture Notes in Computer Science*, pages 95–104, Rennes, France, July 1986. Springer-Verlag. (24, 176)

[102] P. W. Dymond and M. Tompa. Speedups of deterministic machines by synchronous parallel machines. *Journal of Computer and System Sciences*, 30(2):149–161, April 1985. (63, 69)

[103] T. Feather. The parallel complexity of some flow and matching problems. Master's thesis, University of Toronto, 1984. Department of Computer Science Technical Report 174/84. (152, 241)

[104] T. Feder. A new fixed point approach to stable networks and stable marriages. *Journal of Computer and System Sciences*, 45(2):233–284, October 1992. (235)

[105] F. E. Fich. The complexity of computation on the parallel random access machine. In Reif [302], chapter 20, pages 843–899. (17, 21, 24)

[106] F. E. Fich and M. Tompa. The parallel complexity of exponentiating polynomials over finite fields. *Journal of the ACM*, 35(3):651–667, July 1988. (231)

[107] A. Finkel, P. Enjalbert, and K. W. Wagner, editors. *STACS 93: 10th Annual Symposium on Theoretical Aspects of Computer Science*, volume 665 of *Lecture Notes in Computer Science*, Wurzburg, Germany, February 1993. Springer-Verlag. (257, 262, 279, 282)

[108] L. R. Ford and D. R. Fulkerson. *Flows in Networks.* Princeton University Press, 1962.   (152)

[109] S. Fortune and J. C. Wyllie. Parallelism in random access machines. In *Conference Record of the Tenth Annual ACM Symposium on Theory of Computing*, pages 114–118, San Diego, CA, May 1978.   (19, 22–24)

[110] M. L. Furst, J. E. Hopcroft, and E. M. Luks. Polynomial time algorithms for permutation groups. In *21st Annual Symposium on Foundations of Computer Science*, pages 36–41, Syracuse, NY, October 1980. IEEE.   (223)

[111] Z. Galil. Two way deterministic pushdown automaton languages and some open problems in the theory of computation. In *15th Annual Symposium on Switching and Automata Theory*, pages 170–177, 1974. Published in journal form as [112].   (14, 179)

[112] Z. Galil. Some open problems in the theory of computation as questions about two-way deterministic pushdown automaton languages. *Mathematical Systems Theory*, 10(3):211–228, 1977.   (14, 179, 264)

[113] M. R. Garey and D. S. Johnson. *Computers and Intractability: A Guide to the Theory of NP-Completeness.* W. H. Freeman and Company, 1979.   (x, 8, 47, 102, 111, 112, 132, 137, 141, 166, 189, 222)

[114] H. Gazit, G. L. Miller, and S.-H. Teng. Optimal tree contraction in the EREW model. In Tewksbury et al. [353], pages 139–156.   (66)

[115] M. Geréb-Graus, R. Paturi, and E. Szemerédi. There are no *P*-complete families of symmetric Boolean functions. *Information Processing Letters*, 30(1):47–49, 16 January 1989.   (16)

[116] A. M. Gibbons. *Algorithmic Graph Theory.* Cambridge University Press, 1985.   (237)

[117] A. M. Gibbons and W. Rytter. *Efficient Parallel Algorithms.* Cambridge University Press, 1988.   (16)

[118] P. B. Gibbons, R. M. Karp, G. L. Miller, and D. Soroker. Subtree isomorphism is in Random *NC*. *Discrete Applied Mathematics*, 29(1):35–62, November 1990.   (223, 242)

[119] G. Godbeer. The computational complexity of the stable configuration problem for connectionist models. Master's thesis, University of Toronto, 1987.   (163, 164, 224, 225)

[120] A. V. Goldberg and R. E. Tarjan. A parallel algorithm for finding a blocking flow in an acyclic network. *Information Processing Letters*, 31(5):265–271, 12 June 1989.   (154, 239)

[121] M. Goldberg and T. Spencer. A new parallel algorithm for the maximal independent set problem. *SIAM Journal on Computing*, 18(2):419–427, April 1989. (128)

[122] L. M. Goldschlager. The monotone and planar circuit value problems are log space complete for *P*. *SIGACT News*, 9(2):25–29, Summer 1977. (14, 79, 122, 123)

[123] L. M. Goldschlager. *Synchronous Parallel Computation*. PhD thesis, University of Toronto, December 1977. Computer Science Department Technical Report 114. (15)

[124] L. M. Goldschlager. A space efficient algorithm for the monotone planar circuit value problem. *Information Processing Letters*, 10(1):25–27, 1980. (124)

[125] L. M. Goldschlager. ϵ-productions in context-free grammars. *Acta Informatica*, 16(3):303–308, 1981. (176, 177)

[126] L. M. Goldschlager. A universal interconnection pattern for parallel computers. *Journal of the ACM*, 29(4):1073–1086, October 1982.
(15, 19, 22–24, 33, 68)

[127] L. M. Goldschlager and I. Parberry. On the construction of parallel computers from various bases of Boolean functions. *Theoretical Computer Science*, 43(1):43–58, 1986. (121)

[128] L. M. Goldschlager, R. A. Shaw, and J. Staples. The maximum flow problem is log space complete for *P*. *Theoretical Computer Science*, 21(1):105–111, October 1982. (16, 122, 152)

[129] G. B. Goodrich. *The Complexity of Finite Languages*. PhD thesis, University of Washington, 1983. (178, 179)

[130] M. T. Goodrich. Triangulating a polygon in parallel. *Journal of Algorithms*, 10(3):327–351, 1989. (201, 233)

[131] R. L. Graham, D. E. Knuth, and O. Patashnik. *Concrete Mathematics: A Foundation for Computer Science*. Addison-Wesley, 1989. (245)

[132] A. G. Greenberg, B. D. Lubachevsky, and L.-C. Wang. Experience in massively parallel discrete event simulation. In *Proceedings of the 1993 ACM Symposium on Parallel Algorithms and Architectures*, pages 193–202, Velen, Germany, June 1993. (220)

[133] R. Greenlaw. *The Complexity of Parallel Computations: Inherently Sequential Algorithms and P-Complete Problems*. PhD thesis, University of Washington, December 1988. Department of Computer Science Technical Report 88–12–01. (94, 96, 137, 146–148)

[134] R. Greenlaw. Ordered vertex removal and subgraph problems. *Journal of Computer and System Sciences*, 39(3):323–342, December 1989.   (133, 136, 139, 224, 225)

[135] R. Greenlaw. A model classifying algorithms as inherently sequential with applications to graph searching. *Information and Computation*, 97(2):133–149, April 1992.   (94, 95, 146, 147, 240)

[136] R. Greenlaw. The parallel complexity of approximation algorithms for the maximum acyclic subgraph problem. *Mathematical Systems Theory*, 25(3):161–175, 1992.   (140, 141)

[137] R. Greenlaw. Towards understanding the effective parallelization of sequential algorithms. In R. Baeza-Yates and U. Manber, editors, *Computer Science: Research and Applications*, chapter 30, pages 395–406. Plenum Press, 1992.   (140, 141)

[138] R. Greenlaw. Polynomial completeness and parallel computation. In Reif [302], chapter 21, pages 901–953.   (17)

[139] R. Greenlaw. Breadth-depth search is *P*-complete. *Parallel Processing Letters*, 3(3):209–222, 1993.   (147)

[140] R. Greenlaw, H. J. Hoover, and W. L. Ruzzo. *Limits to Parallel Computation: P-Completeness Theory* . Computing Science Series, editor Z. Galil. Oxford University Press, 1995. THIS WORK.
              (84, 109, 110, 123, 148, 169, 178, 180, 208, 211, 217, 232)

[141] R. Greenlaw and J. Machta. The parallel complexity of algorithms for pattern formation models. In *Canada/France Conference on Parallel Computing*, volume 805 of *Lecture Notes in Computer Science*, pages 23–34, Montreal, Canada, May 1994. Springer-Verlag.   (218)

[142] R. Greenlaw and J. Machta. The parallel complexity of Eden growth, solid-on-solid growth and ballistic deposition. In *Second European Symposium on Algorithms*, volume 855 of *Lecture Notes in Computer Science*, pages 436–447, Utrecht, The Netherlands, September 1994. Springer-Verlag.   (218)

[143] D. Y. Grigoriev and M. Karpinski. The matching problem for bipartite graphs with polynomially bounded permanents is in *NC*. In *28th Annual Symposium on Foundations of Computer Science*, pages 166–172, Los Angeles, CA, October 1987. IEEE.   (242)

[144] D. Y. Grigoriev, M. Karpinski, and M. F. Singer. Fast parallel algorithms for sparse multivariate polynomial interpolation over finite fields. *SIAM Journal on Computing*, 19(6):1059–1063, December 1990.   (242)

[145] T. Hagerup. Planar depth-first search in $O(\log n)$ parallel time. *SIAM Journal on Computing*, 19(4):678–704, August 1990.   (146)

[146] P. Hajnal and E. Szemerédi. Brooks coloring in parallel. *SIAM Journal on Discrete Mathematics*, 3(1):74–80, 1990.   (132)

[147] M. A. Harrison. *Introduction to Formal Language Theory.* Addison Wesley, 1979.   (180)

[148] J. Hartmanis, P. M. Lewis, II, and R. E. Stearns. Hierarchies of memory limited computations. In *Conference Record on Switching Circuit Theory and Logical Design*, pages 179–190, Ann Arbor, MI, 1965.   (70)

[149] J. Håstad. *Computational Limitations of Small-Depth Circuits.* MIT Press, 1987. ACM Doctoral Dissertation Award Series (1986).   (126)

[150] J. Håstad. One-way permutations in NC^0. *Information Processing Letters*, 26(3):153–155, 23 November 1987.   (126)

[151] X. He. Efficient parallel algorithms for solving some tree problems. In *Proceedings, Twenty-Fourth Annual Allerton Conference on Communication, Control and Computing*, pages 777–786, Monticello, IL, September 1986.   (66)

[152] X. He and Y. Yesha. A nearly optimal parallel algorithm for constructing depth first spanning trees in planar graphs. *SIAM Journal on Computing*, 17(3):486–491, 1988.   (146)

[153] D. Helmbold and E. W. Mayr. Perfect graphs and parallel algorithms. In *International Conference on Parallel Processing*, pages 853–860. IEEE, 1986.   (156)

[154] D. Helmbold and E. W. Mayr. Fast scheduling algorithms on parallel computers. In *Advances in Computing Research*, volume 4, pages 39–68. JAI Press, 1987.   (101, 102, 155, 156)

[155] F. Henglein. Fast left-linear semi-unification. In S. G. Akl, F. Fiala, and W. W. Koczkodaj, editors, *Advances in Computing and Information – ICCI '90*, volume 468 of *Lecture Notes in Computer Science*, pages 82–91, Niagara Falls, Ont., Canada, May 1990. Springer-Verlag.   (173, 174, 227)

[156] J. Hershberger. Upper envelope onion peeling. *Computational Geometry: Theory and Applications*, 2(2):93–110, October 1992.
                                                                   (203, 204)

[157] J.-W. Hong. Similarity and duality in computation. *Information and Control*, 62(1):109–128, 1984.   (67)

[158] H. J. Hoover. Feasible real functions and arithmetic circuits. *SIAM Journal on Computing*, 19(1):182–204, February 1990.   (206)

[159] H. J. Hoover. Real functions, contraction mappings, and *P*-completeness. *Information and Computation*, 93(2):333–349, August 1991.   (206, 207)

[160] H. J. Hoover, M. M. Klawe, and N. J. Pippenger. Bounding fan-out in logical networks. *Journal of the ACM*, 31(1):13–18, January 1984.   (29)

[161] J. E. Hopcroft and J. D. Ullman. *Formal Languages and their Relation to Automata*. Addison-Wesley, 1969.   (58)

[162] J. E. Hopcroft and J. D. Ullman. *Introduction to Automata Theory, Languages, and Computation*. Addison-Wesley, 1979. (58, 179, 180)

[163] E. Horowitz and S. Sahni. *Fundamentals of Computer Algorithms*. Computer Science Press, 1978.   (146)

[164] R. A. Howard. *Dynamic Programming and Markov Processes*. MIT Press, 1960.   (185)

[165] O. H. Ibarra, T. Jiang, and J. H. Chang. On iterative and cellular tree arrays. *Journal of Computer and System Sciences*, 38(3):452–473, June 1989.   (182, 183)

[166] O. H. Ibarra and S. M. Kim. Characterizations and computational complexity of systolic trellis automata. *Theoretical Computer Science*, 29(1,2):123–153, 1984.   (182)

[167] O. H. Ibarra, S. Moran, and L. E. Rosier. A note on the parallel complexity of computing the rank of order n matrices. *Information Processing Letters*, 11(4-5):162, 12 December 1980.   (188)

[168] N. Immerman. Number of quantifiers is better than number of tape cells. *Journal of Computer and System Sciences*, 22(3):384–406, 1981.   (129)

[169] N. Immerman. Languages that capture complexity classes. *SIAM Journal on Computing*, 16(4):760–778, 1987.   (129)

[170] Institute for New Generation Computer Technology (ICOT), editor. *Fifth Generation Computer Systems 1988: Proceedings of the International Conference on Fifth Generation Computer Systems 1988*, Tokyo, Japan, November-December 1988. OHMSHA, LTD./Springer-Verlag.   (275)

[171] A. Itai. Two–commodity flow. *Journal of the ACM*, 25(4):596–611, 1978.   (151, 153)

[172] J. JáJá. *An Introduction to Parallel Algorithms*. Addison-Wesley, 1992.   (17)

[173] M. Jerrum and A. Sinclair. Conductance and the rapid mixing property for Markov chains: The approximation of the permanent resolved. In *Proceedings of the Twentieth Annual ACM Symposium on Theory of Computing*, pages 235–244, Chicago, IL, May 1988. (143)

[174] D. B. Johnson. Parallel algorithms for minimum cuts and maximum flows in planar networks. *Journal of the ACM*, 34(4):950–967, 1987.
(153)

[175] D. B. Johnson and S. M. Venkatesan. Parallel algorithms for minimum cuts and maximum flows in planar networks (preliminary version). In *23rd Annual Symposium on Foundations of Computer Science*, pages 244–254, Chicago, IL, November 1982. IEEE. (153)

[176] D. S. Johnson. The *NP*-completeness column: An ongoing guide (7th). *Journal of Algorithms*, 4(2):189–203, 1983. (21)

[177] D. S. Johnson. A catalog of complexity classes. In van Leeuwen [360], chapter 2, pages 67–161. (14, 17, 51, 247, 251)

[178] D. S. Johnson, C. H. Papadimitriou, and M. Yannakakis. How easy is local search? *Journal of Computer and System Sciences*, 37(1):79–100, 1988. (158, 159, 161)

[179] N. D. Jones. Space-bounded reducibility among combinatorial problems. *Journal of Computer and System Sciences*, 11:68–85, 1975. (14)

[180] N. D. Jones and W. T. Laaser. Complete problems for deterministic polynomial time. In *Conference Record of Sixth Annual ACM Symposium on Theory of Computing*, pages 40–46, Seattle, WA, April-May 1974. (14)

[181] N. D. Jones and W. T. Laaser. Complete problems for deterministic polynomial time. *Theoretical Computer Science*, 3(1):105–117, 1976.
(14, 54, 167, 170, 171, 176, 177, 196, 208)

[182] Y. Kaji, R. Nakanishi, H. Seki, and T. Kasami. The universal recognition problems for parallel multiple context-free grammars and for their subclasses. *IEICE Transactions on Information and Systems*, E75-D(4):499–508, July 1992. (176)

[183] P. C. Kanellakis and S. A. Smolka. CCS expressions, finite state processes, and three problems of equivalence. *Information and Computation*, 86(1):43–68, May 1990. (183)

[184] R. Kannan, G. L. Miller, and L. Rudolph. Sublinear parallel algorithm for computing the greatest common divisor of two integers. *SIAM Journal on Computing*, 16(1):7–16, February 1987. (229, 230)

[185] W. M. Kantor. Sylow's theorem in polynomial time. *Journal of Computer and System Sciences*, 30(3):359–394, 1985. (232)

[186] M.-Y. Kao. All graphs have cycle separators and planar directed depth-first search is in *DNC*. In Reif [301], pages 53–63. (146)

[187] M. Karchmer and J. Naor. A fast parallel algorithm to color a graph with Δ colors. *Journal of Algorithms*, 9(1):83–91, 1988. (132)

[188] H. J. Karloff. A Las Vegas *RNC* algorithm for maximum matching. *Combinatorica*, 6(4):387–391, 1986. (241)

[189] H. J. Karloff. An *NC* algorithm for Brooks' Theorem. *Theoretical Computer Science*, 68(1):89–103, 16 October 1989. (132)

[190] H. J. Karloff and W. L. Ruzzo. The iterated mod problem. *Information and Computation*, 80(3):193–204, March 1989. (188, 189)

[191] H. J. Karloff and D. B. Shmoys. Efficient parallel algorithms for edge coloring problems. *Journal of Algorithms*, 8(1):39–52, 1987. (132, 223, 240)

[192] N. Karmarkar. A new polynomial-time algorithm for linear programming. *Combinatorica*, 4(4):373–395, 1984. (150, 151)

[193] R. M. Karp. Reducibility among combinatorial problems. In R. E. Miller and J. W. Thatcher, editors, *Complexity of Computer Computations*, pages 85–104. Plenum Press, New York, 1972. (47, 139–141)

[194] R. M. Karp. Talk at the University of Toronto, 1984. (128)

[195] R. M. Karp and V. Ramachandran. Parallel algorithms for shared-memory machines. In van Leeuwen [360], chapter 17, pages 869–941. (17, 21, 33, 36, 62, 66, 80, 93)

[196] R. M. Karp, E. Upfal, and A. Wigderson. Constructing a perfect matching is in Random *NC*. *Combinatorica*, 6(1):35–48, 1986. (149, 152, 224, 241, 242)

[197] R. M. Karp, E. Upfal, and A. Wigderson. The complexity of parallel search. *Journal of Computer and System Sciences*, 36(2):225–253, April 1988. (40, 91, 93)

[198] R. M. Karp and A. Wigderson. A fast parallel algorithm for the maximal independent set problem. *Journal of the ACM*, 32(4):762–773, 1985. (128, 132)

[199] M. Karpinski. Boolean circuit complexity of algebraic interpolation problems. In E. Börger, H. Kleine Büning, and M. M. Richter, editors, *CSL '88: 2nd Workshop on Computer Science Logic*, volume 385 of *Lecture Notes in Computer Science*, pages 138–147. Springer-Verlag, Duisburg, Germany, October 1988. (242)

[200] M. Karpinski and K. W. Wagner. The computational complexity of graph problems with succinct multigraph representation. *Zeitschrift für Operations Research*, 32(3):201–211, 1988. (241, 242)

[201] T. Kasai, A. Adachi, and S. Iwata. Classes of pebble games and complete problems. *SIAM Journal on Computing*, 8(4):574–586, 1979. (213, 214)

[202] S. Kasif. On the parallel complexity of some constraint satisfaction problems. In *Proceedings, AAAI-86: Fifth National Conference on Artificial Intelligence*, pages 349–353, Philadelphia, PA, August 1986. American Association for Artificial Intelligence. (168, 169, 208)

[203] S. Kasif. On the parallel complexity of discrete relaxation in constraint satisfaction networks. *Artificial Intelligence*, 3(45):275–286, October 1990. (168, 170)

[204] S. Kasif. Analysis of local consistency in parallel constraint satisfaction networks. In *Symposium: Constraint-Based Reasoning*, Spring Symposium Series, pages 154–163. AAAI, March 1991. (Extended Abstract). (170)

[205] D. Kavadias, L. M. Kirousis, and P. G. Spirakis. The complexity of the reliable connectivity problem. *Information Processing Letters*, 39(5):245–252, 13 September 1991. (135)

[206] P. Kelsen. On computing a maximal independent set in a hypergraph of constant dimension in parallel. In *Proceedings of the Twenty-Fourth Annual ACM Symposium on Theory of Computing*, pages 339–369, Victoria, B.C., Canada, May 1992. (225)

[207] L. G. Khachian. A polynomial time algorithm for linear programming. *Doklady Akademii Nauk SSSR, n.s.*, 244(5):1093–1096, 1979. English translation in *Soviet Math. Dokl. 20*, 191–194.
(150, 151, 153)

[208] S. Khuller. On computing graph closures. *Information Processing Letters*, 31(5):249–255, 12 June 1989. (142, 224)

[209] S. Khuller and B. Schieber. Efficient parallel algorithms for testing k-connectivity and finding disjoint $s-t$ paths in graphs. *SIAM Journal on Computing*, 20(2):352–375, April 1991. (134)

[210] G. A. P. Kindervater and J. K. Lenstra. An introduction to parallelism in combinatorial optimization. In J. van Leeuwen and J. K. Lenstra, editors, *Parallel Computers and Computation*, volume 9 of *CWI Syllabus*, pages 163–184. Center for Mathematics and Computer Science, Amsterdam, The Netherlands, 1985. (17)

[211] G. A. P. Kindervater and J. K. Lenstra. Parallel algorithms. In M. O'hEigeartaigh, J. K. Lenstra, and A. H. G. Rinnooy Kan, editors, *Combinatorial Optimization: Annotated Bibliographies*, chapter 8, pages 106–128. John Wiley & Sons, Chichester, 1985. (17, 21)

[212] G. A. P. Kindervater, J. K. Lenstra, and D. B. Shmoys. The parallel complexity of TSP heuristics. *Journal of Algorithms*, 10(2):249–270, June 1989. (138)

[213] G. A. P. Kindervater and H. W. J. M. Trienekens. Experiments with parallel algorithms for combinatorial problems. Technical Report 8550/A, Erasmus University Rotterdam, Econometric Inst., 1985.
(17)

[214] L. M. Kirousis, M. J. Serna, and P. G. Spirakis. The parallel complexity of the connected subgraph problem. *SIAM Journal on Computing*, 22(3):573–586, June 1993.
(134)

[215] L. M. Kirousis and P. G. Spirakis. Probabilistic log-space reductions and problems probabilistically hard for P. In R. Karlsson and A. Lingas, editors, *SWAT88. 1st Scandanavian Workshop on Algorithm Theory*, volume 318 of *Lecture Notes in Computer Science*, pages 163–175, Halmstad, Sweden, July 1988. Springer-Verlag. (125, 135)

[216] P. N. Klein and J. H. Reif. Parallel time $O(\log n)$ acceptance of deterministic CFLs on an exclusive-write P-RAM. *SIAM Journal on Computing*, 17(3):463–485, June 1988.
(176)

[217] D. E. Knuth, C. H. Papadimitriou, and J. N. Tsitsiklis. A note on strategy elimination in bimatrix games. *Operations Research Letters*, 7(3):103–107, June 1988.
(212)

[218] K.-I. Ko. Binary search for roots of real functions. In S. R. Buss and P. J. Scott, editors, *Feasible Mathematics*, pages 239–257, A Mathematical Sciences Institute Workshop, Ithaca, NY, 1990. Birkhäuser.
(207)

[219] S. R. Kosaraju. On the parallel evaluation of classes of circuits. In K. V. Nori and C. E. Veni Madhavan, editors, *Foundations of Software Technology and Theoretical Computer Science, Tenth Conference*, volume 472 of *Lecture Notes in Computer Science*, pages 232–237, Bangalore, India, December 1990. Springer-Verlag. (124)

[220] S. R. Kosaraju and A. L. Delcher. Optimal parallel evaluation of tree-structured computations by raking. In Reif [301], pages 101–110. (Extended Abstract).
(66)

[221] D. C. Kozen. Complexity of finitely presented algebras. In *Conference Record of the Ninth Annual ACM Symposium on Theory of Computing*, pages 164–177, Boulder, CO, May 1977. (194, 195)

[222] M. W. Krentel. On finding and verifying locally optimal solutions. *SIAM Journal on Computing*, 19(4):742–749, August 1990. (158)

[223] C. P. Kruskal, L. Rudolph, and M. Snir. The power of parallel prefix computation. In *International Conference on Parallel Processing*, pages 180–185, 1985. (64, 103)

[224] G. M. Kuper, K. W. McAloon, K. V. Palem, and K. J. Perry. A note on the parallel complexity of anti-unification. *Journal of Automated Reasoning*, 9(3):381–389, 1992. (172)

[225] R. E. Ladner. The circuit value problem is log space complete for P. *SIGACT News*, 7(1):18–20, January 1975.

(14, 18, 59, 60, 72, 121, 179)

[226] R. E. Ladner and M. J. Fischer. Parallel prefix computation. *Journal of the ACM*, 27(4):831–838, October 1980.   (35, 64)

[227] E. L. Lawler. *Combinatorial Optimization: Networks and Matroids.* Holt, Rinehart and Winston, New York, 1976.   (92)

[228] F. T. Leighton. *Introduction to Parallel Algorithms and Architectures: Arrays, Trees, Hypercubes.* Morgan Kaufmann, 1992.

(6, 17, 19, 21)

[229] T. Lengauer. VLSI theory. In van Leeuwen [360], chapter 16, pages 837–868.   (27)

[230] T. Lengauer and R. E. Tarjan. Asymptotically tight bounds on time-space trade-offs in a pebble game. *Journal of the ACM*, 29(4):1087–1130, October 1982.   (69)

[231] T. Lengauer and K. W. Wagner. The binary network flow problem is logspace complete for P. *Theoretical Computer Science*, 75(3):357–363, 1 October 1990.   (129–131, 152)

[232] A. K. Lenstra, H. W. Lenstra, Jr., and L. Lovász. Factoring polynomials with rational coefficients. *Mathematische Annalen*, 261(4):515–534, December 1982.   (234)

[233] H. R. Lewis and C. H. Papadimitriou. Symmetric space-bounded computation. *Theoretical Computer Science*, 19(2):161–187, August 1982.   (130)

[234] P. M. Lewis, II, R. E. Stearns, and J. Hartmanis. Memory bounds for recognition of context-free and context-sensitive languages. In *Proceedings of the Sixth Annual Symposium on Switching Circuit Theory and Logic Design*, pages 191–202. IEEE, 1965.   (176)

[235] S. Lin and B. W. Kernighan. An effective heuristic algorithm for the traveling salesman problem. *Operations Research*, 21(1):498–516, January-February 1973.   (164)

[236] Y. Lin. *Parallel Computational Methods in Integer Linear Programming.* PhD thesis, The City University of New York, 1991. (188, 189)

[237] Y. Lin-Kriz and V. Pan. On parallel complexity of integer linear programming, GCD and the iterated mod function. In *Proceedings of the Third Annual ACM-SIAM Symposium on Discrete Algorithms*, pages 124–137, Orlando, FL, January 1992.   (151, 189, 230)

[238] S. Lindell. A logspace algorithm for tree canonization. In *Proceedings of the Twenty-Fourth Annual ACM Symposium on Theory of Computing*, pages 400–404, Victoria, B.C., Canada, May 1992.   (223, 242, 243)

[239] K. Lindgren and M. G. Nordahl. Universal computation in simple one-dimensional cellular automata. *Complex Systems*, 4(3):299–318, 1990.   (216, 217)

[240] A. Lingas. A note on a parallel heuristic for minimum vertex cover. *Bulletin of the European Association for Theoretical Computer Science*, 42:174–177, October 1990.   (137)

[241] A. Lingas and M. Karpinski. Subtree isomorphism is *NC* reducible to bipartite perfect matching. *Information Processing Letters*, 30(1):27–32, 16 January 1989.   (223, 242)

[242] J. Lipscomb. On the computational complexity of finding a connectionist model's stable state vectors. Master's thesis, University of Toronto, 1987.   (163)

[243] R. J. Lipton and Y. Zalcstein. Word problems solvable in log space. *Journal of the ACM*, 24(3):522–526, 1977.   (189)

[244] *Logic and Algorithmic*, An International Symposium Held in Honor of Ernst Specker, Zürich, February 5–11, 1980. Monographie No. 30 de L'Enseignement Mathématique, Université de Genève, 1982.
                                                        (258, 260, 283)

[245] P. M. Long and M. K. Warmuth. Composite geometric concepts and polynomial predictability. *Information and Computation*, 113(2):230–252, September 1994.   (204)

[246] M. Luby. A simple parallel algorithm for the maximal independent set problem. *SIAM Journal on Computing*, 15(4):1036–1053, 1986.
                                                    (93, 128, 131, 164)

[247] M. Luby. Removing randomness in parallel computation without a processor penalty. In *29th Annual Symposium on Foundations of Computer Science*, pages 162–173, White Plains, NY, October 1988. IEEE.   (160)

[248] G. S. Lueker, N. Megiddo, and V. Ramachandran. Linear programming with two variables per inequality in poly-log time. *SIAM Journal on Computing*, 19(6):1000–1010, December 1990.   (227)

[249] J. Machta. The computational complexity of pattern formation. *Journal of Statistical Physics*, 70(3-4):949–966, February 1993.
                                                            (217, 218)

[250] J. Machta and R. Greenlaw. The parallel complexity of growth models. Technical Report TR 94-05, University of New Hampshire, 1994.   (218)

[251] L. Mak. Are parallel machines always faster than sequential machines? Submitted for publication, August 1993.   (63)

[252] L. Mak. Parallelism always helps. Submitted for publication, August 1993. (63)

[253] E. W. Mayr. The dynamic tree expression problem. In Tewksbury et al. [353], pages 157–179. (66, 124)

[254] E. W. Mayr. Parallel approximation algorithms. In Institute for New Generation Computer Technology (ICOT) [170], pages 542–551 (Volume 2). (112, 155, 156, 189)

[255] E. W. Mayr and A. Subramanian. The complexity of circuit value and network stability. *Journal of Computer and System Sciences*, 44(2):302–323, April 1992. (235–238)

[256] W. F. McColl. Planar crossovers. *IEEE Transactions on Computers*, C-30(3):223–225, 1981. (124)

[257] N. Megiddo. A note on approximate linear programming. *Information Processing Letters*, 42(1):53, 27 April 1992. (151)

[258] G. L. Miller, V. Ramachandran, and E. Kaltofen. Efficient parallel evaluation of straight-line code and arithmetic circuits. *SIAM Journal on Computing*, 17(4):687–695, August 1988. (124)

[259] G. L. Miller and J. H. Reif. Parallel tree contraction and its applications. In *26th Annual Symposium on Foundations of Computer Science*, pages 478–489, Portland, OR, October 1985. IEEE. (66)

[260] G. L. Miller and J. H. Reif. Parallel tree contraction, Part 1: Fundamentals. In S. Micali, editor, *Advances in Computing Research, Volume 5: Randomness and Computation*, pages 47–72. JAI Press Inc., Greenwich, CT, 1989. Series Editor, F. P. Preparata. (66)

[261] G. L. Miller and J. H. Reif. Parallel tree contraction, Part 2: Further applications. *SIAM Journal on Computing*, 20(6):1128–1147, 1991. (66)

[262] M. Minsky. *Computation: Finite and Infinite Machines*. Prentice Hall, 1967. (217)

[263] S. Miyano. Parallel complexity and *P*-complete problems. In Institute for New Generation Computer Technology (ICOT) [170], pages 532–541 (Volume 2). (128, 139)

[264] S. Miyano. A parallelizable lexicographically first maximal edge-induced subgraph problem. *Information Processing Letters*, 27(2):75–78, 29 February 1988. (143, 226)

[265] S. Miyano. The lexicographically first maximal subgraph problems: *P*-completeness and *NC* algorithms. *Mathematical Systems Theory*, 22(1):47–73, 1989. (91, 128, 139, 143, 225, 226)

[266] S. Miyano. Systematized approaches to the complexity of subgraph problems. *Journal of Information Processing*, 13(4):442–448, 1990.
(139)

[267] S. Miyano and M. Haraguchi. The computational complexity of incomplete table recovery. Research Report 100, Kyushu University Research Institute of Fundamental Information Science, September 1982.   (175)

[268] S. Miyano, S. Shiraishi, and T. Shoudai. A list of *P*-complete problems. Technical Report RIFIS-TR-CS-17, Kyushu University 33, Research Institute of Fundamental Information Science, 1989. Revised, December 29, 1990. 68 pages.   (17, 175)

[269] A. Monti and A. Roncato. On the complexity of some reachability problems. In M. Bonuccelli, P. Crescenzi, and R. Petreschi, editors, *Algorithms and Complexity: Second Italian Conference, CIAC '94*, volume 778 of *Lecture Notes in Computer Science*, pages 192–202, Rome, Italy, February 1994. Springer-Verlag.   (182)

[270] K. Mulmuley. A fast parallel algorithm to compute the rank of a matrix over an arbitrary field. *Combinatorica*, 7(1):101–104, 1987.
(188)

[271] K. Mulmuley, U. V. Vazirani, and V. V. Vazirani. Matching is as easy as matrix inversion. *Combinatorica*, 7(1):105–113, 1987.
(149, 241, 242)

[272] J. Naor. A fast parallel coloring of planar graphs with five colors. *Information Processing Letters*, 25(1):51–53, 20 April 1987.   (132)

[273] Y. P. Ofman. On the algorithmic complexity of discrete functions. *Soviet Physics Doklady*, 7(7):589–591, 1963.   (64)

[274] W. F. Ogden, W. E. Riddle, and W. C. Rounds. Complexity of expressions allowing concurrency. In *Conference Record of the Fifth Annual ACM Symposium on Principles of Programming Languages*, pages 185–194, Tucson, AZ, January 1978.   (184)

[275] C. N. K. Osiakwan and S. G. Akl. The maximum weight perfect matching problem for complete weighted graphs is in *PC*. In *Proceedings of the Second IEEE Symposium on Parallel and Distributed Processing*, pages 880–887, Dallas, TX, December 1990. IEEE. (242)

[276] V. Pan and J. H. Reif. Fast and efficient parallel solution of dense linear systems. *Computers and Mathematics with Applications*, 17(11):1481–1491, 1989.   (188)

[277] C. H. Papadimitriou. Efficient search for rationals. *Information Processing Letters*, 8(1):1–4, 1978.   (151)

[278] C. H. Papadimitriou, A. A. Schäffer, and M. Yannakakis. On the complexity of local search. In *Proceedings of the Twenty-Second Annual ACM Symposium on Theory of Computing*, pages 438–445, Baltimore, MD, May 1990. (Extended Abstract).   (160, 161, 163)

[279] C. H. Papadimitriou and J. N. Tsitsiklis. The complexity of Markov decision processes. *Mathematics of Operations Research*, 12(3):441–450, 1987.   (185–187)

[280] I. Parberry. Parallel speedup of sequential machines: A defense of the parallel computation thesis. *SIGACT News*, 18(1):54–67, Summer 1986.   (68)

[281] I. Parberry. *Parallel Complexity Theory*. Research Notes in Theoretical Computer Science. Pitman/Wiley, 1987.   (63, 68, 121)

[282] M. S. Paterson and L. G. Valiant. Circuit size is nonlinear in depth. *Theoretical Computer Science*, 2(3):397–400, 1976.   (63)

[283] W. J. Paul, R. E. Tarjan, and J. R. Celoni. Space bounds for a game on graphs. *Mathematical Systems Theory*, 10(3):239–251, 1977. Correction, *ibid.* 11(1):85, 1977.   (69)

[284] N. J. Pippenger. Fast simulation of combinational logic networks by machines without random-access storage. In *Proceedings, Fifteenth Annual Allerton Conference on Communication, Control and Computing*, pages 25–33, Monticello, IL, September 1977.   (71)

[285] N. J. Pippenger. On simultaneous resource bounds. In *20th Annual Symposium on Foundations of Computer Science*, pages 307–311, San Juan, Puerto Rico, October 1979. IEEE.   (15, 33, 66, 67)

[286] N. J. Pippenger. Pebbling. In *Proceedings of the Fifth IBM Symposium on Mathematical Foundations of Computer Science*. IBM Japan, May 1980.   (69)

[287] N. J. Pippenger. Pebbling with an auxiliary pushdown. *Journal of Computer and System Sciences*, 23(2):151–165, October 1981.   (69)

[288] N. J. Pippenger. Advances in pebbling. Research Report RJ3466, IBM Research Division, Thomas J. Watson Research Center, Yorktown Heights, NY, April 1982.   (69)

[289] N. J. Pippenger and M. J. Fischer. Relations among complexity measures. *Journal of the ACM*, 26(2):361–381, April 1979. (14, 67)

[290] D. A. Plaisted. Complete problems in the first-order predicate calculus. *Journal of Computer and System Sciences*, 29(1):8–35, 1984.   (168)

[291] G. Pólya, R. E. Tarjan, and D. R. Woods. *Notes on Introductory Combinatorics*. Birkhäuser, Boston, 1983.   (237)

[292] E. L. Post. *The Two-Valued Iterative Systems of Mathematical Logic.* Number 5 in Annals of Math. Studies. Princeton University Press, 1941.   (122)

[293] V. R. Pratt and L. J. Stockmeyer. A characterization of the power of vector machines. *Journal of Computer and System Sciences,* 12(2):198–221, April 1976.   (19)

[294] S. Rajasekaran and J. H. Reif. Randomized parallel computation. In Tewksbury et al. [353], pages 181–202.   (93)

[295] V. Ramachandran. The complexity of minimum cut and maximum flow problems in an acyclic network. *Networks,* 17(4):387–392, 1987.
                                                                                           (152)

[296] V. Ramachandran. Fast and processor-efficient parallel algorithms for reducible flow graphs. Technical Report UILU-ENG-88-2257, ACT-103, University of Illinois at Urbana-Champaign, 1988.   (140, 141)

[297] V. Ramachandran. Fast parallel algorithms for reducible flow graphs. In Tewksbury et al. [353], pages 117–138.   (140, 141)

[298] V. Ramachandran and L.-C. Wang. Parallel algorithms and complexity results for telephone link simulation. In *Proceedings of the Third IEEE Symposium on Parallel and Distributed Processing,* pages 378–385, Dallas, TX, December 1991. IEEE.   (235, 238)

[299] J. H. Reif. On synchronous parallel computations with independent probabilistic choice. *SIAM Journal on Computing,* 13(1):46–56, February 1984.   (63)

[300] J. H. Reif. Depth-first search is inherently sequential. *Information Processing Letters,* 20(5):229–234, 12 June 1985.   (16, 145)

[301] J. H. Reif, editor. *VLSI Algorithms and Architectures, 3rd Aegean Workshop on Computing, AWOC 88,* volume 319 of *Lecture Notes in Computer Science,* Corfu, Greece, June-July 1988. Springer-Verlag.
                                                                                       (269, 272)

[302] J. H. Reif, editor. *Synthesis of Parallel Algorithms.* Morgan Kaufmann, 1993.   (17, 258, 263, 266)

[303] J. H. Reif, J. D. Tygar, and A. Yoshida. The computability and complexity of optical beam tracing. In *Proceedings 31st Annual Symposium on Foundations of Computer Science,* pages 106–114, St. Louis, MO, October 1990. IEEE.   (232)

[304] S. P. Reiss. Rational search. *Information Processing Letters,* 8(2):87–90, 1978.   (151)

[305] J. A. Robinson. A machine oriented logic based on the resolution principle. *Journal of the ACM,* 12(1):23–41, 1965.   (171)

[306] W. L. Ruzzo. Complete pushdown languages. Unpublished manuscript, 1979. (180)

[307] W. L. Ruzzo. Tree-size bounded alternation. *Journal of Computer and System Sciences*, 21(2):218–235, October 1980. (65, 176)

[308] W. L. Ruzzo. On uniform circuit complexity. *Journal of Computer and System Sciences*, 22(3):365–383, June 1981.
(15, 29, 32, 33, 53, 65)

[309] W. Rytter. On the recognition of context-free languages. In A. Skowron, editor, *Computation Theory: Fifth Symposium*, volume 208 of *Lecture Notes in Computer Science*, pages 318–325, Zaborów, Poland, December 1984 (published 1985). Springer-Verlag. (176)

[310] W. Rytter. Parallel time $O(\log n)$ recognition of unambiguous context-free languages. *Information and Computation*, 73(1):75–86, 1987. (176)

[311] S. Sairam, J. S. Vitter, and R. Tamassia. A complexity theoretic approach to incremental computation. In Finkel et al. [107], pages 640–649. (236)

[312] Sang Cho and D. T. Huynh. The complexity of membership for deterministic growing context-sensitive grammars. *International Journal of Computer Mathematics*, 37(3-4):185–188, 1990. (178)

[313] Sang Cho and D. T. Huynh. The parallel complexity of coarsest set partition problems. *Information Processing Letters*, 42(2):89–94, 11 May 1992. (183)

[314] Sang Cho and D. T. Huynh. The parallel complexity of finite-state automata problems. *Information and Computation*, 97(1):1–22, 1992. (228)

[315] J. L. C. Sanz, editor. *Opportunities and Constraints of Parallel Computing*. Springer-Verlag, 1989. Papers presented at a workshop, December 5–6, 1988, at the IBM Almaden Research Center, San Jose, CA. (10)

[316] R. Sarnath and X. He. A P-complete graph partition problem. *Theoretical Computer Science*, 76(2,3):343–351, 21 November 1990. (160, 164)

[317] J. E. Savage. Computational work and time on finite machines. *Journal of the ACM*, 19(4):660–674, October 1972. (14, 67)

[318] J. E. Savage and M. G. Wloka. A parallel algorithm for channel routing. In J. van Leeuwen, editor, *Proceedings of the International Workshop on Graph-Theoretic Concepts in Computer Science*, volume 344 of *Lecture Notes in Computer Science*, pages 288–303, Amsterdam, Netherlands, June 1988 (published 1989). Springer-Verlag. (166)

[319] J. E. Savage and M. G. Wloka. On parallelizing graph-partitioning heuristics. In M. S. Paterson, editor, *Automata, Languages, and Programming: 17th International Colloquium*, volume 443 of *Lecture Notes in Computer Science*, pages 476–489, Warwick University, England, July 1990. Springer-Verlag.   (159, 161, 162)

[320] J. E. Savage and M. G. Wloka. Parallelism in graph-partitioning. *Journal of Parallel and Distributed Computing*, 13(3):257–272, November 1991.   (159, 161, 162)

[321] J. E. Savage and M. G. Wloka. The parallel complexity of minimizing column conflicts. In N. Sherwani, editor, *Proceedings of the Second Great Lakes Symposium on VLSI, Design Automation of VLSI Systems in the 90's*, pages 30–34, Kalamazoo, MI, February 1992. IEEE.
(166)

[322] W. J. Savitch. Relationships between nondeterministic and deterministic tape complexities. *Journal of Computer and System Sciences*, 4(2):177–192, 1970.   (65, 129)

[323] W. J. Savitch and M. J. Stimson. Time bounded random access machines with parallel processing. *Journal of the ACM*, 26(1):103–118, 1979.   (19)

[324] A. A. Schäffer and M. Yannakakis. Simple local search problems that are hard to solve. *SIAM Journal on Computing*, 20(1):56–87, February 1991.   (159–164, 251)

[325] C. A. Schevon and J. S. Vitter. A parallel algorithm for recognizing unordered depth-first search. *Information Processing Letters*, 28(2):105–110, 24 June 1988.   (146)

[326] M. J. Serna. *The Parallel Approximability of P-Complete Problems*. PhD thesis, Universitat Politecnica de Catalunya, Barcelona, 1990.
(111, 125, 134)

[327] M. J. Serna. Approximating linear programming is log-space complete for *P*. *Information Processing Letters*, 37(4):233–236, 28 February 1991.   (125, 126, 151)

[328] M. J. Serna and P. G. Spirakis. The approximability of problems complete for *P*. In H. Djidjev, editor, *Optimal Algorithms, International Symposium Proceedings. Varna, Bulgaria.*, volume 401 of *Lecture Notes in Computer Science*, pages 193–204. Springer-Verlag, 29 May–2 June 1989.   (111, 134, 167, 170, 171)

[329] D. Shallcross, V. Pan, and Y. Lin-Kriz. The *NC* equivalence of planar integer linear programming and Euclidean GCD. In *Proceedings 34th Annual Symposium on Foundations of Computer Science*, pages 557–564, Palo Alto, CA, November 1993. IEEE.   (226, 229, 230)

[330] S. Shimozono and S. Miyano. Complexity of finding alphabet indexing. Manuscript, 1994. (219, 220)

[331] T. Shoudai. The lexicographically first topological order problem is *NLOG*-complete. *Information Processing Letters*, 33(3):121–124, 30 November 1989. (139)

[332] T. Shoudai. A *P*-complete language describable with iterated shuffle. *Information Processing Letters*, 41(5):233–238, 3 April 1992. (184)

[333] A. R. Smith, III. Simple computation-universal cellular spaces. *Journal of the ACM*, 18(3):339–353, 1971. (216)

[334] J. R. Smith. Parallel algorithms for depth first searches I: Planar graphs. *SIAM Journal on Computing*, 15(3):814–830, 1986.
(146, 240)

[335] J. Sorenson. The *k*-ary GCD algorithm. Technical Report 979, University of Wisconsin, Madison, WI, April 1991. (230)

[336] J. Sorenson. Two fast GCD algorithms. Manuscript, Department of Mathematics and Computer Science, Bulter University, Indianapolis, IN, January 1992. (230)

[337] P. G. Spirakis. The parallel complexity of deadlock detection. *Theoretical Computer Science*, 52(1,2):155–163, 1987. (215, 216)

[338] P. G. Spirakis. Fast parallel algorithms and the complexity of parallelism (basic issues and recent advances). In G. Wolf, T. Legendi, and U. Schendel, editors, *Parcella '88. Fourth International Workshop on Parallel Processing by Cellular Automata and Arrays Proceedings*, volume 342 of *Lecture Notes in Computer Science*, pages 177–189, Berlin, East Germany, October 1988 (published 1989). Springer-Verlag. (21)

[339] C. Stein and J. Wein. Approximating the minimum-cost maximum flow is *P*-complete. *Information Processing Letters*, 42(6):315–319, 24 July 1992. (153)

[340] I. A. Stewart. Complete problems for symmetric logspace involving free groups. *Information Processing Letters*, 40(5):263–267, 13 December 1991. (189)

[341] I. A. Stewart. Refining known results on the generalized word problem for free groups. *International Journal of Algebra and Computation*, 2(2):221–236, June 1992. (189)

[342] I. A. Stewart. On parallelizing a greedy heuristic for finding small dominant sets. *BIT*, 33(1):57–62, 1993. (137)

[343] I. A. Stewart. On two approximation algorithms for the clique problem. *International Journal of Foundations of Computer Science*, 4(2):117–133, 1993. (128, 129)

[344] L. J. Stockmeyer and A. R. Meyer. Word problems requiring exponential time. In *Conference Record of Fifth Annual ACM Symposium on Theory of Computing*, pages 1–9, Austin, TX, April-May 1973.   (14)

[345] L. J. Stockmeyer and U. Vishkin. Simulation of parallel random access machines by circuits. *SIAM Journal on Computing*, 13(2):409–422, May 1984.   (30, 36)

[346] A. Subramanian. A new approach to stable matching problems. Technical Report STAN-CS-89-1275, Stanford University, Department of Computer Science, 1989.   (235, 237, 238)

[347] A. Subramanian. *The Computational Complexity of the Circuit Value and Network Stability Problems*. PhD thesis, Stanford University, 1990. Department of Computer Science Technical Report STAN-CS-90-1311.   (235)

[348] I. H. Sudborough. On the tape complexity of deterministic context-free languages. *Journal of the ACM*, 25(3):405–414, 1978.   (179)

[349] S. Sunder and X. He. Scheduling interval ordered tasks in parallel. In Finkel et al. [107], pages 100–109.   (156)

[350] R. E. Tarjan and U. Vishkin. Finding biconnected components and computing tree functions in logarithmic parallel time. In *25th Annual Symposium on Foundations of Computer Science*, pages 12–20, Singer Island, FL, October 1984. IEEE.   (98)

[351] R. E. Tarjan and U. Vishkin. An efficient parallel biconnectivity algorithm. *SIAM Journal on Computing*, 14(4):862–874, November 1985.   (98)

[352] S.-H. Teng. Matching randomly in parallel. Department of Computer Science CMU-CS-89-149, Carnegie Mellon University, Pittsburgh, PA, 1989.   (143)

[353] S. K. Tewksbury, B. W. Dickinson, and S. C. Schwartz, editors. *Concurrent Computations: Algorithms, Architecture, and Technology*. Plenum Press, 1988. Proceedings of the 1987 Princeton Workshop on Algorithm, Architecture and Technology issues for Models of Concurrent Computation, September 30 – October 1, 1987. (264, 275, 278)

[354] M. Tompa. Unpublished notes on *NC* reductions among problems in *RP*, 1983.   (230, 231)

[355] J. D. Ullman and A. Van Gelder. Parallel complexity of logical query programs. *Algorithmica*, 3(1):5–42, 1988.   (173)

[356] L. G. Valiant. Parallel computation. Technical Report TR-16-82, Harvard, Center of Research in Computing Technology, April 1982. Presented at the 7th IBM Symposium on Mathematical Foundations

of Computer Science, Hakone, Kanagawa, Japan, May 24–26, 1982.
(88)

[357] L. G. Valiant. Reducibility by algebraic projections. *L'Enseignement Mathématique*, XXVIII:253–268, 1982. Also in [244, pages 365–380].
(16, 150, 151)

[358] L. G. Valiant, S. Skyum, S. Berkowitz, and C. W. Rackoff. Fast parallel computation of polynomials using few processors. *SIAM Journal on Computing*, 12(4):641–644, November 1983.   (124)

[359] P. van Emde Boas. The second machine class: Models of parallelism. In J. van Leeuwen and J. K. Lenstra, editors, *Parallel Computers and Computation*, volume 9 of *CWI Syllabus*, pages 133–161. Center for Mathematics and Computer Science, Amsterdam, The Netherlands, 1985.   (21)

[360] J. van Leeuwen, editor. *Handbook of Theoretical Computer Science*, volume A: Algorithms and Complexity. M.I.T. Press/Elsevier, 1990.
(17, 269, 270, 273)

[361] S. Vavasis. Gaussian elimination with pivoting is *P*-complete. *SIAM Journal on Discrete Mathematics*, 2(3):413–423, 1989.
(99, 187, 188, 229, 230)

[362] H. Venkateswaran. Two dynamic programming algorithms for which interpreted pebbling helps. *Information and Computation*, 92(2):237–252, 1991.   (69)

[363] H. Venkateswaran and M. Tompa. A new pebble game that characterizes parallel complexity classes. *SIAM Journal on Computing*, 18(3):533–549, June 1989.   (69)

[364] U. Vishkin. Synchronous parallel computation — a survey. Preprint, 1983. Courant Institute, New York University.   (21, 24)

[365] S. Vishwanathan and M. A. Sridhar. Some results on graph coloring in parallel. In F. A. Briggs, editor, *Proceedings of the 1988 International Conference on Parallel Processing*, pages 299–303, volume 3, University Park, PA, 15-19 August 1988. Pennsylvania State University.   (133, 136)

[366] J. S. Vitter and R. A. Simons. New classes for parallel complexity: A study of unification and other complete problems for *P*. *IEEE Transactions on Computers*, TC-35:403–418, May 1986. Reprinted in [370, pages 135–150].   (103, 122, 146, 171, 172)

[367] B. von Braunmühl, S. A. Cook, K. Mehlhorn, and R. Verbeek. The recognition of deterministic CFL's in small time and space. *Information and Control*, 56(1-2):34–51, January/February 1983.   (67, 260)

[368] J. von zur Gathen. Parallel algorithms for algebraic problems. *SIAM Journal on Computing*, 13(4):802–824, November 1984.
(229, 234, 235)

[369] J. von zur Gathen. Computing powers in parallel. *SIAM Journal on Computing*, 16(5):930–945, October 1987.   (231)

[370] B. Wah and G. J. Li, editors. *Computers for Artificial Intelligence Applications*. IEEE Computer Society Press, Washington, DC, 1986.
(283)

[371] C.-C. Wang, E. L. Lloyd, and M. L. Soffa. Feedback vertex sets and cyclically reducible graphs. *Journal of the ACM*, 32(2):296–313, April 1985.   (139, 140)

[372] A. Wigderson. Improving the performance guarantee for approximate graph coloring. *Journal of the ACM*, 30(4):729–735, 1983.   (137)

[373] R. Wilber. White pebbles help. *Journal of Computer and System Sciences*, 36(2):108–124, April 1988.   (69)

[374] H. Yasuura. The reachability problem on directed hypergraphs and computational complexity. Yajima Lab. Research Report ER 83-02, Department of Information Science, Kyoto University, November 1983.   (130)

[375] H. Yasuura. On parallel computational complexity of unification. In Institute for New Generation Computer Technology (ICOT), editor, *Fifth Generation Computer Systems 1984: Proceedings of the International Conference on Fifth Generation Computer Systems 1984*, pages 235–243, Tokyo, Japan, November 1984. OHMSHA, LTD./North-Holland.   (171)

[376] T. Zeugmann. Computing large polynomial powers very fast in parallel. In B. Rovan, editor, *Mathematical Foundations of Computer Science 1990: Proceedings, 15th Symposium*, volume 452 of *Lecture Notes in Computer Science*, pages 538–545. Springer-Verlag, Banská Bystrica, Czechoslovakia, August 1990.   (231)

[377] T. Zeugmann. Highly parallel computations modulo a number having only small prime factors. *Information and Computation*, 96(1):95–114, 1992.   (230, 231)

[378] S. Zhang and S. A. Smolka. Towards efficient parallelization of equivalence checking algorithms. In *Fifth International Conference on Formal Description Techniques for Distributed Systems and Communications Protocols — FORTE '92*, pages 121–135, Perros-Guirec, France, October 1992 (published 1993).   (181)

[379] Y. Zhang. *Parallel Algorithms for Problems Involving Directed Graphs*. PhD thesis, Drexel University, 1986.   (146)

Problem List

Here is a complete list of the *P*-complete and open problems given in Appendices A and B, in order of appearance, with problem name and page number. Problems are also listed alphabetically in the Index by name and acronym.

Index

This index contains entries for authors, concepts, and problems. Concept entries are in lower case, problems are capitalized. Problems are indexed in three ways. The first two forms indicate where the problem is defined in Part II: indexed by full title, along with the problem number in parentheses; and indexed by acronym, also with the problem number in parentheses. The third form, indexed by problem acronym only, gives the pages which make a reference to the problem, either by use in a reduction or as related information. See for example, 3OWPP and MVCP below.